THE PET BIZ SERIES COLLECTION

COMPLETE COLLECTION OF BOOKS 1-3

WENDY VAN DE POLL

Spirit Paw Press, LLC

CONTENTS

PET BLOGGING 101

Copyright 3
Introduction 7

Part I
CREATING YOUR BLOG

1. Courage and Inspiration 13
2. Finding Your Niche and Appealing to Followers 24

Part II
SETTING UP YOUR BLOG

3. Finding a Home for Your Blog 49
4. WordPress Bootcamp 65
5. Creating Winning Content 87

Part III
GROWING YOUR BLOG FOR SUCCESS

6. Getting Social with Social Media 111
7. Get Them to Come Back! 126
8. Monetizing Your Blog 137

Pep Talk! 152
Glossary 154
Resources 158
Thank You! 162

PET JOBS 101

Introduction 167

Part I

IN PERSON PET JOBS

1. Pet Photographer 173
2. Professional Pet Sitter 177
3. Dog Trainer 182
4. Groomer 187
5. Pet Bakery 192
6. Animal Energy Practitioner 197
7. Kennel Owner 202
8. Pet Massage Therapist 207
9. Doggie Day Care Owner 211
10. Veterinarian 216
11. Veterinary Technician 221
12. Barn Manager 225
13. Veterinary Acupuncturist 229
14. Veterinarian Chiropractor 234

Part II

VOLUNTEER

15. Humane Society/Rescue Volunteer 241
16. Service Animal Trainer 246
17. Prison Dog Trainer/Handler 252
18. Foster Parent 256
19. Wildlife Rehabilitator 261

Part III

JUMPSTART YOUR PET BUSINESS

20. Deciding What You Want to Do 269
21. Getting Started 277
22. Creating Your Website 293
23. Developing Your Website 298

Part IV
CUSTOMER SERVICE TIPS
24. Handling Aggressive and Difficult Animals 309
25. Handling Difficult People 314
26. Building Customer Loyalty 321

Pep Talk! 330
Glossary 332
Resources 336
Thank You! 343

PET AUTHORPRENEUR 101

Part I
GET READY TO WRITE
1. What do You Want to Write About? 355
2. Create Your Avatar 367
3. Mind Mapping Techniques 380
4. Outlining Your Manuscript 394
5. Character Profiles For Fiction 400

Part II
READY. SET. WRITE.
6. Make Time for Writing Every Day 409
7. Motivation, Inspiration, and Procrastination 423
8. Your Rough Draft 438
9. Clean up Your Rough Draft 447

Part III
WHAT'S NEXT FOR SUCCESS
10. Find Your Editors 463
11. Design Your Book 470
12. Create a Website and Landing Page 480
13. Build a Launch Team 492

14. Kindle Direct Publishing 503
15. Internet Marketing 509
16. In Person Marketing 520

Pep Talk! 528
Glossary 531
Resources 536
Acknowledgements 543
About the Author 545
Thank You! 548
Also by Wendy Van de Poll 549

PET BLOGGING 101

How to Start a Riveting Pet Blog and Gain Loyal Followers

The Pet Biz Series, Book 1

WENDY VAN DE POLL

INTERNATIONAL BESTSELLING AUTHOR

Pet Blogging 101:
How to Start a Riveting Pet Blog and
Gain Loyal Followers

Published by Spirit Paw Press, LLC, Concord, NH, 03303

Publisher's Cataloging-in-Publication Data
provided by Five Rainbows Cataloging Services

Names: Van de Poll, Wendy, author.
Title: Pet blogging 101 : how to start a riveting pet blog and gain loyal followers / Wendy Van de Poll.
Description: Concord, NH : Spirit Paw Press, 2019. | Series: Pet business, bk. 1. | Also available in ebook format.
Identifiers: ISBN 978-1-7324375-3-1 (softcover)
Subjects: LCSH: Blogs. | Pets. | Online authorship. | WordPress (Electronic resource) | Small business--Management. |

BISAC: COMPUTERS / Web / Blogging. | PETS / General. | BUSINESS & ECONOMICS / Small Business.
Classification: LCC PN171.O55 .V36 2019 (print) | LCC PN171.O55 (ebook) | DDC 302.23/1--dc23.

For all the animals that grace my life. You are behind this mission as you are with all of my work.

INTRODUCTION

Do you have the yearning to start a blog about pets, but don't know where to begin? Would you like to know how to get from your awesome idea to creating a successful blog? Is the thought of getting started overwhelming you?

The truth is that your idea is the seed that can grow into something great if you plant it.

You already made the first step by picking up this book. This book is your ultimate starting point. It contains what you need to know about starting your pet blog. I have outlined the steps from SEO to WordPress to affiliate marketing that you must take to make your blog a reality.

Don't feel that you lack the knowledge or skills to be a successful blogger, because I have included what you need to know to get started in these pages. If you follow the chapters from start to finish, you will have created a unique brand that will inspire you.

But first you may be wondering what a blog is and how it is different than a website.

A *blog,* according to Merriam-Webster Dictionary, is a website that contains online personal reflections, comments, and often hyperlinks, videos, and photographs provided by the writer. A *website* is a group of World Wide Web pages usually containing hyperlinks to each other and made available online by an individual, company, educational institution, government, or organization. Websites host blogs.

These are terms often used interchangeably. But for the purpose of this book, I will use blog. My advice is to not get distracted by the correct use of blog or website.

As a professional pet blogger for twenty-plus years and the founder of five blogs (two of which I created and then sold), I have the experience necessary to teach you how to blog.

Blogging is one of my passions, and helping people start their pet blog is inspiring. Guiding people who have the passion to share their ideas, knowledge, and expertise to help animals and pet lovers is an amazing experience. I want to help you feel the same.

If you want to create a blog, then you can do it. With this book, you will be able to create a riveting blog that will reach and attract many readers.

As you grow your readership, you will also grow as a person. I cannot stress enough how rewarding blogging is, as you reach people and change their lives.

You will meet many great people, you will make a difference in many lives, and you may even generate a nice income. Blogging is worth it. It just takes a few skills and some hard work to get going.

The most important thing is to be yourself. Find your voice and write what you want to write about. Share the photos that you love. Even feel free to make some mistakes and learn from them.

As you start this journey, you will learn many things, and you will perform the necessary research that will make you an expert in your particular pet niche. Be open to growth and you will find that your blog is a fantastic vehicle to things you never imagined learning and accomplishing.

My twenty-year success rate with pet blogging has enriched my professional and personal life on many levels. My sites have rated well with Google, my client base increased whenever I posted an article, and I am seen as an expert in the pet loss genre.

When I created and sold my two sites: natural-pet-essentials.com and chronic-pain-management.com (not a pet site), the pet industry was gaining momentum. I saw the potential for growth in the pet blogging industry. I didn't quit. I kept going.

My hope is that you keep going with your idea. With this book, you will be able to create your riveting and unique blog that will help people and animals around the world. You will change lives and gain an online community that will enrich your life by doing something meaningful.

Don't wait for this opportunity. Are you ready to start your pet blog? Then let's get started!

Affiliate links are present at the end of this book. This means if you purchase the product, I receive a small commission (which helps me greatly as an author.) You are not charged more because of the affiliate link. In fact, sometimes there is even a small discount. I have personally tested all affiliate products mentioned. I would never recommend something I didn't love.

PART I
CREATING YOUR BLOG

1

COURAGE AND INSPIRATION

Fortune sides with him who dares. — Virgil

You want to start a pet blog. I can't commend your bravery enough. It takes a lot of courage to put yourself out there in front of fans and critics alike, to share your thoughts with a blog, and to try to generate income in a nonconventional way. But that courage pays off, and the rewards of writing a pet blog can be monumental.

All pet lovers share something in common: a deep love for pets and a desire to be good pet parents. As you start your blog, you will realize you have a larger audience than you may have previously thought.

The Internet Age has made it possible to connect with other similar people more easily than ever. Your blog will have a home in an online pet community, where other people will warm your heart with their stories and pictures, just as you warm theirs.

It is normal to be anxious whenever you attempt something new. As you begin your blog, you may wonder, "Will anyone care what I have to say? Do I even have the skills to do this? What the heck am I getting myself into?" You may also wonder, "What should I write about?"

WILL ANYONE CARE?

First, there is no need to worry. People *will* care about what you have to say. Pet lovers are forever researching and looking to connect with like-minded people.

You will have an audience of dedicated readers, as long as you stay true to your voice and focus on delivering meaningful pet-related content. This book will show you how to find a niche that you can use to reach followers, as well as how to appeal to your readers by being yourself.

The Internet is quite saturated with content, and you will have competition. But if you stay true to your unique voice, you will stand out from the crowd naturally.

No one can offer just what you have to offer. Being unique is critical. You must offer readers something that they can't get in other blogs.

When I got started with natural-pet-essentials.com twenty years ago, I was scared to put myself out there. I was an animal lover with no official nutritional training.

However, what I had going for me was I lived a natural and holistic lifestyle. I was a canine and equine massage therapist, I prepared my dogs' food (before raw feeding was discovered), and I treated them with acupuncture, herbs, and homeopathy.

I researched everything I could find about taking care of the body, mind, and spirit of animals. And this, my friends, was the material for my blog. I used my unique voice and my passion for a holistic lifestyle to make my blog successful.

My site gained momentum fast. I was affiliate marketing, offering freebies (Chapter 8), and producing a new article every day.

When I sold this site, I was very proud of what I created.

DO YOU HAVE THE SKILLS?

You already possess some of the skills necessary for launching a successful pet blog. Your love for pets, your knowledge, and your life experiences—these are three skills that will make your blog flourish.

You don't have to be some rock-star writer with twenty published books or a pet expert with a veterinary degree to make it as a pet blogger. As long as you deliver on your idea and research your claims, your blog will be able to offer something to the world.

Think about the stories you want to share. No one else on this planet possesses those exact stories. No one has your pets, or your pictures, either. Sharing these snippets of your life with your pets and creating a little (or big) community of pet lovers will brighten the lives of so many people.

If you know about home remedies and tricks for caring for pets, how to run a business, or like to review products, you already have tons of useful content that other pet owners will want (Chapters 5 and 8).

Whatever your blog is about, this is your space to share what you have to offer others. Make it yours and truly yours!

Computer skills can scare some people off from blogging. If you know how to visit websites and type, that is a good start. You don't need to know fancy code to create a blog. I will teach you how to basically use the software that I love that handles all of the complex back-end stuff for you.

All you have to do is download the software, pick your design, input your content, and register and publish the blog. The rest is handled for you by your host and your WordPress suite (Chapter 4).

Owning your voice is the single most important thing you can do to stand out from the competition. However, there is obviously more to it.

No one will read your blog if no one knows about it. You can have the most wonderful content, but if you don't put it in front of people, you won't get readers.

Never fear, though, because this book will show you how to rank higher on search engines, how to use social media to build a brand people know about, and how to reach and incur followers. You must put in the work to put yourself out there, but I can promise you it is worth it.

WHAT ARE YOU GETTING YOURSELF INTO?

Yes, a blog is hard work. As a blogger, I cannot lie and claim that blogging is easy, passive income. You must post often, you must market yourself, and you must create an attractive site that is both convenient and accessible for readers.

Creating your blog is probably the most time-consuming part. A blog also requires ongoing upkeep and maintenance.

But all of this is work that can be both rewarding and relatively straightforward. You get to write about what you love! You can work from anywhere, anytime! And you can find new colleagues through the community you create. Your blog will be a reflection of what you love to do. And that is—talk about animals!

Blogs do require some patience, as well. It can take a while to build a following. Don't let impatience get the best of you because all good things come with time.

If you are dedicated and keep working, you will see a return. You might have zero readers for your first post; keep posting. You might not get anyone signing up for your email list; revisit your blog and tweak your description or content to offer your readers more of what they want.

To make money through your blog, you can use several different avenues. I cover many of them in Chapter 8. You can use the blog to market your own line or business, or you can use affiliate marketing to get paid by companies when readers click on your links. You will find that this is an excellent revenue stream. Once you get yourself in front of readers, you open the doors to many potential lucrative moneymaking opportunities.

When I first started writing, I started on a whim. I wasn't sure if anyone would want to read my work or if anyone would care about what I had to say. My blog took off, however, and I was shocked to discover that one day I was very successful.

Treating your blog as a whim is a good way to start because it removes the fear. Don't think of it as a matter of life or death. Think of it as a fun new venture. You will be surprised by the success that makes all of your hard work and writing pay off.

It is a shame to let your dream die because you are afraid. It is far better to try; the only failure is not trying at all! While you may not know what you are getting into, I promise it is fun and rewarding. Try it out and maybe you will find that starting a blog is something you enjoy.

WHAT SHOULD YOU WRITE ABOUT?

Now that you have the courage to make your blog a success, you need to work on finding inspiration. You are likely already inspired to create a blog and make money through it. But what if you lack inspiration on what to write about?

It is okay to feel uninspired sometimes. Inspiration can come from many places. Read other blogs or books. Watch a movie or take a walk. Talk to people about ideas. Think about causes you care about and things you would like to change in the pet world through education. Ideas will come to you.

Be sure to write all of your ideas down so you don't forget anything. It is a common saying that if you forget an idea, it wasn't that good of an idea to begin with. In the flurry of busyness that is my life, I cannot say that is true at all.

It is easy to forget things when you are busy or when you have many ideas, but each idea can become something great if acted upon. Always carry a little notebook with you and jot down ideas as they come to you.

My inspirations come when I am walking my dog in nature. Nature clears my mind and allows me to think creatively. I record my ideas on my phone when I get an idea or a brainstorm.

Using your pets as inspiration is also a great way to find things to write about. Think about your love for them and what you want to share with the world about them. Think about how you can make a difference for other people and other pets. That love will show in your writing and your photos, which can certainly appeal to followers.

Do not be scared to put your ideas out there. Do not feel that something you want to write about is stupid or a poor idea. And certainly, do not throttle your ideas by worrying about whether or not they appeal to followers!

This blog is your little space in the world. You can fill it with whatever you want. Someone will appreciate it.

The most successful blogs offer useful information. You might offer reviews of pet products to help other pet owners research and buy products. Companies will also pay you to review their products, and you will get tons of free products from sponsors!

Or you might offer instructional videos, such as how to potty train your puppy or how to get pet odors out of carpets. You might offer very specific educational information on certain breeds of lizards and how to care for them.

Drawing on your expertise and life experiences, documenting your trial-and-error discoveries, and passing on research you have performed can make you extremely successful.

This is because you are teaching people things they don't know. When they scour the Internet for answers or start preliminary research before they bring a new pet into their home—they will find you and you will will be there to help them.

However, there are also many successful blogs dedicated to simply warming people's hearts. These blogs share stories about the joys and trials of pet ownership.

Think of the book and movie *Marley and Me,* wherein the author documented his experience with a very rambunctious puppy. The book became a bestseller, and the movie grossed millions.

Just sharing your stories and photos will appeal to many readers who want to find someone to relate to. Pet lovers around the world will enjoy reading what you have to share.

There is no need to find something that is trending and then force yourself to fit into that little box. You can operate on a completely original idea and find great success. You never know what people will like until you try it.

Cramming yourself into a niche that you don't actually like will not bring the rewards that creating your own niche or writing in a niche that you enjoy will bring. Don't just do what is popular. Do what is you!

WRAP-UP

In this chapter, you have learned how to find courage and inspiration. You have also learned some answers to your biggest anxiety questions.

The basic message is this: You can do it! And once you do, you will be very happy with the results. A blog is extremely rewarding. You will find that your blog is a place to express yourself, make a difference in the world, and maybe make you some passive income.

Don't worry about not being good enough. You are good enough. What you don't know, you can learn. Many more people will love your voice than you realize.

Just be yourself and write about what you enjoy. Don't be afraid to share your thoughts with the world. You will gain an audience because you will stand out from the competition with the inherent uniqueness of your brand.

Plus, you will learn a lot and grow as a person. You will virtually meet many great people, many of whom will become great lifelong followers. All of these things make blogging an enriching and rewarding undertaking that anyone can accomplish.

Use the action steps at the end of this chapter to get you started with finding your courage and inspiration.

The next chapter will focus on finding your niche and appealing to followers. You will learn about your niche, how to title your blog, how to write to your demographic, and how to stand out from the competition. In addition, I provide the bare-bones basics of SEO, though I cover this more extensively in Chapters 3 and 6.

YOUR FIRST THREE ACTION STEPS

> *Listed are the steps I covered in this chapter. Use the action steps as a checklist as you proceed with creating your blog. Refer back in this chapter to gain more detail when you are ready for the tasks outlined below.*

STEP 1: GATHER COURAGE

Let go of fear, and let courage fill your soul. This blog is your baby. You don't need to be some expert or a professional writer to make it beautiful. Your knowledge and experience are already enough. The rest you can learn with this book.

STEP 2: SEEK INSPIRATION

Draw on your love of pets or your enthusiasm for pet care. Look to your experiences and stories. Consider the change you wish to make in the pet world. Your love of pets, your life experiences, and your passions are all valuable sources of inspiration that can get you far.

STEP 3: SET A CLEAR PURPOSE IN MIND

This step comes in handy as you move to the next chapter. You must determine what your blog will be about and what you want to achieve with it. That will drive everything you do in your blog, and it will also help you find a niche and a readership. Plus, having a purpose helps motivate you, so even when you feel like giving up, you keep going to reach that big goal in your mind.

2

FINDING YOUR NICHE AND APPEALING TO FOLLOWERS

If everybody is doing it one way, there's a good chance you can find your niche by going exactly in the opposite direction. — Sam Walton

When starting a blog, you need to establish a niche, or a purpose. Think of it as if you are etching out your own little part of the blogging world, a place where your followers and you feel comfortable.

Your niche needs to be something that you can write about with confidence. It needs to be something that enriches the lives of your followers, making them want to come back for more. Furthermore, it needs to be something that you enjoy writing about and your readers enjoy reading about.

After all, you won't want to stick to writing a blog on topics that you find boring, and your lack of enthusiasm will show to your followers.

Every blog needs a definitive purpose to drive its content and attract followers. The purpose needs to be reflected in your title and your overall content. This hardly means that you need to stick to writing about one specific brand of pet food, because you will rapidly run out of content that way.

It just means that your articles should reflect the purpose overall, such as a series of articles about home remedies for common pet maladies or a blog focused on providing pet product reviews.

This brings me to a very important point: Don't pigeonhole yourself! Picking a topic that is too narrow will consequently narrow down your readership. A blog about one type of turtle food is a good example of how you can pick a topic that is just too specific.

With your content and your title, you attract readers. If you pick a topic that is too small, you run out of things to write about and people lose interest as they realize they have reaped all of the information your blog has to offer.

Then, if you try to expand your topic, you find that you don't attract readers because your title and previous content makes them expect only one thing. Avoid being too specific. Leave some wiggle room to expand into new realms of content to appeal to more people.

However, you also don't want to pick a topic that is too broad. "All things pets" could be too broad, for instance. If you have too general or broad of a topic, your readers won't know what to expect. They will ask, "Will this blogger ever post anything relevant to me? I can't tell, so I'm going to move on to a more specific blog."

Make it clear that your blog is about dogs, or turtles, or pet product reviews. Show readers exactly what to expect and then deliver.

For instance, my blog, Center for Pet Loss Grief, has a specific theme: the grief that comes with losing a pet. It is reflected clearly in the title. People know what to expect when they read my blog, and they choose to come to my blog when they need support after losing a pet.

This topic is not too broad, but it encompasses a wide variety of points and subtopics, which make it an engaging resource to my readers. It appeals to a big demographic, as well, since many people go through the tragic loss of a pet in their lifetime. More on demographics later in this chapter.

The adage, "Write what you know," does have some truth to it. You don't want to write about something you have no idea about because you won't be able to offer as much information to your readers or engage yourself.

However, I don't think this is always true. Life is about learning and broadening your horizons. You can always do research and learn more about new topics that you can then share with your readers.

Make your blog a place where you learn and grow with your followers, creating a harmonious educational space that brings you and your readers together into a community.

Start with a topic that you know something about and want to write about; then expand it with research, interviews, and enlightening links to other articles.

The best way to find your niche is to draw from your own life experience, strengths, and interests. If you are an avid amphibian owner, you probably want to write about caring for amphibians. You already know a lot about the topic and have some personal stories to share with readers.

But you also have a lot that you can learn on the topic. Look at what you love about pets, what you want to share with the world, and what you feel you can comfortably write about. Chances are, you already have an idea of the topic you want to write about. Now it's time to determine how to present that topic in a palatable way that is neither too vague nor too specific.

If you are like me, you are an idea person. I am always full of dynamic ideas, and I sometimes find myself waking up at night and scrambling out of bed to jot some new idea down before it is lost in the haze of sleep. That is always a great quality, but sometimes you have to write your ideas down and then pare them down to find the one that fits a solid purpose.

If your mind is swirling with ideas for your blog, write them all down and sort them into categories based on the overall topic. Figure out the purpose of your blog and then only expand on the ideas that fit into that purpose.

Ideas that are too incongruent with your niche should probably get a separate blog of their own. It would be odd to start a blog on canine nutrition, only to throw in a series of articles about snake handling.

There is no reason why you can't have several blogs on different topics! But it is a mistake to jumble tons of different topics and ideas into a single blog. It appears disorganized and, again, too broad.

It all boils down to readership, the main reason you are blogging in the first place. You want to appeal to specific people and appear in the search engine list when people search for a certain topic that applies to their needs. Fitting into a good, solid niche that certain people find relevant will earn you more loyal followers.

FINDING YOUR PEOPLE

A major part (perhaps the main part) of deciding your niche and directing the content of your blog involves finding your demographic. Who are you writing to?

Obviously, you are writing a pet blog, so your audience will be comprised of pet owners. But you must go a little deeper than that.

Most pet blogs appeal to a large demographic. You can strip away demographic divisions such as age, gender, and income when you are writing about a general pet topic that many different people will find relevant.

A lot of the content you create will likely appeal to a general audience, so just write in a way you think pet owners would relate to. The kind of pet you are writing about and the purpose of the information you are sharing will just naturally attract the kinds of people who can relate.

I once read somewhere that all of your writing should be on a fifth-grade level. This may not be true for dense research articles, but in the case of a blog, I think it is quite applicable. If a ten-year-old can read and understand what you are talking about, then you can appeal to a wide demographic.

However, maybe your topic in itself appeals to a very particular demographic. A blog about apartment living with a big dog would only appeal to a specific category of people; a lot of people with different living circumstances or small dogs will not find your topic at all relevant.

Therefore, you must always write to this specific category of people. Focus your content on what they would care about. Use language that they can understand and relate to, and share stories about your experiences that they will likely identify with.

Always tailor your writing to your demographic.

- Are they going to be pet lovers looking for something lighthearted and cheerful?
- Are they going to be people suffering from serious pet-related issues, looking for help or grief support?
- Does the topic you are writing about in a particular post fit in with this demographic, or should it get a separate blog with a separate audience of its own?

Ask yourself, "Will this fit in with what my demographic is looking for?" Figure out what your target demographic wants and use that to drive your content.

Information-rich articles supported by scientific research will appeal to those seeking education on pet health or nutrition, step-by-step listicles with pictures will appeal to those looking for instructions, and lighthearted personal stories with a few pictures will appeal to those looking for heartwarming pet stories to brighten their day. Your content must align with your niche, and your niche must align with your target demographic.

You might consider tweaking a blog post to appeal more to your demographic if you see that you are getting little traffic or earning negative comments.

Often, you won't know what people like until you try something out and get feedback. Don't take negative feedback personally; use it constructively and grow from it.

Once, I was very hurt by a comment in which a woman complained that I did not offer much information in a post. Then I realized, "She is just expressing a need for more information. I can add more depth to my posts and thus appeal to more people."

By taking her comment as constructive criticism, I was able to formulate the writing style I use to this day. Blogging is a learning and growth experience for all of us!

You should read some pet blogs to see what they are doing. This can serve as inspiration for your own blog. Call it market research and look into what people want from pet blogs. However, keeping your own voice is essential. Your voice is what makes your blog uniquely yours. Don't just copy what others are doing. Stand out by doing your own thing.

You may find something is trending and you want to hop on the bandwagon. That is always a good short-term strategy which can really work to drive traffic.

However, in time, that topic will no longer be trending. Having a solid niche that will endure through time will ensure loyalty from your readers for years to come. Don't just do what everyone else is doing.

You can stand out and leave your impression on the blogosphere by creating something that will stay relevant.

For instance, writing about feeding your dog grain-free may be a great one-time post that fits in with the big trend on the Internet right now, but offering other content on doggie nutrition will endure long after that fad has passed and pet owners start seeking a different feeding regimen.

CHOOSING YOUR BLOG TITLE

Once you have decided on your niche, you must think of a title that accurately reflects your niche. The title of your blog is so important because it contains keywords relating to your topic, making it possible for people to find it when they Google something. Plus, people are going to click on your blog when they see that the title is relevant to them.

Too many details and unnecessary words in your title can make someone lose interest rapidly. The average attention span of a person racing through a long list of websites on a Google search is about three seconds. This is not much time for someone to process an excessively wordy title.

Short and sweet is the name of the game. Consider these two examples: "rorysblogaboutturtlesandotherthings.com" versus "rorysturtlesandmore.com." Which one of these titles would you be more inclined to click on?

In a copywriting course, you learn to condense long-winded sentences into a few snappy words that sum up the entire message in a neat little package with a bow on top. That's why ads have little sentence fragments that roll off the tongue easily, rather than sentences befitting a dissertation.

The elements of copywriting apply to your blog's title, since the title is essentially selling your blog in a few words. It can be helpful to write a complete, lengthy sentence expressing your blog's purpose. Then pare it down to the few words that really matter. Read them aloud in different ways until you find a pleasing combination that works.

Something fun is always attractive to readers. Say you are writing a dog food review blog. You could title it "feedingdogs.com" or "caninenutrition.com," but that's a bit boring. You will appeal to more people if you came up with something creative and cute, like "feedingfido.com" or "thedoggiebowl.com."

Once you have an idea, go back to the sentence you have pared down to a few words and see if you can replace any common or boring words with more interesting ones. A thesaurus is always a helpful reference.

Remember, pet owners love their pets. They want to read blogs that use fun, affectionate, enthusiastic language to reflect that love. Calling dogs "doggies"—or my favorite, "doggo"—is one way to express the fondness you share with your readers and for the canine species.

Return to your sentence one last time and see if you can replace a word with something a bit more affectionate, silly, or fun. For instance, in my travels I saw a business called "Fish and Phips," and they run a fascinating blog by the same name.

By using the slang word for amphibians, they managed to create a business name and blog title that is far more appealing to amphibian owners.

Plus, "Fish and Phips" rolls off the tongue a bit more pleasingly than the clunky and boring "Fish and Amphibians."

Alliteration and rhyming are both aesthetically and sonically appealing. Creating a title that uses one or both of these elements creates something that people can remember.

This is why you should read your title aloud several times. See if it clicks nicely with your brain, or if it seems awkward and stilted.

Of course, you may not want to use silly or fun words in a blog about a more serious topic. My pet grief support blog addresses a topic that carries deep gravity. I wouldn't want to make light of it, so my title uses serious words that relate directly to my topic.

It all boils down to the niche you are filling. If you are writing about a serious topic, there is still no reason to come up with a name that does not read nicely. You can find new words to replace ones that don't sound so good.

You can trim unnecessary "fat," so to speak, from long-winded titles, too. A serious topic still should not have a boring title.

If you own a business and wish your blog to center around it, then a logical title would be your business name. That way, when people look you up, they will locate your blog. Having your blog on your website (Glossary) is a great way to drive sales. I'll talk about that more in Chapter 8.

When you register your blog, you will have to put in your title (Chapter 3). Condense the title of your blog into all lowercase and follow it with ".com." Should your chosen title be taken, don't try changing it from ".com" to ".org" or ".net." If you do, your title is not unique and may be confused with the other blog site.

THE CRUCIALITY OF SEO

SEO, or search engine optimization, can be the bane of any new blogger's existence because it calls for using a lot of the same words, which can feel tedious. But in time, you will realize how essential it is to ranking higher in searches.

The more you use keywords (Glossary and Chapter 6) for your different articles and the more often you use them within each article, the more likely a search engine will pull up your page to the front when someone searches for a specific thing.

When you Google something, you probably just type in a few words. Then your Google search populates with related sites and you can easily retrieve the information you seek.

You probably don't even bother clicking past the first page, or even the first five or so sites on the list, because what you need is right there on top. That means that the sites on the top of the list get far more traffic than those that hide beyond the first page. You want to be on that first page!

The secret to getting to the top of all of those sites involves inputting the keywords someone is likely to enter in the search bar into your blog. Therefore, you must determine a set of keywords that relate to your blog and your content. You must do this for your page, your title, and each post that you create.

Come up with as many as you can to fit into the most possible searches. You could write a good number of blog posts about frog habitats. Each article would need one specific keyword about frogs, frog habitats, and so on.

Sometimes you may know the specific terms for something, while the average layman does not. A reader might Google "warm rock for lizards" when the technical term is "heating rock." So, you want to optimize your page to respond to common layman's requests, not just the technical name.

Otherwise, fewer people will discover your post on rock heaters. Therefore, do some keyword research and find out what trending keywords are. Great tools for this include Google Keyword Planner, Wordtracker, and Ubersuggest.

Another key part of learning about how to use SEO is researching your competitors. Search for keywords and visit the blogs that pop up on top. How are they different from your blog? Take note of the keywords they use, the way they structure their sites, and the way they use keywords in titles.

Visit their social media pages to glean some clues about how they market themselves and how consumers respond. While you don't want to copy anybody, you can certainly learn a few tips from the pros who already rank highly on search engines.

Research keywords and create a chart with your highest ranking, mid-ranking, and lower ranking keywords. Make sure you add both short-tailed keywords and long-tailed keywords (Glossary). Put this list aside for later.

Once you have your keywords, you need to enter them for your site. On your blog's host, you will have a place where you enter a description of your site. Input your keywords here. Also, if you can, work those keywords into your title.

When you create a post, you will need to enter a meta description. The meta description tells search engines how to present your page, or in other words, what keyword needs to be entered in the search engine in order to retrieve your page.

Always use your keyword, and make it very specific what your post is about. Google and other search engines will then know what to do with it. Don't be shy about telling search engines what to do.

SEO does not necessarily mean that you need to use the same words over and over in your blog post; that is a common misunderstanding that many new bloggers have, and you will get into trouble with the search engines. But do try to use them as much as possible. That way, the bots employed by big search engines will locate these words within your blog when someone types those same words into a search. Then, like magic, your site ranks on top and gets more traffic.

Ensuring that your metadata keyword matches the content of your post will also ensure that your site ranks highly because the search engine will find your site and display it based on the match between someone's search and your meta description.

You might add some additional related keywords that someone is likely to use in a search to your metadata, too, even if you don't use them in the blog post itself.

Once you have figured out your keywords and input them, you can use a variety of tools to ensure that your blog is optimized, or using your keywords in a suitable way. These tools will search your site and make sure that your keywords are used enough. They will also provide useful suggestions for how to improve titles and where to enter meta descriptive data.

Some are plug-ins that you can use from your blog, such as WordPress SEO by Yoast. This is my favorite because Yoast lets you know if you used your keyword appropriately, if your post is easy to read, and gives you suggestions on how to improve your article.

If you use Wix, there is a built-in SEO Optimizer. Others, such as Google Keyword Planner or Keyword Tool, allow you to search keywords and see how they rank.

I do most of my keyword research myself, but I also use Fiverr (Resources). I have hired various freelancers that have provided very useful lists when I am feeling pressed for time. These lists have been extremely useful and successful for me.

Finally, don't forget to use your keywords on your social media posts. That helps them rank higher in searches, while also communicating what your blog post is about to users. Using them as relevant hashtags (Glossary) can help you accomplish higher rankings on social media, as well. If you are posting ads, be sure to use keywords in them, as well.

SEO is a huge topic, and I can't cover it all in this book. Conducting your own research is essential to being a successful pet blogger with many loyal followers. This is a good introduction on how to use them in your blog. Also, see Chapters 3 and 6 for more extensive information on SEO.

POST REGULARLY

To stay relevant, you must post regularly. Every day may be a bit much to ask of any busy person, but set a schedule for weekly posts. Having a certain day that you publish a new post can appeal to people, since they know when to visit your blog for new content.

You will also find that posting on a certain day allows you to automate emails to people who have signed up for your blog's email list, notifying readers of new content when you post it.

Imagine visiting a blog and finding that the blogger has not posted anything for six months. How likely are you to follow this blog?

You will probably read one or two posts that apply to you and then move on. You assume that this blog is going defunct and nothing new will appear, so you don't bother following or revisiting. You don't want people to treat your blog like this.

Posting regularly helps people see that you are an active member of the little online community you have created, and so they want to join in.

Time moves fast on the Internet. Old posts rapidly get buried by newer posts. Have you ever found a great blog post, forgot to bookmark it, and then failed to ever find it again when you search for it because hundreds of new sites have leapt up higher in the search engine ranking?

This can happen to your blog before you know it. To stay at the top of your SEO ranking, you must keep posting.

Last but certainly not least, not posting regularly will cause a decline in followers, as readers realize you are not offering them anything new. To keep followers, you want to engage your readers with new content.

You also want to offer various ways for readers to follow you so that they know when you post something new. Posting links to new content to your social media feeds and sending emails to people who have signed up for your email list will accomplish this.

There are tools that enable you to automate these social media posts and emails within WordPress and other blogging software.

We all need a vacation, and sometimes unexpected things come up. If something happens and you can't post, notify your followers that you will be taking a brief hiatus but you will be returning.

Provide a date when they can expect new content. Even send everyone on your email list an email notification to ensure they know why they haven't heard from you in a while. That way, you don't lose followers who think you have simply stopped writing.

DARE TO BE DIFFERENT

I cannot stress it enough: The real key to getting followers is appealing to them. And the only way to appeal to people is to have your blog with your own unique spin on your theme.

There are other people in your niche; how do you stand out from them and get people to follow you? The answer is being bold and offering readers something different from what they can get from competitors.

You may even have an idea that allows you to create your own niche that no one has done before; it may not trend, but it is worthwhile to take a risk and try anyway.

You may have many followers who subscribe to other blogs in your niche. You can't expect to have exclusive loyalty with every person who follows your blog.

However, if you can offer readers something that stays with them even as they peruse other blogs of the same nature, you will give them something that makes them stick around and keep reading.

Do something bold and memorable. A certain adorable story, a powerful backstory in your "About Me" section (Chapter 4), an article with some rare information or impactful points that you don't see in your competitors' posts: these are all viable ways to win and maintain loyalty amongst your followers. Even just a really creative title will make you stand out from the competition (Chapter 5).

Be sure to stay true to yourself and you will stand out from competitors regardless, simply because every blogger is different.

If you are a humorous writer, add some humor and jokes to your blog. If you like to muse, ask a question and then invite your readers to chime in on the comments. If you are great at research or if you can offer interesting perspectives on issues, then do that as much as applicable in your blog.

Your readers will fall in love with your voice. They feel that they connect with you in some way. The little glimpses you offer them into your own mind generates a sense of fellowship and a bond that attracts and maintains followers. So be unique to give people a reason to want to read what you have to say.

Your blog is also a community. As you post your thoughts, people respond in comments. If you have guest bloggers or run the blog with other writers, you have even more people joining in the community. By actively engaging with your readers, you create kinship and a sense of personal connection that people like. This makes people feel more loyal to your blog.

You are already part of a community of other pet owners; putting yourself out there with a blog and engaging personally with your readers helps you draw upon those bonds that are already in place.

Dr. Robert Cialdini talks about commitment and consistency in his book *Influence: Science and Practice.* Once someone commits to a brand or cause, they generally stay consistent with it.

You can get people to commit to your blog by giving them things to love about your blog, things that the competitors don't offer in quite the same way, if at all. Unless you give followers a reason to ditch your blog, you will find that they stay loyal. Consistently deliver what you have to offer and you will find fans consistently enjoy your content.

The important thing is to give people something different with your own unique spin on your niche of choice. Then engage with them and build an online community. From there, you will build a loyal following and a robust email list that only grows.

WRAP-UP

You have learned about picking a niche. Your blog needs a definitive purpose. Draw from your inspiration and look to the changes you want to make in the pet world.

Don't pigeonhole yourself with a topic that is too narrow, but don't pick something so broad that your readers won't know what your blog is about.

You have learned how to tie up your purpose in a title that expresses what your blog is about. Your title says who you are. Pick a short and concise one that sums your purpose up neatly. A course in copywriting can be helpful.

Consider this a brief introduction to SEO for your site. Do some research on keywords using handy keyword tools so that you rank higher in searches. That will drive more traffic to your blog.

You don't want to be hiding on some back page of a Google search; your goal is to appear on the first page when your readers search for relevant keywords.

Posting regularly is key. Don't let your blog fall to the wayside. If you are going to be gone for a while, let your readers know.

Finally, find your unique voice. Stand out from the crowd. The only way to attract a readership is to offer them something the competition doesn't. You might fret that you have nothing to offer, but you do with your ideas. No one else has the same ideas as you.

Use the three action steps at the end of this chapter to help you find your niche, choose your name, and figure out your keywords. This will help you plan and organize your blog.

Now, read on to learn more about hosting. This next chapter will show you the secrets to finding a domain name and a place for your blog on the Internet. It really isn't as hard as it seems! I will show you how to use my favorite host and get your blog up and running in no time.

ACTION STEPS

Listed are the steps I covered in this chapter. Use the action steps as a checklist as you proceed with creating your blog. Refer back in this chapter to gain more detail when you are ready for the tasks outlined below.

STEP 1: FIND YOUR NICHE

Look into your heart and locate the one thing you are most passionate about in the pet world. That should be your niche.

Check out my book *Pet Jobs 101: How to Choose Your Dream Job and Jumpstart Your Business for ideas* for finding your niche.

On a piece of paper, jot down all of your ideas for blog posts. Narrow them down to a few that fit into the overarching purpose of your blog.

It is also helpful to write down your niche in clear language for future reference. Should you have lots of ideas that don't fit into one niche, you could consider opening more than one blog.

Based on your niche, also figure out what your audience, or demographic, will be. Use this to drive your content and your language. It should even drive your title and your chosen WordPress theme (Chapter 4).

STEP 2: CHOOSE YOUR NAME

On a piece of paper, write down the overall purpose of your blog in a long sentence, using as many words as you want.

Then start to trim unnecessary words until you're down to a nice, short title. Replace boring words with more interesting ones. Think of something snappy and cute. Read your title aloud to see if it sounds good.

STEP 3: FIGURE OUT YOUR KEYWORDS

You will do your SEO optimizing later in the blogging process, but now is a good time to figure out your SEO keywords.

That way, you can easily retrieve them as you write. You want to create a chart with highest ranking, middle ranking, and lowest ranking keywords.

PART II
SETTING UP YOUR BLOG

3

FINDING A HOME FOR YOUR BLOG

The magic thing about home is that it feels good to leave, and it feels even better to come back. — Wendy Wunder

You have drummed up your courage, tapped into your inspiration, conceived the topic of your blog, picked a great title, determined some keywords, and possibly even created some content. But what do you do with it? Well, now it's time to go public!

To launch your blog, you first must find a host. A host is essentially the home wherein your blog dwells on the Internet. Hosting servers are companies that keep your blog running and maintain your domain name for varying fees.

There are many, many hosts out there, but the best one, in my opinion, is SiteGround (Resources). With their amazing customer service, I have no complaints. Another popular one is BlueHost, though I did not have the best experiences with them.

You should avoid GoDaddy since you are an animal lover; the CEO is a trophy hunter who proudly displays his kills on the Internet.

Some people may think of hosting as the hard part. I can't promise you it will be easy because everyone has a different skill set when it comes to technology. But if you are adventurous, I urge you to try.

I will show you how to basically use SiteGround. If you want more detailed instructions, please go to their website and contact customer care, as they are extremely helpful. I will also briefly talk about two free server options, as well.

If you choose a different hosting service, it should be self-explanatory if you are computer savvy. If you are not so tech savvy, watch a YouTube tutorial on how to use the service. You will be amazed at the number of instructional posts you can find on YouTube.

STEP 1: GET READY FOR SITEGROUND

Are you ready to take the plunge into your first blog? Okay, here we go!

Visit SiteGround and pick a plan. Currently, there are three plans.

The first (and cheapest) is called StartUp. It offers you one site, ten gigabytes of storage, and ten thousand monthly visits. It comes with all of the features you need for a basic blog, including: free SSL certificates, unmetered traffic, daily backup, and 24/7 support.

The thirty-day money back guarantee is also great, in case you don't like SiteGround and want to move hosts. This plan might be a great option if you are intending on starting only one blog. You can always start with this and then upgrade later on if you need more storage, more visits, or more sites.

However, I wanted a little more wiggle room to grow as a blogger, plus I have three websites, so I went with the middle option.

This is called GrowBig, and it is tailored to those who want to grow on the web. It offers multiple websites, twenty thousand visits per month, and twenty gigabytes of storage.

This should be more than enough for your needs as a blogger starting out. You will get the room to grow that you need, and you will also have plenty of visits and storage. As you get started, you won't have that many visits.

Don't get discouraged about this, as that will change if you put in the work!, and twenty thousand is more than enough when you are starting out. Again, you can always upgrade if you need.

The main thing I like about this middle plan is that it boasts premium features for just a few dollars more than the StartUp plan.

Premium features include site transfer, which is great if you already have a site on a different server. You get priority technical support, so your emails will be answered first. There is SuperCacher, which makes your site run faster. And you get free backup restores. That is a great deal and makes the few dollars extra worth it!

There is still another tier. GoGeek is "for the real web geeks." This is the one for you if you are looking to start several sites with advanced features. You get thirty gigabytes of storage, a hundred thousand monthly visits, and essential, premium, *and* "geeky advanced" features.

What are these "geeky advanced" features? You get fewer accounts on the server, which can make your sites run and load faster. You get WordPress and Joomla! staging; in other words, you get dummy sites where you can test out new features before you actually publish them into your real site.

You also get PCI-compliant servers, which basically means that you can safely accept payments from users of your site as a merchant. You get a one-click git repo creation, or basically a storage cache of files that change over time called a "repository."

Finally, you get free backups. All of these features are necessary to host a merchant site or a constantly evolving site, but they are not so necessary for the average blogger. You may not need this plan, depending on your niche.

I am not going to talk about fees in this book, simply because fees change and you may find different rates in the future. However, these plans go up by a few dollars for each tier.

You essentially get what you pay for. I think the lowest tier, or the cheapest plan, is sufficient; the middle plan is ideal; and the top one is probably more than you need.

STEP 2: REGISTER YOUR DOMAIN

Once you pick your plan, click or tap on the big "Order Now" button. This takes you to a page asking you to register your domain. You can choose "register a new domain" if you don't already have a blog. Otherwise, click "I already have a domain." Then enter your domain name in the bar underneath your selection.

Click "Proceed" and you are taken to a page that asks you to review and complete your submission. This is where you get to enter your email, your chosen password, your address, and your payment information.

You also get to select the time duration in which you will use the service. I just left it at "twelve months," the default option.

You can renew within a year easily. SiteGround will automatically notify you as soon as your expiration date draws near.

Now, let's say you enter your domain name, and the site says that this name is not available for registration. In Chapter 2, I discussed tweaking your domain name. If someone already has your domain name registered, you can add or take away little words. But I don't suggest changing the .com to .org or .net or .info, as this is not considered a unique domain name.

Your blog name is part of who you are, and it speaks to your readers, so having a name too similar to another site is a bad idea. It is best to find something unique. Someone can easily get confused if your site is funwithfido.net and someone else already has funwithfido.com.

STEP 3: TRANSFER A DOMAIN

In a different direction, if you already have a domain name, you need to transfer it. SiteGround handles the transfer so you don't have to communicate with your old host and your new one at the same time. It is very easy. Simply go to your user area and tap the green "Get" button next to "Domain Transfer."

Next, you're going to see a "Product Information" box, where you can type your domain name in the box. The system will automatically detect and notify you of the status of your domain and whether or not you can transfer it.

The most common issue you may find here is that your domain is locked in its server. You have to go into your old host and unlock the domain from your control panel.

To find out how to do this, look at tutorials for unlocking within your specific host server. Usually, it's pretty easy and straightforward.

Your domain also has to be active, meaning that it is published and running on the old host. It has to have been published and active for more than sixty days, and it can't be less than fifteen days from expiring on your old server.

Furthermore, you must obtain your authorization code, or your EPP code, from your old server in order to prove ownership and authorize the transfer. You can find your EPP by going into your old server and looking it up.

If you have met all of the requirements, then the transfer will be straightforward. SiteGround will tell you so and load a box where you enter your EPP code. Once you enter the code, SiteGround will begin the transfer.

Sit back and enjoy some tea while you wait. You might expect an email from your old server, asking for you to confirm the transfer. Be sure to confirm it or the transfer won't take place.

SiteGround will send you an email welcoming you when the transfer is completed. You're in!

STEP 4: FILL IN YOUR WHOIS INFORMATION

WHOIS (Glossary) is the information about you and how to contact you. You must keep it accurate and up to date for your site to work properly. SiteGround may suspect your site if your information falls out of date.

First, go to your user area. From here, go to the domain you want to edit (This is very easy if you have only one domain.) and click "Manage" to the right. A page full of your information then pops up. Edit the information that needs to be updated.

You can also ask your former server to send that information through your EPP code if you have transferred a domain.

Now that you have done that, you should look into the SiteGround privacy tool. For most sites on SiteGround, you have to order this additionally. This tool masks all of your information and enters SiteGround's information instead so that hackers won't be able to retrieve your address or email. Your email won't get harvested and added to millions of spam lists.

To add this privacy tool, go to your user area again, find your domain, and click on "Add ID Protect," which is on your far right.

STEP 5: SET UP YOUR SITE

Now, here's the fun part. You will be building your site using WordPress, which I cover in more detail in the next chapter. Then you must upload it to SiteGround using a handy wizard within the server.

Enter your user area. A wizard will pop up, inviting you to start a new website, transfer a website, or "Don't need help now." Click on starting a new website if you haven't started your own yet.

Then you will see a list of website-building software. You can select any one you would like, but I use and recommend WordPress. It should be your first option. Joomla! is another popular one.

Select the software you want and hit "Confirm" at the bottom. It will start setting up your new software. Now you can use it right away. You can also select "I do not want to set up now. Remind me next time I log in."

If you select that option, SiteGround will pause the setup and save it for up to thirty days. You can start the setup whenever you are ready by simply logging in.

If this doesn't work for you for some reason, you can contact SiteGround through their support. Request help downloading the software of your choice. You will encounter a list of common support topics. Select "Install WordPress" or any other option that applies to you.

The support team will happily assist you. I have had excellent experiences using the SiteGround support, which is why I favor it as a host server over others.

Now, if you have already created a website, don't select "Start a new website." Click on "Transfer a website" instead. Then hit "Confirm." The SiteGround support team will then handle the transfer for you so you don't have to build a whole new site.

The best part of this is that you can order a site transfer for a small fee if you have the StartUp plan, but you get one free transfer with your GrowBig plan.

The team can transfer every part of your old website if you were operating it on cPanel (see Glossary), from email accounts to configurations. Otherwise, the team can only copy over most elements of your old site, minus your email accounts and configurations.

It is also possible to transfer your site manually, though it is more difficult and time-consuming. You need to use a file transfer protocol between your previous host and SiteGround. Then you need to move your database over.

Finally, you need to reconfigure your whole application. I think it is far better to just let SiteGround do all of that for you!

STEP 6: CREATE EMAIL ACCOUNTS

For numerous reasons, you don't want your personal email receiving all correspondence from your blog. First, it looks more professional to have a contact email that uses your blog's name, such as susan@susanspetblog.com.

Second, you can stop email harvesting and hacking with this extra security measure, and you can block spam using SiteGround's built-in spam filter. Finally, you can keep everything organized nicely.

Your SiteGround plan (regardless of which one you choose) comes with unlimited free email accounts. The different plans do put limits on how much space you get with your email account, however. Be mindful of that, and be sure to clean out old emails to conserve space.

Visit your user area. Click on "My Accounts" and then "Go to cPanel" and "Mail section." There, you should find an email icon and the name "Email Accounts." Click on that. Some text fields should pop up, asking for your email name, your password, and your chosen mailbox quota.

The mailbox quota is just how much space you want to dedicate to your email storage. The quota can't exceed the space you are allotted with your plan. StartUp is 2000 MB, GrowBig is 4000 MB, and GoGeek is 6000 MB. To simplify things, I just specified the limit for my plan, 4000 MB, and left it at that.

After you have filled everything in, hit "Create Accounts." Your email account is instantly generated. Now you can get correspondence through your blog!

It is critical to install the email to your phone and computer so that you can stay on top of your emails. Or you can direct your business email to your personal email using the prompts in SiteGround.

If you want to install the email to your phone and computer, enter your email account on your phone and select "Add Account." Then configure the account using the requested information.

On your computer, you can do the same and configure your account with your desktop email application. That way, you can get notified of emails whenever and wherever you are away from your desk.

STEP 7: SET UP YOUR SSL CERTIFICATE

Your SSL certificate is your ticket to safety on the Internet. It is a bit of data that locks your site to an https encryption.

This keeps your site secure and enables people to navigate your site without their browsers blocking it due to security risks. A bad SSL configuration will make most browsers block your site, simply because your site has "holes" that allows viruses to infect others and hackers to retrieve information.

First, go to your user area and click on "cPanel." Hit the "Security" tab and then "Let's Encrypt." This brings up a list of your domains on SiteGround. Select the one you are working with and hit the "Install" button at the very bottom of the page. This installs encryption and keeps your site safe.

It also automatically renews every three months, so you don't have to remember to do so yourself. The best part is that it is free.

Wildcard is another encryption solution to your site. It is ideal if you have subdomains. Or you can try Extended Validation SSL if you are running a site that needs top-level encryption for processing cards and storing user information. Both of these are paid.

You can also enter SSL certificates yourself if you obtain them through other means. Go to "cPanel" and then select "Security" and find the tab with "SSL/TLS Manager." You will find a variety of settings here.

For further security, you need to configure your SSL certificate to work on every part of your site. Once again, go to your user area and select "cPanel." Then hit "Let's Encrypt" and peruse the "Action" dropdown menu. Tap on "HTTPS Settings." A new window pops up, asking if you want to allow redirections and other such things. Be sure to toggle each option on.

You can also install the SG Optimizer plug-in within WordPress. This accomplishes the same thing within your site. It is all easy enough, even if you don't understand all of the computer jargon.

STEP 8: LEARN THE SITEGROUND TOOLS

The tools within SiteGround help you master your site and offer a wide range of useful features. Getting to know them is imperative to operating your site. Fortunately, most of the tools are very intuitive. SiteGround offers tutorials on each one.

Support through SiteGround is also very helpful in all situations. We all know how fickle technology and software can be. You are likely to run into some sort of problem. Support is always available, 24/7/365, and they truly care. You can get answers to your questions and help solving issues within your site very quickly.

FREE OPTIONS

If you are not interested in paying for your domain, you can explore certain free options. These options offer you a basic website and a domain name that combines your blog's name with the server's name.

For instance, your free domain would be something like wendysblog.wix.com. This does not look as professional or as polished as having your own domain, but if you want to save money, it is a great option.

Probably the best free host would be Wix. Visit wix.com and create an account. Start a site and design it using the Wix in-site tools. Once your site is completed to your liking, you can publish it and enter your domain name. For a fee, you can upgrade to your own domain name, as well.

Other free options include weebly.com and webs.com. These sites work just like Wix. They have fewer design options in the site, however.

CONGRATULATIONS!

Believe it or not, you are now the official owner of a real blog. You are no longer fantasizing about starting a blog someday; you have actually started one! With your own site, you have taken the second huge step toward success as a pet blogger.

It can only get better from here. You have done the first hard part, navigating the technical part of launching a website. Now you have just one more technical part, where you create your blog on WordPress, and then you are ready to launch your blog.

After the next step, you will have an operational blog on the Internet, and you can start creating your online community and posting content from your heart. You did it!

I think some congratulations are in order. Take yourself out and celebrate! You are now on your way to becoming a blogger!

WRAP-UP

You have learned all about starting up on SiteGround. You have learned how to pick a plan, register your domain, transfer your site, start your site with WordPress, verify encryption, and create email accounts.

It is all straightforward, even if you are not a computer whiz, because SiteGround automates everything for you, and their customer service is excellent.

With your site up and running, it is time to create your actual content. You will do this using WordPress, or any other software of your choice. Because WordPress is the most common and the most popular (for good reason), I will only cover using WordPress in the following chapter.

If you pick a different software, look up tutorials on how to use it. SiteGround offers you the freedom to download different software for this purpose.

It is time to pat yourself on the back. Having completed these steps, you officially own your very own blog. You have etched out your little personal space in the blogosphere, and you have taken one more step than most people, who only dream of starting a blog but never take the initiative to actually start one.

You may have noticed this chapter consisted of action steps, but I have still outlined the steps for you to use as a checklist to get your site up and running without missing anything.

The fun part has just begun! Are you ready to create the content that makes your blog its own beautiful creation? Then read on!

ACTION STEPS

Listed are the steps I covered in this chapter. Use the action steps as a checklist as you proceed with creating your blog. Refer back in this chapter to gain more detail when you are ready for the tasks outlined below.

Step 1: Sign Up With Siteground (or another host)

Step 2: Register Your Domain

Step 3: Fill in WHOIS Information

Step 4: Set Up Your Site With Wordpress (or another platform)

Step 5: Create Your Email Accounts

Step 6: Set Up Your SSL Certificate

Step 7: Learn the SiteGround Tools

4

WORDPRESS BOOTCAMP

Your limitation—it's only your imagination. — Anonymous

In the last chapter, you learned about setting up your site with SiteGround. But now you need to actually create your site. You will do this using the WordPress software application within SiteGround.

Here's a little boot camp to get you up and running with WordPress. Keep in mind, I couldn't possibly cover all the aspects of using WordPress in this book, but I will point you in the right direction to get further help.

SET UP WORDPRESS

To get WordPress, access your user area on your SiteGround account and find your accounts. Locate the domain you are customizing with WordPress. Hit the "Manage Account" button on the far right next to your domain name. Now you'll see a few tabs on top. Select the orange one that says, "Go to cPanel."

A pop-up will appear asking if you're sure. Select "Access cPanel Securely." A page appears with a lot of options. At the bottom, there should be a section called "Autoinstallers." You'll see the WordPress icon here. Click on that.

Another pop-up will appear. At the bottom left-hand corner, there is a button that says, "Install Now." Select that. Now you come to a software setup page. On the right-hand side, there is a dropdown menu. Select the "HTTP" option with your mouse and then enter your domain name in the blank. If you have your SSL certificate set up, select the "HTTPS" option.

You will also see a blank for "In Directory." Leave this part blank.

Now, on this same exact page, you'll see a place asking for your site name and your site description. This is where that handy SEO introduction in Chapter 2 comes into play.

You should already have your title picked out and your site description. Enter them in the appropriate slots.

Don't just enter something like "my site" in the title slot. Enter your actual blog name, as this will recall your blog in searches. Under description, use tons of keywords as you fill out a sentence that perfectly describes your blog's purpose.

Spare no details. A long description that hits lots of keywords is better than something short that maybe hits one possible keyword.

Finally, enter your username and your password. You can use your personal email or your SiteGround email. I use my Site-Ground email for this part. Pick a strong password and write it down. You will need it every time you access WordPress to write a post. Choose your language from the dropdown menu. Hit "Complete."

SiteGround should generate a success page. It will say, "Congratulations, the software was installed successfully." This page has a key piece of information: your site URL. It will be your domain name plus "/wp-admin/." Definitely save this URL!

Now copy and paste this URL into your browser. It will take you to a WordPress page where you can enter your username and password. Log in, and you're ready to start creating your masterpiece.

GET FAMILIAR WITH WORDPRESS

WordPress is relatively easy to use. Once you become familiar with it, you will have very few problems with it. However, it involves a learning curve. Before you even start writing posts, you should take some time to play around with WordPress and find out how to use it.

When you first enter your WordPress, you will be met by a stark white page. On the right-hand side, you will see a search bar, a section for posts, and a section for comments. On the left-hand side, you will see a blank post. "Welcome to WordPress. This is your first post. Edit or delete it, then start writing!"

Start by visiting your dashboard. This is where you control every part of your blog. Get familiar with the buttons and where they go. You'll see a list of options on the left of your page, posts, media, pages, comments, and appearance.

ADD AVADA THEME

Yay! This is where you get to find yourself and express yourself through your blog. I found customizing my site's appearance to be my favorite part of the whole process. It is super fun.

I love the Avada theme. Super easy. It is the best-selling WordPress theme because it makes everything easy for the user. You don't need to learn how to code, as Avada does it for you. It generates a powerful and customizable theme that allows you to design your site as you see fit.

I'm going to talk about Avada here, but if you want to install your own theme, you can shop for themes on WordPress. With over six thousand themes on WordPress, you are sure to find something you like. Many are free, though some cost money.

To get them, go to "Appearance" on your dashboard and then click on "Add New" and click on themes. You can hover your mouse over the theme you like to see two buttons, "Preview" and "Install." Preview everything to ensure you like it.

Remember, you can customize most things within a theme, such as your colors or your title fonts. The overall layout will primarily stay the same based on the theme. When you find a theme you love, click on the "Install" button.

HOW TO INSTALL AVADA

You can install Avada from within your WordPress dashboard. I will cover how you can get started, but I recommend the website Avadaphile.com, where you can find helpful and detailed tutorials.

First, you must get Avada. There is a beginner package that you can download. Be sure to save the downloaded files into your "Downloads" or somewhere else so that it is easy to find. You'll need to be able to retrieve the downloaded files for your WordPress upload.

Second, go to "Appearance." Click on "Add New" and then the "Upload Theme" button. Click on "Choose File." Find your theme file and click on it. It will then upload.

If you are uploading the full package, you first have to right click on the file in your computer and unzip it. It will display several files. Click on the second one in the list when you go to upload it through WordPress.

Now go back to your themes page on your WordPress dashboard. Find the theme and click "Activate." This part is essential or your theme won't run!

Once you activate it, you will be redirected to a welcome page. You can install all of the necessary plug-ins from within Avada and begin customizing your site from here.

Some people get an error. This is because your host has placed a limit on the files you can upload and won't accept your theme. That's when you have to use FTP to upload Avada to WordPress. Let's go over that.

You should use a service like FileZilla for this. Log in to your server installation. Now unzip your Avada file and use the second one to upload it to the *wp-content* > *themes* folder on the server.

That's it! All you have to do is go into your WordPress themes and click the "Activate" button for the Avada theme. It should already be sitting there in your themes, waiting to be activated. If it isn't, try refreshing the page.

A FEW TIPS FOR YOUR SITE'S APPEARANCE

Strive to make your site simple and clean. No one is going to have the patience to read a convoluted blog with tons of links everywhere and no clear organization.

Using Avada, display all of your pages in a menu bar, organize your content into neat individual containers, and provide everything in a layout that trains the eye on one thing at a time.

Colors should not be distracting, and you should not pick font colors that are hard to read against the background. Your pictures should not take away from the fonts, either.

Another thing that is crucial is making your site responsive. With more and more people using their phones to search the Internet every day, you want your blog to be adaptable to mobile viewing. People will lose interest in your site if they can't load it on any device. Simple and responsive themes are critical in this era.

Furthermore, your blog should be compatible with different browsers, or at least the main ones (Google Chrome, Firefox, Internet Explorer, and Safari). Some themes display perfectly on Firefox but break on Chrome. Therefore, you lose every single person who uses Chrome, which represents a significant number of potential followers.

Most themes will say that they have been tested on different browsers, but you can also run the theme yourself by installing it and then checking out your domain from different browsers. A theme that runs smoothly and quickly on each browser is ideal.

Make sure your blog's appearance is congruent with your blog's purpose. A fun blog about how to care for a dog would feature lighthearted images of dogs, bright colors, and fun language.

A blog about pet grief would be more serious, perhaps with blue or gray colors. It would be odd to have a sad theme and serious language in a blog that is supposed to make people feel happy, or vice versa.

Really think about your niche and your demographic to find the best theme. Realize that you can customize colors and fonts and language, but the overall layout will stay the same.

Visit Pinterest and type in your keywords. See what comes up. This can give you some great ideas for how to customize your blog once you register it. You can also visit pixabay.com for free images that appear professional and high quality (Resources).

USING AVADA

Once you have activated Avada, you can enter it to build your site. You can easily create pages, insert headings, and add pictures and portfolios.

You can also avoid using extra WordPress plug-ins, which can majorly slow down your site, by using the ones inside the theme. Furthermore, there are free demos that show you how to use the theme, or you can go to Avadaphile.com (Resources) for excellent tutorials.

CREATE ESSENTIAL PAGES

Posts are different from pages. Posts are your blog articles, and a page is a separate part of your blog. You will want to create pages for different things within the blog. Here are a few pages you must have:

- Author bio
- Contact form
- Blog
- Products or services, if applicable
- Information page about a cause you are supporting, if applicable.

STEPS TO CREATE A PAGE ON YOUR BLOG:

Step 1: Go to the "Pages" tab in WordPress and click "Add New."

Step 2: Title your page in the "Title" field on top.

This is not where you have to get fancy. You can make the title of the page clear and concise. "Contact Me" for a contact page, "About Me" for an author bio page, and so on is sufficient.

Once you title the page, the permalink will appear, generated by the title you entered. You can always edit this from your editor if you need.

Usually, you can just leave this alone. You would only want to edit it if you wanted to make it more keyword-rich or specific.

Step 3: Change the parent settings and template from your "Page Attributes" box.

This is where you set up everything that governs how your page looks.

Page templates help you set up your pages as you want them. You can adjust width to affect the display. You should still find plenty that are both responsive and possible to use on many different browsers.

Parent settings help you create a "Side Navigation" page. This allows you to put a lot of content on one page. It is essential for online stores, product reviews, and blog pages.

All you have to do is go to your "Page Attributes" box and select "Side Navigation" page under templates. Add all of your pages to it.

They will be set up alphabetically in the side menu bar, but you can reorder them by inserting a new order in the "Order" field. Then select if the sidebar will be on the right or left. Publish each page and you are done!

Step 4: Add content to your page.

In the editor part of the page, you can enter images and text. Design the page you want. Use the settings on the right side to change fonts, sizes, colors, and layout.

You can even upload images to rest behind your text. Fusion Builder using the Avada theme helps you add different things you may need to your page, as well.

Containers are a convenient way to organize things on your blog. If you are writing a column, don't just make columns in your editor. Use a column container from Avada.

Go to "Builder Containers" and pick one appropriate for your layout on a particular part of your page. Then customize the settings to make it look just the way you want.

When you are finished with your page design, be sure to click the blue "Publish" button on the top of the page. This makes your page public. But it may or may not add the page to your navigation menu.

You must ensure the page is added to this menu to make it easy for site visitors to find it. Go to your home page and ensure that your page is there. If it isn't, a second step is necessary.

Click on "Appearance" on your left menu bar, and then click on "Menus." Your menu should be there by default. If you don't see one, you will have to add one. You can select a menu style from here.

Next to this on your left sidebar, you will see a "Pages" list. Click the box beside the pages you want on your menu. Ideally, all of your pages should be on your menu, unless there's a page you haven't finished creating yet. Then hit the blue "Save Menu" button on the bottom right-hand side and you are done!

To make the blog a cohesive whole that users can easily navigate, I recommend adding as many internal links (Glossary) as you can. That way, a person doesn't have to scour your site to find something you are talking about. They can simply click on your easy-to-read links and go directly to the desired content.

For example: Say you reference a previous blog entry in a post. Don't make a reader go through all of your previous posts to find the entry. Instead, link to it.

Another example for an internal link is when you invite people to contact you in a post. Don't make them skip over to your "Contact Me" page. Offer a link to your "Contact Me" page or a clickable button that says, "Contact Me!" that leads them to the contact page or pulls up a contact form.

To internal link, all you have to do is highlight the text you want to turn into a link with your mouse and then hit the link button at the top of your editor. The link button looks like two chain links hooked together.

A small window will open up asking for the link. Copy and paste the link. This could be a link to an outside webpage or to one of your pages. Just copy and paste the permalink from your other page here if you are linking within your site.

Buttons are great to add. They are clear and grab readers' attention. Plus, they look attractive. Avada has a variety of buttons you can choose from to direct readers where they may want to go.

Large, colorful buttons that clearly say what you want the reader to do are great. "Click to Follow Me on Social Media!" is an example.

Step 5: Set Your Theme Fusion settings.

In your "Fusion Page Options" box, you will see various settings. Use these to customize your page. Theme Fusion is where the magic happens. You can adjust SEO, responsiveness, your logo, your footer and header, your typography, your background, etc. These settings are all located in logical tabs so that you can easily locate them. Be sure to mess with these settings to make your page awesome!

You can also use these settings to add the plug-ins that you would normally get through WordPress. For instance, there is a "WooCommerce" plug-in that lets you set up an online store. There is a portfolio option to display your work, such as pet photography or pictures of your grooming.

ABOUT THE AUTHOR

Using the instructions above, create a page dedicated solely to you. Call this page something like "Meet the Author" or "About Me." This page is going to be your autobiography.

It should show the world who you are with a few sentences and a picture or two. If you are on a team of writers, you might consider a page for each contributor, or a page featuring a list of the contributors and their names, short bios, and pictures. Everyone who writes on this blog needs a bio.

The reason for this is simple. Since your blog is basically selling your voice and your opinions, you want to show readers who you are. You can connect with readers on a more personal level by featuring a picture of your face and a bio highlighting who you are. Prove to them that you are a real person.

For the photo, be sure to include one that is both flattering and appropriate. A picture of your face, or a picture of you with your pets, is ideal here.

The picture needs to show your face clearly. Don't hide it behind hair, hats, sunglasses, or even your pet. Gaze directly at the camera with a warm, inviting smile. Be sure to have lighting behind you, or be in a well-lit area, to make the picture clear.

Don't stand before a cluttered background, such as a busy intersection or a wall painted violent orange, as the background can distract viewers from what is important, your face.

A full body shot is probably not necessary here. Focus on above the shoulders. However, if you want to upload a picture of your full body while you are playing with your pets toward the bottom of your page, that is fine.

Try to feature your pet in the photo for obvious reasons. You might be holding her or standing next to her at a dog show. You might be engaged in an activity with her. Say you are writing a blog on agility for dogs.

A logical good picture would be one of you with your agility dog holding a trophy or one of you with your dog on an agility course.

On the other hand, if you are writing a blog about spiders, you might want to pose with your tarantula and a big smile. Make the photo express who you are and what your blog is about.

Since you are running a pet blog, you should focus a lot on your experience with pets and the pets you own in your bio. Include some pictures of them. If you run a business, or used to run a pet business, be sure to mention that.

Your goal is to establish yourself as an authority on the topic you are writing about. Your experience and your love for pets will prove that you know what you're talking about.

No one is going to read a blog about fish from some guy who has never owned fish; however, they will eagerly pay rapt attention to a blog written by an aquarium owner or someone who has kept saltwater fish for fifteen years.

Think of something else unique about yourself. If you lived in Paris for five years, that is maybe worth mentioning. Mention some of your hobbies and your major accomplishments. While the main focus of your bio should be on your relevant experience with pets and your love for them, you can veer off that topic to give people a more well-rounded glimpse of who you are.

People tend to connect on similarities. Therefore, you want to find things in common with your readers. You will attract and maintain followers based on these common points of interest. Mentioning things you are into or have done can make people identify with you more readily.

CASE STUDY

I have the pleasure of knowing an excellent resource and expert on spiders, Amanda. Amanda was an entomology major who specialized in identifying spiders and advocating for their preservation in ecosystems.

She is a huge contributor on a local Facebook site, where people post photos of spiders they find in their homes to learn what species the spiders are and whether or not they are venomous.

When Amanda started a blog on spiders, she completely omitted a bio. I advised her to create one, so she wrote a sentence about her age and her love of spiders. "That's good," I told her, "but what about your degree? What about all of your experience with identifying spiders and your conservation work?"

Amanda then constructed a wonderful bio, in which she discussed her authority on the subject. She established that she was an expert that people could trust based on her educational background and many years of experience working with spiders.

That bio helped readers trust her words, and it made people want to follow her for accurate information on spiders and their care.

ADD YOUR CONTENT

Go to your dashboard. Click on "Posts" and then select "Add New." A blank post page appears, where you can enter your content. This page is called the "editor" hereafter.

Now, bad things happen all of the time. I'm talking about slow Internet, hard drive crashes, and the like. That's why I like to create my blog posts in a Microsoft Word document that is automatically set to upload to OneDrive.

That way, I can work offline anywhere and my work is backed up when I'm online to protect against computer malfunctions, the bane of any writer. I can also sync Word across many devices so that I can add ideas to my post when I'm on the go or on a different computer. Then, I copy and paste these posts into my WordPress "Add New."

When you make a post, you must always title it. Your title can be long or short, but it needs to state your point. Have your main keyword in it. The top of the editor will feature a bar that says, "Title." Type your title here.

On the right column, scroll down to "Featured Image." This is the thumbnail that goes with your blog post. It will display on your blog and on searches.

You want to use at least one image per blog; the more the merrier! You should always select a relevant featured image, as well. Stock images work wonders, so familiarize yourself with "Librestock," "Pixabay," and other stock image sites that offer free high-quality images (Resources).

Next, scroll down to "Yoast SEO," which I recommended installing in Chapter 2. Fill in your "Focus Keyword" and "Snippet Preview." Your SEO title should contain the title of your post, which includes the keyword and your name and title.

HERE IS AN EXAMPLE OF MINE:

How to Start a Pet Blog | Wendy Van de Poll, Author, Writing Coach

Next, check your slug, which is your post title with dashes: *how-to-start-a-pet-blog*. WordPress will automate this for you based on your article's name, just double-check to see that everything matches up.

Your last step is customizing your "Meta Description." This box must be filled out if you want to rate well on Google. It contains a brief description about your article. You don't get that many words, so make sure you use your keywords and a blurb that entices your reader.

When you are finished writing, set your categories and tags. Go ahead and hit "Publish" at the top of the editor. Once published, you'll be taken to your "Posts" page where you can see your post. Here, you can edit categories and tags.

Keep in mind these are the basics to setting up your first blog. There are many other options you can enhance, but that would take an entire book on the subject. My goal is to get you started right away with the basic information you need. It will be up to you to go further with learning about SEO, etc.

CATEGORIES VERSUS TAGS

With your first post written, you now must sort it into a category and tag it. This part allows for SEO optimization, which makes your site more discoverable by search engines.

The category is the basic and broad grouping that your posts fits into. If you are writing about grooming a dog, you can put it into the category "pets." WordPress has a list of common categories that you must select from a dropdown menu.

You want to pick one or two categories that you generally write in. Sort posts into these categories. Don't have thirty possible categories for your blog and only have one post in each.

Each post should fit into only one category. A good idea is to start with an umbrella category that applies to your niche. Pets or dogs are good ones, for instance.

Now that you have your category, sort your posts into subcategories under that. If you have a lot of posts dedicated to "grooming" and a lot dedicated to "feeding," these could be your subcategories. Some people choose to forego subcategories and simply add tags, however. It is up to you.

Tags use specific details from your post and convert them into keywords. You want to use as many tags as possible. If you are writing about dog grooming, you want to add tags like dog shampoo, canine shampoo, shampoo safe for pets, pet shampoo, and bathing dogs.

These are just examples, but they illustrate how you should identify and list as many possible tags as you can think of. That way, search engines locate your site more often as people enter different search terms.

Everybody is different, and they will enter different terms, but some are more common than others. That's why researching keywords is critical.

SEO THE HECK OUT OF EACH PAGE AND POST

As you already know, SEO is your leg up as a blogger. Not using or understanding SEO can be the death of a blog because you're not able to place your blog in front of people who will read it. You must use SEO in every part of your blog to rank higher in searches and reach more people.

When you create a page, make sure its slug is the primary keyword. Also, be sure to use lots of keywords in your meta description, including the primary.

Whenever you create a post, be sure to add tons of tags. Also, use specify common keywords that relate to your post's topic and repeat them throughout the post, as well as in titles. This will make your post appear in searches.

As more people visit particular posts, they will also feel inclined to check out the rest of your blog and possibly sign up for your email list. I will cover that more in Chapters 7 and 8.

For now, think of every visitor as a potential lead or customer, and strategize how to get them to come back. I will show you how later, but as long as you have this mentality, you will hopefully be on your way to making money with your blog.

Don't let SEO blind you. Some bloggers make their blogs all about SEO and forget to focus on the number one priority: the readers. SEO is important, but if using keywords makes your blog read in a funky way that isn't appealing, then don't use it.

You want your blog to read smoothly. You want it to be a good experience for your readers. Cater to them more than the SEO-feeding search bots.

A balance of SEO and great language written to your readers is an ideal way to keep a popular, high-ranking blog. The plug-in "Yoast" is an excellent tool to keep your SEO in line.

WRAP-UP

In this chapter, you learned about WordPress and the Avada theme. From setting it up to creating pages and tagging posts, you know the basics of WordPress now. With time, you will learn and become comfortable using this software.

Pages, plug-ins, and posts. You don't need to know code to create and use them. WordPress and Avada does it all for you.

From within your WordPress menu, you can create an amazing blog that is both visually appealing to visitors and convenient to navigate with a menu and cross-links or buttons. Certain plug-ins will make your site interactive, as well.

Keep it clean with what you need. When running a blog, the adage, "Less is more," is always applicable!

Like the previous chapter, I have listed these action steps as a reminder for you as you navigate WordPress."

Now, I think it may be time for you to go have a spa day or enjoy some time with friends or something else you enjoy. You deserve to reward yourself. The "hard part" is now over.

You own and run a blog that looks and runs the way you want. You are a winner!

Ready to start actually blogging? Then read on for ideas and tips on how to make enlightening blog posts that keep your readers coming back for more in the next chapter.

ACTION STEPS

> *Listed are the steps I covered in this chapter. Use the action steps as a checklist as you proceed with creating your blog. Refer back in this chapter to gain more detail when you are ready for the tasks outlined below.*

Step 1: Install WordPress through SiteGround. This part is really easy.

Step 2: Install the Avada theme. You can do this separately and then upload it to your WordPress site.

Step 3: Create pages. Definitely feature an "About the Author" page. Also, feature a shop if you are selling something. Feature a blog page for your blog content.

Step 4: Add your content. Don't let SEO blind you.

5

CREATING WINNING CONTENT

Believe in yourself. You are braver than you think, more talented than you know, and capable of more than you imagine. — Roy T. Bennett

Your site is up and running. You have designed your pages and selected a great theme. Everything looks great. Now what?

Now it's time to publish that content that makes your blog!

Blogs run on the content that they generate. If you are a blogger, then your content comes from the meaningful ideas, suggestions, and stories that you give other people.

Whether your blog is based on providing helpful tips or offering unbiased product reviews, you must put out content to bring in the followers and money.

An empty blog won't get many followers. A blog populated with lots of posts made on a schedule is going to be more successful. That means that you must post, and you must post often.

I will share later in this chapter what tools I use to create well-written articles. For now, I want to concentrate on your awesome ideas for articles, as well as suggestions to make your blogging efforts successful.

LOGO

Your logo is part of your brand. It represents you and makes you easy to recognize. A creative yet effective logo is imperative to your brand. Before you start posting content, be sure to create one.

I recommend PicMonkey. This platform lets you create a free logo that fits your brand. Using their templates, designs, and fonts, you can make something awesome for your blog.

I also have great luck on Upwork.com with finding logo artists. My logo for wendyvandepoll.com cost me $20, and people always comment how perfect it is for my brand.

My logos for Center for Pet Loss Grief and Center for Animal Communication cost me more. But when I ordered them, I didn't know about Upwork.

Proudly display your logo on your blog where visitors can see it. You can feature it next to your title and on your home page. The bottom of your page, known as the footer, or the end of your posts are also great places. Find somewhere it stands out.

A visual double entendre is a great place to start. This is where two images come together to make one statement. For instance, a hair brush and a dog imposed over each other could be great for a grooming business, while a snake wrapped around the title of a blog could be great for a snake shop.

Also, use negative space. That's blank space in your logo. It makes the viewer focus upon your actual logo content more.

Symmetry is often vital. A symmetrical image is visually pleasing to people. When you look at it, it should have a nice shape, and its different components should line up or fit together nicely. Custom type that follows the same rules of symmetry is a great way to sum up your blog name in a nice little logo that stands out.

Colors are even more vital. Colors represent messages to people. With a pet blog, figure out the colors that best represent your blog's purpose. If you are writing about animal abuse, red for anger and passion might be appropriate, or gray for sadness and seriousness. Pastel or cartoon designs with bright colors would suit lighter topics.

If you are not a master artist, never fear. You can stick with something simple. Think of the Nike swish: a simple swish design has become one of the most famous logos in history. A simple shape or cartoon is sufficient.

You can also hire a logo designer online or locally and have a professional artist create something more beautiful and complex, if you so desire.

Don't just do what everyone else is doing. You want something recognizable. When people see it, they think of you. Think of some popular logos, like the Starbucks mermaid or the Evernote elephant head. Both are clear, and both are recognizable. Your logo should be like that.

Adding motion or activity is also great. More active logos inspire action in viewers. A cartoon dog who is clearly running is an example. Maybe show a cat meowing, indicated by noise lines or a cartoon speaking bubble over its head.

Fill a few notebooks with sketches. Look at other pet bloggers' logos to ensure you are not copying anyone. Once you find something unique and symmetrical, you can design it.

STICK TO YOUR NICHE

Since you have already established your niche, you want to generally stay within it. You will throw readers off if they follow you for excellent dog advice and you start writing about cats. You can even lose readers if they feel that your information is too off-topic and they are no longer getting what they signed up for.

When you get an idea for a blog post, think about whether or not it relates to your niche and furthers your blog's purpose. You can do things a bit differently now and then, but you can generally find the most success by delivering on what you originally promised readers you would.

If you decide to shake things up, be sure to say in the intro to your post, "I'm doing something a bit different today!"

Incongruent ideas don't have to be rejected. Maybe you should create another blog for them. Just don't jumble tons of unrelated ideas in the same blog, or you will confuse and lose your readers.

START WRITING

Don't know what to write about? Get a blank page. Then start writing words that come to mind. Eventually, an idea will take shape. This works almost every time for me.

I like to collect ideas in a notebook or record them on my phone. When I'm out of things to write about, I revisit my old ideas and expand on them, turning them into blog posts. Never let an idea go to waste. Always document it for later.

When I'm truly dry in the idea well, which is rare, I like to go do something or talk to someone for inspiration. New experiences give you unique stories. Maybe volunteer at the shelter, watch a pet movie, or visit a friend. Look into trends and read about current disagreements on issues that have people talking. These things can give you inspiring topics to research.

FIND TRENDING TOPICS

If something is trending, that means everyone is looking it up. It would be wise to hop on the bandwagon. However, don't base your blog solely on a trend, since trends fade away. A few posts dedicated to a trend should be good enough to draw in new readers.

You can tell something is trending when you see it time and again on other blogs and in social media. Your social media groups will reference it. Your other pet friends will mention it. You can also look at hashtags (Glossary) on Facebook and Twitter to see if any current trending ones relate to your niche.

A still current yet long-term trend is feeding a raw diet to our dogs and cats. Maybe feature an article on this or offer some reviews of popular books on the topic by the experts.

Another big trend involves huskies, after Game of Thrones. Appeal to the Game of Thrones pet lovers and new or aspiring husky owners by writing about how many people don't know how to properly care for huskies and how the number of unwanted huskies going to shelters is rapidly rising. Feature an article on how to care for huskies the right way.

The trend should obviously fit into your particular niche in the pet industry, of course. Writing about huskies in a fish blog is obviously not appropriate. Find trends in your own niche and you will have a wealth of things to write about.

Maybe every month, look into new trends and dedicate at least one post to it. That way, you stay current with the times and continue to produce content that readers find relevant. Be flexible and open to the changing times, and then your blog will weather the test of time!

PERSONAL STORIES

My favorite thing to do while blogging is sharing my own pet stories. As a pet lover, your ticket to many readers is relating to them on the nuances and joys of pet ownership. Sharing your stories will most definitely appeal to people and incur readers!

Photos or videos accompanying these posts are even more winning. A photo of your naughty dog after she ate the trash, followed by an amusing anecdote about the incident and how you subsequently remedied her trash-eating behavior, is great.

A little story about your lizard's finicky treatment of crickets, followed by a photo of her in her cage with live crickets hopping around before your review of a certain lizard feeding method or food product, is another great example.

Accompany a post with a story about how the topic is relevant to you. Share your experiences with said topic. Give readers something person to relate to. Then they feel more inclined to read on because they think, "This is like something that happened to me!" Even just bringing a smile to someone's face will make readers read on.

I like to begin a post with some sort of relatable story. As I relate the story, readers feel hooked to read on because they want to know the ending. The ending can be the overall point you want to make.

You can show how you made a mistake with your pet and what you learned, or what you did that worked in your favor. You can share research you performed to figure out how to surmount some new challenge with a pet. You can recommend products that address the main problem in your story.

Your personal story should have some basic point. Otherwise, readers will wonder, "Why did I just waste so much time reading this for nothing?" Have an introduction, a problem, and a remedy. Use that to lead into the topic you are writing about in your post.

Some blogs are built entirely on sharing amusing stories. You can build a readership just by sharing funny pictures, videos, memes, and stories about your pets or your experiences with pets.

If you do this, however, you must dedicate the blog to that. Throwing in random articles about other topics will throw off readers who feel committed to reading about your pet and only your pet.

These blogs thrive because people love animals. As they follow your blog, they feel as if they are part of your pet's life. They become emotionally invested. That is how you keep readers coming back, by creating emotional investment.

Regular updates and sharing cute stories will make them keep reading. When your pet passes away, they will grieve with you. You can create a massive support community based on your pet, with people sharing their own stories and expressing lots of love for your pet.

One thing I really love to do is illustrate how I made a mistake and how I learned from it. Readers love this because you show your vulnerability—you are not some perfect, untouchable pet guru, but rather a real person who is capable of making mistakes and bouncing back.

People will find that far more relatable, and they will derive comfort from the fact that you made the same mistake they have made. Show people that they can recover and learn from mistakes by describing how you did.

RHETORICAL APPEAL

Any writer can benefit from a crash course on ethos, pathos, and logos. These three elements of rhetoric are taught in basic English classes, then quickly forgotten. However, they are key to creating written content and pictures that people become invested in. To keep readers coming back, you should employ these elements in your posts. That is how you become *riveting*!

Ethos

Ethos involves appealing to the ethics of readers. As a pet writer, your readers are going to care most about the ethical implications certain people or practices have regarding animals.

Bringing attention to the harm certain training or feeding trends has on animals can persuade readers to find something better. Calling out some organization for animal testing or cruelty is another way to convince readers to boycott that company.

Don't just point out the dismal unethical treatment of roosters in cock fighting rings, for example. Point out a solution. Highlight an organization or product that helps.

Help people see how they can right an ethical wrongdoing. Readers will become hooked, as they want to read how to solve an ethical problem they care about.

For instance, if you are writing about how hitting your puppy during house training is wrong, point out why it hurts a puppy's psychology and his bond with his owner, and then offer a different way to train using positive reinforcement.

Pathos

Pathos is the emotional side of your writing. You want to make readers feel what you are writing about. If you are raising awareness about how important it is to neuter and spay, you should invoke emotions in pet owners. Prove to them that pets suffer from overpopulation.

A picture of an overcrowded local shelter, a moving paragraph about the lack of funding and suffering animals endure in shelters, and a bit about how pets are euthanized due to overpopulation will make pet owners feel horrible for other animals. They will then be more inclined to neuter or spay. Pathos is how you can make a difference.

Pathos doesn't have to be all negative. You can make people feel warm and fuzzy inside, which in turn drives them to keep reading to brighten their days. You can make people feel like good pet owners. That praise can make them want to return to your blog for more. Offer something emotional and you will get readers.

Logos

Logos is logic. The logical side of anything involves the facts, the research, the statistics. Some people find logic more appealing than emotions. But even people who are more invested in your blog emotionally can benefit from some solid facts.

Providing advice, statistics, facts, and research results can educate readers and show them what to do. Direct them toward a product or cause that you may be supporting by using pathos or ethos or both, suggesting a solution, and then showing the evidence supporting a solution.

For instance, if you are pushing for people to donate to the Humane Society, you should combine these three elements. Show how pets suffer from abuse to appeal to both pathos and ethos. Then make people feel good by showing them what the Humane Society does. Then break it down into math, or logos, by showing how much money the Society needs to raise for something and where that money goes.

START WRITING

Before you even begin to write your post, you must brainstorm what it will be about. Ideally, you have a topic picked out. But now you must ask yourself, "What do I want my readers to know after reading my post?"

A blog can flop horribly if the writer doesn't think of this. People don't want to waste their time reading meandering posts that never teach anything or make any solid points.

They also get frustrated if the blog makes a point, jumps to a wildly different point, circles back to the first point, comes out of left field with some odd bit of information, and goes on and on, jumping around between topics.

To make your blog post worth reading, decide on at least four takeaways the reader should gain from your blog (more is better!). These are four things you want your readers to learn or do. Write them down. If one takeaway is unrelated to the overall topic of the post, cut it. Your post needs to stay on topic and not shift to other things, or you could lose the reader.

For example, if you are discussing natural flea treatments for a kitty, you want to come up with the four basic takeaways relating only to feline flea treatments: natural products don't harm your pets as much as chemicals; flea treatments are necessary only when your cat has a flea infestation; which products are best to use; how effective these products are and any tips you may have for using them.

After you have outlined your takeaways, you can add more information with your research, knowledge, and tips in more detail. This way, you know when and where to insert certain information in a logical way.

Also, consider how each subtopic ties into the next. That way, you can create a nice flow for your post. It would be most logical to start by talking about what flea dips are and how they contain dangerous chemicals, which you can then segue into an introduction to natural products.

Since you are still trying to convince readers to use a natural product over a dangerous chemical, you should probably place the takeaway about effectiveness here. Then go into how often you should dip and which products to use. Include tips with each product you feature.

Do you see how flow can be achieved by logically linking the different main points of your post? Think of how one topic relates to another to create flow.

Also think where in the post a topic may be most effective. Least important points should go toward the end, while more important ones (or ones "selling" an idea to the readers) should go toward the top.

Finally, decide on headings for each takeaway. Break the takeaway into different paragraphs, with a clear heading that uses a keyword and describes the point of the paragraph.

Separating paragraphs with headings is a great way to sneak in some SEO and give your post a clean appearance.

OVERALL BLOG POST LAYOUT

Before you start writing, you can generate an outline that organizes your points into a neat structure that readers can easily follow. You can rearrange the outline as needed until the post has a logical flow.

It's always better to have one topic lead into the next, such as a paragraph about training your puppy to come to his name followed by one about how to accomplish that. If you use a logical sequence, where one topic builds upon the previous one, you create a post that is easier to read.

You don't have to follow an outline format to the letter. But having a formula for how you usually lay out your posts can be extremely helpful, especially on those days when you're crunched for time but you have to post something.

It prevents you from missing key elements of your post or skipping over important parts. You also don't have to think as hard when you post.

HERE'S WHAT THE TYPICAL OUTLINE SHOULD LOOK LIKE:

- **Introduction**

Here is where you state what your post is going to be about. You want to introduce the topic to readers in a way that hooks them to read more.

Use some keywords and some sort of lead-in. I love to use a question like, "What do you do when your new puppy pees in the house?"

The introduction should also make some sort of promise. "In this post, I'm going to show you how to house train your new puppy effectively and humanely." Share what you have to offer and why readers will benefit if they read on.

Always focus on what readers have to gain from reading your post! It is shameless self-advertising that puts you out there.

Finally, use a call to action. This may be something like "Read on to find out more!" or "Let's end this abuse now!" The call to action makes readers want to take action by reading more, in order to make some sort of change or solve a problem.

Think of introductions like this: A reader is skimming the intro, wondering if he or she should dedicate time to finishing the post. You must make the reader want to finish it.

Therefore, your intro must "sell" the rest of the post. A clear statement of the subject, a promise for how this post will help readers, and a call to action are how you do this.

- **First Topic**

Separate your first paragraph from your introduction using a heading. Then launch into your first, and most important, subtopic. Offer as many details and facts as you can.

Images and videos are often attention-grabbers. Plus, people prefer shorter paragraphs. Don't have long paragraphs with more than four sentences. Once you start a new train of thought, definitely start a new paragraph.

- **Second Topic**

Separate your second subtopic from the first with another heading. Then repeat. Keep doing this for each new subtopic. Make your main points and focus on providing one of the takeaways you outlined with each subtopic.

- **Conclusion**

In my writing experience, most people have the most trouble with conclusions. But conclusions are actually very easy to write! All you have to do is sum up everything you just said in a neat little sentence or two.

Then invite readers to chime in or encourage them to tell you about their results with the last sentence. Three to four sentences are sufficient.

You must include a conclusion with each post. It reminds readers of what you just said, and it leaves them with a sense of completion. Some people only read conclusions as a way to rapidly get information about the whole post.

USE CONSTRUCTIVE FEEDBACK

As you gain a following, you might get lots of requests. "I want to know more about..." or "Could you post more about...?" These comments are the most valuable tools you have as a blogger.

They can hurt, sure. You want people to just accept what you have to say, and you don't like being told that they want something else.

But as a blogger, the only way to grow your business is by giving your followers answers to what they are asking. So, if your readers are clamoring for something, or voicing complaints, you can use that feedback to power new content.

The great thing about blogs is that they are malleable to change with the times. The blog that endures the test of time is the one that is flexible to change. You would be wise to make adjustments where they are needed.

If something doesn't fly with readers, you can remove it. If readers want more of something, give it to them. Make the changes that people want to see.

Now, if you have one bizarre suggestion from one person, and no one else says the same thing, then you can safely disregard it. Don't do things that disagree with you emotionally or morally, or that seem outlandish or ill-fitting for your blog. Don't do things that seem totally unnecessary or incongruent with your niche, either. You don't have to cater to each and every single reader of your blog. Stay true to yourself.

In the blogging world, you can encounter some weird things. Some people are trolls, only out to hurt others with mean-spirited comments. Other people have strange ideas that they insist you use.

Yet others don't seem to actually read your content before they post totally irrelevant comments. Be sure to take everything you read on your blog's comments with a little caution.

But popular opinion, or the majority vote, can really suggest a change is in order. If most readers are somehow dissatisfied with something you have posted, then you should take that into consideration. Use it as a chance to help yourself elevate your blog.

For example, maybe you post a recipe for doggie biscuits. A ton of users complain that they can't find a specific ingredient in their local grocery stores, or they complain that the instructions didn't work. You may need to revise the recipe to fit the needs of the majority. Add a more common ingredient or post where people can order the rare ingredient online. Clarify instructions or find where you went wrong.

You may have people asking lots of questions that your blog post should have answered. If lots of people don't seem to be getting what you say, it may be time to clarify a few points with more specific language, or even bolding a part so that readers pay attention to it.

People may complain that your post did not provide enough information. It can't hurt making another post addressing the information that people want. Prove to your readers that you listen and you care by addressing their concerns.

PROOFREAD WITH SOFTWARE

I am an advocate for intuitive writing. This is where you write without pausing to fix grammar or criticize yourself. Doing this lets you get your ideas out. You don't ever stop yourself to fix a spelling error, or else you throttle the flow of ideas.

The problem with this is that your writing may come out jumbled, phrased oddly, and full of errors. That's okay, though. That's where editing comes in.

Before you post something, you must edit it. Poor writing is frustrating to read. You can lose followers if your posts are not high quality. Therefore, you must polish your posts after you write them to ensure that they read nicely, with no distracting errors.

It can be easy to overlook simple mistakes if you are the author of a post. You know what you meant to say in your mind, so you skip over flaws in your writing, missing words, or even misspellings. That is where an editing software comes in handy.

I use ProWritingAid (Resources). It is a plug-in that you can add to your browser, Google documents, and Microsoft Office. It also has a desktop application where you can edit documents from your computer.

ProWritingAid checks for spelling and grammar errors in your writing and offers suggestions for improvement. You even get notifications about run-on sentences and improper verb tenses!

My advice is to create your blog posts in a word processor. Then run it through ProWritingAid. The result will be a polished post that you can then copy and paste into your post editor on WordPress.

PUBLISH YOUR CONTENT

This is your last step to creating great content: publishing it!

The sense of bravery and accomplishment you feel when you make your first post public is exhilarating. You just became a part of the Internet. Thousands, even millions, of people can now see what you have written.

You just put yourself out there and started growing your own Internet community. You are reaching out to others and making yourself known. Plus, you are one step closer to gaining followers and monetizing your blog!

WRAP-UP

In this chapter, you learned about creating a riveting blog post. You must find inspiration and begin organizing your thoughts. Put them into a logical outline. Then let the words flow.

Afterward, you can use a proofreading software to correct your piece. You can also make sure it logically fits in with your post's theme and uses ethos, pathos, and logos.

Once you have written your piece, publish it. Then use the feedback you get to improve your blog. You should stay true to yourself, but also hear what your readers have to say. Your readers are the ones who promote your blog and make you money, so give them what they really want!

Use the action steps at the end of this chapter as a checklist for getting your article written and ready for your followers.

In Chapter 6, you will learn how to pair social media with your blog to increase your readership and gain more followers.

Social media offers you free and paid advertising options that are extremely effective. Read on to learn how to create your very own brand on social media!

ACTION STEPS

Listed are the steps I covered in this chapter. Use the action steps as a checklist as you proceed with creating your blog. Refer back in this chapter to gain more detail when you are ready for the tasks outlined below.

Step 1: Create a Logo

Step 2: Gather Inspiration

Step 3: Brainstorm and Create an Outline

Step 4: Write Intuitively

Step 5: See if it Fits Your Niche

Step 6: Proofread it

Step 7: Listen to Critics and Fans Alike

Step 8: Publish!

PART III
GROWING YOUR BLOG FOR SUCCESS

6

GETTING SOCIAL WITH SOCIAL MEDIA

Friendship is born at that moment when one person says to another, What! You, too? I thought I was the only one. — C.S. Lewis

Think about the brands that you know. What makes you buy them again and again? Probably the quality, the customer service, the company's values, and even the marketing. Prices and availability probably also factor into your brand loyalty.

When it comes to your blog, you are a brand yourself. You offer people information. If you do so in a way that people find trustworthy and appealing, more people will trust your brand and follow you for years!

They will follow you because of the confidence you developed with them, and they will sign up for the products or courses you offer.

Now why do you ditch brands? The main reason is probably a decline in quality, availability, or even company values and customer care. The same goes for your brand. If your blog dips in quality or anything else that you have promised your readers, you will start to lose people.

It is important to roll with the times. But don't change so much that old fans lose interest. Always keep an element of what you started with, whatever makes your blog unique.

To cement your brand and raise awareness about it, you should use social media to connect with potential readers. Social media allows you to build an online personality and presence that readers can identify with.

It helps promote you as an online influencer, or person that people want to follow. Your blog shows your voice; your social media shows your presence. Often, no one will ever discover your blog unless you promote it with social media.

THE IMPORTANCE OF SOCIAL MEDIA TRAFFIC

Why all this fuss about social media, you wonder? Well, the more people who visit your blog, the higher your blog ranks in searches.

That means you reach more people, make more of a difference, and start getting enough attention to monetize your blog, which is covered more extensively in Chapter 8. As you reach people, your readership and your email list will grow.

Social media is a great way to reach more people and start to drive traffic to your blog. It puts your brand in front of people.

Many of your readers will come from social media. As they see you on social media, they feel inclined to click on your posts, which takes them to your blog. Your following on various social platforms directly translates to people visiting your blog.

Social media followers are in addition to your email list when you consider the number of people following you. Just because someone isn't on your list doesn't mean that they don't still keep an eye on you through social media.

As people see your promotions and new posts, they access your content, just as someone who receives your emails does. You get attention and reach many people this way. The goal, however, is to get the folks on social media to sign up for your newsletter.

A social media presence also puts you in the center of activity relating to your niche. You get to connect with people who love pets as much as you do. You can take part in fun social media groups, where you can garner attention for your blog with authoritative posts.

In addition, you get to meet other bloggers, some of whom can become lifelong colleagues. When new trends or content enter the Internet world, you can be among the first to learn about them and feature them in your blog. Comments on social media can tune you into trends, as well as what your readers think of your posts.

CREATING SOCIAL MEDIA PAGES

To thrive in the blogosphere, you must create pages on the main social media giants right now. These are Twitter, Instagram, Tumblr, LinkedIn, and Facebook. Less than a decade ago, Myspace was big, but now it is obsolete.

Maybe one day, Twitter and Facebook will become obsolete as users drift to another social media trend, so stay on top of this. Whatever social media becomes hot in your niche, make sure you have a presence on it!

If you don't already have accounts on these social media companies, create ones now. You can build a business page from your personal account on Facebook. Otherwise, you can create new accounts for your blog.

You have two options here. You could create an account under your name or under your blog name. It is best to create one dedicated solely to your business, unless your personal name and your business name are clearly linked.

For instance, my blog's URL is wendyvandepoll.com, and my name is Wendy Van de Poll. It is obvious that I am the same person. However, with my blog centerforpetlossgrief.com, it wouldn't make sense to link people to social media pages bearing my personal name.

Obviously, you don't want to link people to your personal social media account, the one you share with friends and family. You want to create a business page dedicated entirely to your business.

The reason for this is twofold: For one thing, you will be connecting with lots of strangers, so you don't want people you don't know personally having access to pictures of your house and your grandkids for security reasons!

Additionally, your followers want to see things relating to your blog, not your personal life. This doesn't mean that you can never put personal posts on your business page. Your followers want to know who the person is behind all your great blogs. Remember to keep it professional and have your "personal" post relate to your brand.

BUILDING YOUR BRAND ON SOCIAL MEDIA

Your social media accounts should bear the same logo and colors and even pictures as your blog. That way, users know that they are in the right place. Consistency in your brand is key. You must keep the same appearance across all interfaces.

On your page, you will have to create your profile. Fill it out with details about your blog and its theme, followed by a paragraph about you.

Tell readers what to expect and why they should trust you as an authority in a particular niche. Use a photo of you as your picture, and create a cover photo using your main blog photo. Write your bio in the same voice that you use in your blog across all social media to build further consistency within your brand.

There will also be a place to enter your URL. You want to first enter your blog's URL. That way, people can find you easily. You can also connect the URLs to other social media accounts.

In addition to decorating your page just like your blog, you should also post about your blog. These posts will generate interest and drive traffic to your blog.

For every post, you should feature the featured WordPress picture, a summary of what your post is about, and an easy link that people can click on to reach your blog.

Don't give away your content for free! Offer a teaser. Say something like, "Make your own dog treats!" Then feature a few lines of the recipe and a link to your blog post. People have to click on it to see more. If you feature the whole recipe, then people won't bother going to your blog post.

Why visit your blog when you feature all of it on social media? Drive traffic to your blog with little teasers that make people want to visit your blog for more.

You can also garner more attention by posting content and links relevant to your brand. Say you run a blog dedicated to ending safari hunting and trophy hunting. Sharing articles about this subject on your social media page can help build awareness about your cause and make more people visit your profile.

As people come to appreciate the content you post, they will be more likely to check out your blog.

Be sure to interact with people, as well. Like and comment on their posts. Post things asking people about their opinions or post surveys and polls to gain information about popular opinions.

Facebook has automated polls, which you can create within a post. The more you interact with people, the more connections you make. These connections draw people to look into your blog.

Join groups on social media. LinkedIn and Facebook are known for groups. When you join groups, become active in them. This establishes you as an authority and makes people aware of who you are.

When you join groups and comment people begin to recognize your page name and feel more familiar with it when they check out your blog. This is just another way to cement your brand on social media.

Facebook and Instagram feature ads. For a small fee, you can appear as an ad on the feeds of social media users. If someone looks up a lot of dog-related information and you run a blog about dogs, Facebook will put you in front of someone's eyes. Running ads is a great way to get people to know about your blog.

Finally, host events. You may host a watch party for a live video where you demonstrate how to groom a cat without getting scratched, for instance. Advertise that watch party on your blog and all of your social media accounts with a link and a time.

You may also host a product review party or a special on some product you sell. You may advertise a free consultation session. Creating public events, such as "Dog Park Day," can help you connect with local people.

I'm going to include some instructions for each social media brand that is big right now. If you are using social media interfaces that I don't cover here, be sure to get comfortable with them and follow similar tips when creating a blog page.

The basic premise is the same: Establish who you are and what your blog is about consistently across all social media to create a recognizable brand that resonates with people.

FACEBOOK

From your personal Facebook account, you can create a business page for your blog. Be sure to add a photo of you as a profile picture and use your blog's name as the page name.

Feature a link to your blog in the "Website" blank and fill out the long and short descriptions of your blog. Under "About Me," talk about why you write this blog, your mission, and how you are qualified.

Use Facebook ads to reach more people. Also, join Facebook groups and get active on relevant content. Post things every day. Post every time you make a new blog post.

Start by inviting your friends to like you. Also, like other blogs on related topics. That way, more people see your blog and are likely to "like" you. Once people like you, they will see your content on their feeds. This is a great promotional opportunity.

TWITTER

Tweet often, and tweet well. Every time you make a new post, be sure to tweet about it.

Make your profile all about your blog. Feature your logo and a description and link to your blog. Also link to all of your other social media accounts.

Inside your blog, feature a link to Twitter with your other social media buttons. Your "Contact Me" page is great for this, as well as the footer of your site.

Follow lots of other active Twitter users in your niche. Refer to your blog in your comments, without making it obvious. For instance, you can say, "I actually wrote about this in my blog recently! I can't agree with you more."

Constantly posting links to your blog can get you banned for spam, but sneaking in references to your blog won't do this. Retweet things major influencers post, as well, to get more attention.

Join Twitter chats. Add valuable input on these chats and you'll make friends and even be invited as a guest on a chat.

Be sure to follow lots of people. That way, people follow you. Expand beyond your circle by following strangers who show an interest in pets.

INSTAGRAM

Instagram is dedicated to photos. To keep your Instagram account going, be sure to post lots of pet pictures with a link to your newest blog posts in the caption. Instagram is a fun platform and very pet friendly.

Also, be sure to use some copywriting techniques by writing short and concise sentences. "Today I'll show you how to make dog cookies!" with a picture of you and your dog in the kitchen is a great example.

Show people what your post is about and how they will benefit from reading it. Make your copy short and sweet and to the point.

In your Instagram profile, feature your logo as the profile picture. Use a handle that is your name or your blog name condensed, like your URL. Finally, be sure to put your blog's URL and write about the things your blog offers under "About Me." Write a bit about who you are and why you are qualified to be running this blog here, as well.

Feature a "Follow Me on Instagram!" button on your blog. This helps people easily connect with you by one click.

And don't forget about hashtags—Instagram allows thirty hashtags (see Glossary).

LINKEDIN

LinkedIn is a social networking site for professionals. To promote your business, definitely create a LinkedIn profile. On the profile, talk about your expertise and feature a link to your blog.

As you add new followers, be sure to send an email greeting each new member by name and then invite them to look at your blog. Talk a bit about what your blog features and how they will benefit from following you.

It is helpful to create a basic email template. Copy and paste that to each new email you send out. Customize the name and you're good to go!

Post every day or every other day. Talk about your newest blog post or some issue that you will be discussing soon. That way, LinkedIn users can follow your content on LinkedIn and tune into your blog when you post something relevant to them.

Add a LinkedIn button to your blog. The bottom of your blog is an ideal place, as well as on your "Contact Me" page. Include the URL to your LinkedIn profile.

SET A SCHEDULE

To remain relevant on social media, you must post often. The easiest way to stay on top of posts is to automate them. But you also want to post personal things directly to add a more relatable human element to your social media brand.

How can you remember to spend all this time posting on social media if you also have to run your blog, answer emails, *and* all the other numerous tasks and events in your busy schedule? I've certainly been there.

Sometimes, you just don't feel that you have the time. However, since social media is so important to building your online brand and web presence, it is worthy of you making time for it.

Set a schedule. Follow it closely. Dedicate maybe an hour a day to posting, chatting, and commenting on your different social media accounts. Consider it all part of a day's work!

AUTOMATE SOCIAL MEDIA POSTS

When you create a new post on WordPress, you can then go and manually post a link to your blog with a teaser on all of your social media accounts. Or, you can save tons of time by automating the social media posting! Never forget to post again, as a handy software can handle all of that for you.

Here's how to automate social media posts from within your blog: Get Agora Pulse. Then set a schedule and link up to six social media accounts across the web. Specify what you want the posts to say.

You can even assign different users if you're working with a team. Agora Pulse does the rest! There is also the option to analyze the success of your posts and get free tips on how to improve your posts.

Agora Pulse is not the only social media posting software out there. You can also try Hootsuite, Buffer, or Crowdfire. They all work in roughly the same way. Try them out and see which ones are easiest for you.

Be sure to add some variety to your automated posts so that your posts seem more personal and your followers don't get bored of the same content over and over. Each post should be unique.

GET FOLLOWERS ON SOCIAL MEDIA

Let's get a little more in depth about how to attract followers on social media.

No one is going to follow you if they don't know you exist. A lack of followers hardly means that your social media brand is lackluster. It just means that you need to put yourself out there a little more and get yourself in front of people.

First, remember the demographic you identified in Chapter 2? That demographic applies to your social media brand, as well. Write to the demographic your niche appeals to with your social posts.

Next, be sure to post meaningful content. No one bothers to read novels on social media. Short, visual posts gain way more attention. A featured photo of a cute pet and a snappy title that summarizes your blog post is great.

But also consider graphs, infographics, or factual videos that offer teasers about your post's content. Sometimes, you can also just post a link to your blog featuring your logo and a teaser like, "Want to learn how to train your dog? Visit my blog!"

Keywords summarized as hashtags will make you appear in social media searches. When someone clicks on a hashtag, they will see your post on the results. Be sure to find relevant hashtags and add them to the end of your posts.

Occasionally, offer a poll. Or offer a contest. “First hundred visitors who sign up for my newsletter get a free gift!” is a good example. This way, you engage readers and give them a reason to visit your blog.

Also, use your keywords generously in your posts. Social media posts on public profiles will show up on search engine searches. Your posts should be retrieved with a keyword. More people will find you if you optimize your posts.

WRAP-UP

Social media is a critical part of getting a readership for your blog. You must feature your blog on all social media. Make it easy for people to follow your accounts from your blog, too.

Engage your audience with meaningful posts. Interact with them through games, contests, polls, and other such posts. Be sure to update them when you post something new to the blog. Posting on a schedule keeps your followers engaged and your social media accounts populated.

Social media lets you find lots of people who may be interested in your blog. You can use it to create your brand, your web presence, and your readership.

Review the action steps for this chapter to keep you on track for your planning.

Now, read on to learn how to retain readers who visit your blog. Getting people to come back to your blog is the foundation for blogging success!

ACTION STEPS

Listed are the steps I covered in this chapter. Use the action steps as a checklist as you proceed with creating your blog. Refer back in this chapter to gain more detail when you are ready for the tasks outlined below.

Step 1: Start social media accounts for your business. Twitter, Facebook, LinkedIn, and Instagram are good places to start.

Step 2: Drive traffic with your social media. Add friends, appeal to followers, and post updates.

Step 3: Set a schedule. You must post in a timely manner to engage with your followers.

Step 4: Get more followers. Offer polls, free gifts, and great content. Use keywords and hashtags to show up higher in searchers. Post in relevant groups to draw attention to your site. Every new follower is a potential lead!

7

GET THEM TO COME BACK!

Every contact we have with a customer influences whether or not they'll come back. We have to be great every time or we'll lose them. — Kevin Stirtz

Recurring readers is a sign that your blog is doing well. If people keep coming back for more, then they are clearly invested in your brand and loyal to you. But how do you get people to come back?

I'm sure you have visited plenty of blogs in your time. You may have liked what you read. However, it was not easy to follow the blog, so you left to visit other sites and you forgot about it.

Then maybe you attempted to look it up again, but it had already become lost in cyberspace, buried by newer posts. If only you could remember its name...

I'm sure you have also visited blogs that you quickly backed out of in search of something better. Maybe the blog was too brief to be informative, or maybe it was poorly written, or maybe its tone just didn't appeal to you.

The key here is to avoid the two scenarios above. To get people to come back, you want to offer a convenient way to sign up and social media links so that people can follow you.

It is important to offer some sort of incentive, such as a discount code or free report, can get more people to give their emails to your ever-growing email list.

You also want to offer content and a layout that makes people stick around to read more. Deliver consistently good, informative, and well-written content, and you get consistently loyal readers.

COLLECT EMAILS

When people visit your blog, you want to have a highly visible place for them to subscribe to your newsletter by giving their email. This is a surefire way to keep putting your content in front of people. By making it easy for people to subscribe to your list, you enable people to actually sign up.

Once someone subscribes to you, this person becomes a lead. Generating leads involves making it easy and convenient for people to subscribe. If you can continue to put meaningful content before them, these leads then become customers.

Also, make it easy for people to follow you on social media. That makes it even more possible to place content in front of them that they will want to read. I recommend placing social media links in handy buttons at the bottom or top of every page on your site.

SharedCounts is a convenient plug-in that places social media buttons of any style you choose wherever you want on your site. Or if you are using Avada (Chapter 4), this is already built in for you.

How do you collect emails? That part is easy! I use ConvertKit (Resources), which is a great way to move visitors into leads. MailChimp is also a great option, with some limitations. MailChimp is free for under two thousand subscribers, but becomes expensive with over two thousand.

That's why I recommend ConvertKit. I also have found that ConvertKit is more robust for a monthly fee. Again, I won't go into fees here since they may change with time, but I find them to be reasonable for the amount of return I get from them!

ConvertKit is actually a WordPress plug-in. Install it from your plug-ins on your dashboard. Once it downloads, hit "Activate."

Now create an account and log in to it to access your API key. Within your account, you will find a button that says, "Show Secret." Click on it and you will retrieve your API key, which you can then copy and paste into the API key blank in your WordPress.

In your settings, you can choose a form and where it appears. You can post one with every blog post, as well as on every page of your blog. You can customize forms to fit different types of posts or different pages, as well.

If you choose to use MailChimp instead, you can also install the plug-in.

With these handy forms, you can get visitors to give you their emails. Then you can send them updates when you post a new thing to your blog, as well as advertisements for different things you may offer, such as coupon codes to an affiliate company or a new course. More on that in the next chapter!

GENERATE DISCUSSIONS

When you are posting, be sure to engage your readers. Interacting with readers helps you establish great business connections, plus it makes your readers feel as if they are actually getting something back from your blog.

Having a great business relationship with your readers inspires a sense of trust, which in turn inspires loyalty!

When you make a post, think of a way to engage your readers. You might host a contest on social media or on your blog. Get people to post pictures with their pets, for instance, and have them vote on pictures to find a winner.

This could even be a weekly thing! The winner could be featured on your home page and receive some sort of gift, such as a coupon code or a free product.

You might ask readers a question and encourage them to answer in the comments. Generate healthy discussions by asking for opinions.

You might tell readers that you will share top comments in your next post. Then, people will comment more meaningful things in order to be featured in your next post.

You can even have a live chat, where you answer questions and comments. You can do this on social media, but be sure to announce it from your blog and let readers know when and where the chat will be online.

Finally, you can offer free (or paid) consultations. If people have pet questions, tell them to please email you. You can email back and forth or set up video conferences where you answer their burning pet questions.

These are just a few ideas. The way you interact with people will depend on your blog and your demographic. Find a way that works for you and makes your blog both interactive and fun.

STAY ON TOP OF COMMENTS

The comments on your articles are a way for you to gain valuable feedback and connect with your readers in a more personal way.

The Internet world can be lonely with no personal communication or it can be warm and full of potential relationships. Replying to comments and engaging with readers personally will make your blog interactive and fun.

Readers will appreciate hearing from you. If you reply to a comment or even email a person back about a comment, you make a personal connection that validates that person's presence on your blog.

Be sure to change your settings to "Approve Comments" so that you can disapprove spam or abusive comments. You don't want your blog becoming cluttered with irrelevant or offensive comments, as that can deter other readers. Always censor comments before you approve them!

To do this, go to your WordPress settings. Click on "Discussion" and then "Before a comment appears." Check the box next to "Comment must be manually approved." Then hit "Save Changes" at the bottom of the page and test it out for yourself by posting a comment. You should get an email asking if you want to approve the comment. Now you have the power to approve or disapprove all comments!

This can get a bit overwhelming when you are running a high-volume blog. If you don't want to spend most of your day sifting through comments, repeat the steps above and be sure to change the settings from "Comment must be manually approved" to "Comment author must have previously approved comment." That automates comment approval from people you know and trust on your blog.

When people post a comment, they will have to enter their email. That makes it easy to add them to your list. You can also send them a Captcha (Glossary) to ensure that they are real people, not bots posting spam on numerous pages.

SET ASIDE TIME FOR EMAILS

As you get personal emails, you must reply to them. You can automate a reply that lets a person know that you have received the email and will respond soon. That reply can make people feel more patient, since they have received something from you.

Set aside some time each day to answer emails. Giving your readers your attention inspires yet more loyalty. You can help people by chatting with them, answering their questions, and getting involved.

Have a goal for the number of emails you answer each day. It can be time-consuming if you get a lot of emails, so start from the oldest and work your way up. Be sure to read each email completely in order to come up with a relevant reply.

Send thoughtful replies with good content, written in the voice you use for your blog. Address each email personally to each person, so that you don't appear cold and impersonal.

Sign them warmly with your blogging name or personal name, depending which one you are using online, and something like "Warmly" or "Wishing the best." You can also ask for updates to inspire a sense of caring in your correspondence.

Stamp your emails with a cute pet-related .gif or your logo. That way, your brand sticks with people and your emails adhere to your blog's voice.

HOW TO AUTOMATE EMAILS

ConvertKit allows you to send beautiful emails on a schedule to keep up with your readers. From within ConvertKit, you can create newsletter forms that you simply fill out. You also can set up automatic emails, such as a welcome email that goes out to new subscribers.

First, set a schedule. Readers love consistency, so sending out emails on a consistent schedule inspires more loyalty. People know when to expect to hear from you. Faithfully stick to this schedule, unless you have a surprise that you must update your readers on.

Second, follow the workflow in your ConvertKit account. This shows you what emails are due. You can click on an item and edit it in the same window. This allows you to edit emails as needed before sending them out.

Third, let ConvertKit handle the rest. You will even see a chart showing how well your emails are doing and how many subscribers are completing steps in the emails.

You can also edit outcomes, events, and actions to automate what your readers are supposed to do. The event could be something like a live video on Facebook that you want your readers to join. An action could be as simple as clicking on a new post or joining an online course you are offering.

HAVE A SURVEY WHEN PEOPLE UNSUBSCRIBE

In a perfect world, no one ever hits "Unsubscribe Here" on your emails. But it can and will happen. The best thing you can do is find out why people do this. That can help you improve your emails and avoid more people from unsubscribing.

A simple automatic email response with a survey is easy to set up within ConvertKit. From there, you can gather data on why people are unsubscribing.

Sometimes, people just don't find your content relevant. If that keeps happening, you may want to reevaluate what you are posting to be more relevant to readers.

Other times, people feel that you send too many emails. Maybe you should scale back. I found that once a week to every other week is ideal for my niche. Too many emails start to overload readers and resemble spam.

Maybe you push selling things a little too hard. I like to provide some valuable content in each email and *then* mention something I'm selling, like a consulting session or a course, at the end. I sell myself by offering good content and thus convincing people to pursue what else I offer.

Finally, maybe you're sending out stuff that has little to do with your blog. This would be a mistake. Don't treat your email list like a group of friends that you should forward every interesting article or funny meme to. Assemble content you want to share that relates specifically to your niche into an email that goes out on a regular schedule.

WRAP-UP

Each person who visits your blog is a potential lead, or customer. To retain people, you must make them value your blog and want to come back to it.

The best way to do this is to get people to sign up for emails so that you can notify them when you post new content and send them marketing emails to get them to spend money on your blog!

Also, create a community. This is where you interact with your readers in some fun way. From contests to simply replying to comments, you will get more loyalty as you engage with people personally.

Stay on top of emails. Send them out on a schedule. ConvertKit can automate emails and create forms that get people to sign up for your emails.

If people do unsubscribe, you want to find out why. That way, you can prevent more people from unsubscribing.

Use the action steps at the end of this chapter as a checklist for getting your article written and ready for your followers.

Now that you know how to retain leads and have a loyal following, you can start to make money off of your blog! Do the five action steps and, to turn blogging into an enriching career, read on!

ACTION STEPS

> *Listed are the steps I covered in this chapter. Use the action steps as a checklist as you proceed with creating your blog. Refer back in this chapter to gain more detail when you are ready for the tasks outlined below.*

Step 1: Make it easy to get subscribers! Use ConvertKit forms or an email provider of your choice to get people to sign up and follow you on social media, as well.

Step 2: Automate emails with ConvertKit or an email provider of your choice. Take the time out of emailing as you generate automatic emails and send out updates or newsletters on a set schedule.

Step 3: Engage your readers. Offer ways for them to interact with you.

Step 4: Always stay on top of comments and emails. When people contact you, get back to them! Show that you are there and you are an active part of their lives.

Step 5: Set up a survey when people unsubscribe. Use that data to improve your emails and to retain more leads.

Remember, if you need more information for your action steps, go back to the beginning of this chapter or watch the videos in ConvertKit.

8

MONETIZING YOUR BLOG

I am open to money coming to me from new ways that I've never imagined. — Anonymous

Monetizing your blog is the process of developing a system to make income from your hard work. Blogs are not get-rich-quick schemes. But with some work and patience, you can start generating excellent income from it!

The most exciting part of blogging is when you start to see a return for all of your efforts. The hours you put in may feel unrewarded at first, but in time, they will start to pay off very well.

The best part is your blog can become a source of passive income that earns money even while you are sleeping. A lot of hard work at the beginning and staying on top of your blog will lead to income that grows with only some emailing and posting on your part in the future.

Your blog is part of a brand. Your brand sells content. Therefore, your customers are the people who visit your blog and use your content. To make money, you must view each person who visits your blog as a customer. Appeal to this customer and you will see money!

Here is what I do to monetize my blogs. My advice to you as you go through this chapter is to have a notebook ready to jot down your ideas on how you want to monetize. You may not implement all your ideas at once, but in the future, you may want to revisit your original ideas.

LEAD MAGNETS

Each person who reads your emails is a potential customer. To get subscribers to spend money at your blog, you want to convert these potential customers, or leads, into real customers.

Lead magnets are simple ways to get people to sign up for your content. Generally, offering someone a free gift of some type is a great lead magnet.

The free gift doesn't need to be something expensive and fancy. I love to offer people special reports on something, such as what dog foods to avoid when I had my natural pet blog. Invite people to take a brief quiz that you design using a plug-in to generate a free report on how they should be feeding their specific breed of dog, for instance.

You can also offer a fifteen-percent-off coupon, or something similar, to new subscribers. This gets lots of people to sign up and redeem their coupons in your store or affiliate links.

You can even send a basic checklist. "Things to get for a new puppy" or "What you need to start your very own aquarium" are examples of checklists. These are easy to create and automate.

Informative newsletters sent out on a schedule are also popular. Offer someone a free subscription to your newsletter if they sign up. Then, send out newsletters on a timely schedule and pack them with great content. Spin them to sell a product or service that you offer, as well.

SELLING CONTENT

When you sell content, you are selling information to people who want to learn more. The most popular forms of content selling include online courses, consultations, information sessions, eBooks, and newsletters. People can sign up for these informational services and pay a fee that you set.

If you can establish yourself as an authority with great, riveting blog content, then people will want to learn everything that you can teach. You can market your information and get many people to sign up. In this day and age, often heralded the "Information Age," selling information is a fantastic way to make money.

To successfully sell information, you must offer something that people can't get on their own. Or at least make people think that they can't get the information on their own. In your marketing, tell people that you have developed a special system for something pet-related.

Always be honest with selling information because you never want to lie to your following. If you do, your followers will figure it out, and their trust will be gone.

Marketing must include video presentations, where you give away about twenty percent of your "system." A great example of information video marketing that I witnessed recently was a vet who created a lengthy video promising to divulge secrets that the pet food industry won't tell you.

He spent a few minutes discussing his veterinary practice and experience, and then he launched into how most dog foods don't offer proper nutrition. He even covered a bit about how canines are meant to eat.

But instead of sharing the true secret of his pet food formula, he instead invited you to sign up for his course on canine nutrition and get twenty percent off of his powdered formula.

People also tend to love systems with steps. "Seven Steps to Reducing Anxiety in Dogs" would be a great example of a course if you decide on offering courses. Breaking things down into a neat system that works is appealing to people. They will be willing to purchase information that can help them tackle problems with their pets in easy-to-follow steps.

Create an organized course where you offer good information and a system. Write the content and add videos. Then market it with a video that gives away a tiny bit of the secret, establishes your authority, and promises people that their pets will benefit enormously from the information contained inside.

Only after all of the marketing should you reveal the price. Make people want the course before you ask for money. People will be more inclined to buy the content if they are already curious about it.

PAID PRODUCT REVIEWS

Free pet products and even payments for posting reviews? Sign me up!

A fantastic way to monetize your pet blog is to offer pet product reviews. Companies will want you to promote their products, as word of mouth works very efficiently as a form of advertising. They will gladly send you free products to review. Many will even pay you to post those reviews!

You can approach companies and ask them about a paid review. Offer to post a flattering review in exchange for a free product, or some other arrangement.

This practice can broach into unethical territory pretty quickly. Don't try a product and then promote it if you didn't like it. Don't promote unsavory companies, either.

It is far better to post positive reviews about products that you have already tried. If you don't like a product some company sends you, you can cancel the deal instead of posting a good review that encourages your reader to buy something horrible.

Your readers trust you and look to you as an authority. Your reviews can drive them to buy something. Please don't violate that trust for money.

Furthermore, you can get into affiliate marketing and use affiliate links in your reviews to drive leads. Read on to see how to transfer reviews into actual money!

AFFILIATE MARKETING

When you post an affiliate link in your blog, you are basically referring people from your blog to another company. As people click on these links and give their business to the companies you refer them to, you make said businesses money.

They will kick you some of the profits in the form of a commission per lead. This is called affiliate marketing, and it is a super common monetization strategy for bloggers.

Another great thing about affiliate marketing is that some companies will give you exclusive discount codes to offer your readers. Everybody loves discounts.

As you advertise a twenty percent off code on your blog, people will be more inclined to click on the link and redeem the code. Therefore, you drive yet more people to an affiliate company.

To get started with affiliate marketing, you want to create affiliations with certain companies. Sometimes, companies will approach you, asking if you might be willing to promote their products on your site. Other times, you can reach out to companies through cold emails and start an affiliation.

Of course, use discernment as you do this. You don't want to be supporting a company that engages in unethical animal treatment or sells lead-poisoned pet products made in unregulated foreign companies, for example.

The companies you work with represent who you are, so a bad company can really sour your reputation online. Be sure to research a company to see if it fits your ethical code before you agree to an affiliation. Look at its reviews, its Better Business Bureau rating, its ingredients, its manufacturing process, and its social media reputation.

You also want to recommend companies that you have actually used. That way, you are posting relevant information about it in your promotions.

If you have never used a product, you should not market it, as you are basically promoting something that you know nothing about. That can easily show in your writing. Plus, you don't want to promote something that doesn't actually work!

Think of a few products that you use. Or think of some that would be in line with your niche that readers could really benefit from. Approach those companies. Usually, on their website footers, you can find a link for "Affiliates" or some such word. If you can't find this, you can send a cold email, which I talk more about in this chapter.

Finally, you can join an affiliate network, which connects you with lots of companies looking for affiliate marketing. ClickBank, Amazon Associates, ShareASale, and CJ Affiliate are a few affiliate networks you can try.

Affiliate marketing generally makes you more money than simply hosting ads. You must partner up with a company's affiliate program and then use your unique ID in posts, banner ads, or newsletter links that you send out. You can also post a product review promoting a product or service with your affiliate link.

In addition, you must create a disclosure page on your blog that tells readers what you are doing and how you are making commission on the companies you promote.

You must also include terms of service and a privacy policy. Simply look up sample pages and add them to your site. All of this legalese is imperative to build trust in your readers and avoid potential legal squabbles.

WordPress does have some restrictions on what products and links you can promote. Check with your platform to ensure that you are allowed to run certain affiliate marketing campaigns.

Also, if you start advertising lots of affiliate businesses, you will find that all of the banners and ads can slow your site down. That's when you should visit your plug-ins menu and find an affiliate plug-in.

This is not necessary if you are just hosting one or two affiliate ads, but if you are hosting more, be sure to get a plug-in to help you stay organized and fast.

COLD EMAILING

If a company does not belong to an affiliate network or have an affiliate key on their website, you can reach out in person.

You really want to sell yourself and your blog to this company so that they want to work with you. Therefore, send a polite and well-written email that you have thoroughly proofread with ProWritingAid (Resources).

At the top, have your name, company, and blog URL. Then begin with "Dear [insert company name]." Doing this shows who you are and that you know who you are writing to.

Below that, write an attention-getting headline. Something controversial can work. Or you can use something friendly, like "Let's Make Each Other Some Money!" Even something cute, like a picture of your pet and a headline about "Your Pet Shampoo Makes My Pooch Happy!"

The last thing you want to do is send an email with a boring headline. The goal here is to get someone's attention!

Next, launch into a story. Talk about how you started from nothing and gained a million followers, or something else relevant. Show this company that your blog is successful, or about to be, and how they can benefit from partnering with you.

Mention your demographic. "To those who live in small apartments with big dogs, I am an advocate that you can do it! I believe you are, too." Show similarities between your demographic and the company's.

You want to personalize the email to show that you did research into the company and you are not just mass emailing —even if you are! Each cold email you send needs to be personally addressed to the company and mention facts you know about it.

Next, offer the company value. Say that you can generate significant traffic on their site with an affiliate link. Maybe mention a problem they have with marketing and how you can help. You want to show a company that you will scratch their backs if they scratch yours.

Finish with a bold call to action. "If you want to make money and gain traffic, you should consider partnering with me!"

Conclude with, "Thank you for taking the time to read this. I can't wait to hear from you." This ending is key. It implies with certainty that you will hear from the company, which makes the recipient of your email more likely to actually write you back. Plus, it makes the recipient feel appreciated for reading your email.

Close with something like "Sincerely" or "Regards." This makes your email professional. Then type your name and add a signature.

ADVERTISING

Companies will pay you to host ads to their businesses or products on your site. Join Google AdSense and post your site's keywords.

Then, merchants can bid on your keywords and pay you every time someone clicks on their ads. Google will take a small cut and send the rest of the money to you.

To add Google AdSense to your blog, follow these steps:

Step 1: Set Up an Account

Visit Google AdSense. If you already have a Gmail account, you can use that to sign up with no hassle. If you already use YouTube or Blogger AdSense, you can get into your account and submit an application with your blog's URL to change it to a WordPress account.

Step 2: My Ads

Click on "My Ads." Then hit the "Add New Ad Unit" button. From there, select the type of ad you want to feature. A video ad, a text ad, an in-article ad—there are a wealth of options here. Text and display ads are ideal.

Step 3: Customize the Ad

Specify the size and colors. Use the "recommended" ones, as these are the ones with typically higher payouts. Then name it. The name really doesn't matter, so use whatever you think will help you remember what the ad is for.

Google will then find an ad for you. If it doesn't, then you can collapse the ad. Then hit save, and you will see a code. Copy and paste this into your notepad on your computer.

Step 4: Add to WordPress

Go to your WordPress dashboard and click on "Widgets." Then drag and drop your "Custom HTML" widget to the appropriate spot on your site and copy and paste the ad code. Save the changes and view your site to ensure that the ad displays correctly.

You can also look into plug-ins that help you place the ad better. Again, I recommend Avada (Chapter 4), as this theme makes it extremely easy to add this step.

Step 5: Don't Click on Your Own Ad

You might be tempted to generate a little extra moolah by clicking on your own ad or getting family and friends to do this for you. But Google has eyes everywhere, and it can tell when you do this. You can get banned from the system for trying to cheat it. Not good!

ONLINE STORE

A blog is a fantastic marketing opportunity if you have a business. Simply create an online store through a WordPress plug-in and promote your store with your blog. Each of your blog posts should mention one of your products or services.

For example, maybe you created your own horse stall bedding. You should create a store that sells your product. Then write articles about horse care and stable maintenance.

Mention your product and include lots of links to your online store throughout these ads. Also, dedicate an entire page to your store and offer videos and articles supporting your product.

I did this for centerforpetlossgrief.com. I created my own store with inexpensive PDFs for people to purchase. I also wrote a number of blogs for each product, and within that blog I provided an internal link (Chapter 4) so the reader would be directed to that particular product in my store.

Or, if you own a store of the brick-and-mortar variety, use your blog to promote it. Include a great "About Us" page (Chapter 4) that highlights your business's purpose, industry, mission, and history. Include business hours, address, social media, and phone on each page. Have a "Contact Us" page, as well. If you can, upgrade your store to include a digital store, as well, in order to reach a broader audience.

Offer subscribers a newsletter. Then, send out relevant content in the newsletter, with a bit about your products or your store at the bottom of each one.

Be sure to mention sales and specials, and try to offer new subscribers a coupon code. That is fantastic marketing that can reach many people.

WRAP-UP

Now you know how to monetize your blog! Blogs require work, but the work can be fun, inspiring, and profitable. By using affiliate links, ads, and an online store, you can generate passive income, even while you watch TV or take a vacation! Put in the work and then see the monetary rewards that pour in.

A monetized blog is truly rewarding. As long as you approach companies about ads and affiliate partnerships, stay on top of marketing emails to your subscribers, offer comprehensive reviews, and promote your own business, you can generate a nice passive income. It is both easy and fun!

You have now created a blog, customized it, worked on gaining a following, and started the process of monetization. Did you ever think you would get this far?

Well, you have! As you reach the end of this book, I hope that you have learned a lot. You have all of the tools and skills necessary to become a blogger. Welcome to the wonderful world of blogging!

But before you go—make sure you check off each action step below. These will keep you on track as you monetize your blog.

ACTION STEPS

> *Listed are the steps I covered in this chapter. Use the action steps as a checklist as you proceed with creating your blog. Refer back in this chapter to gain more detail when you are ready for the tasks outlined below.*

Six Steps to Monetizing Your Blog

Step 1: Send out lead magnets to your email subscribers. Offering something free makes people want to spend more!

Step 2: Sell what you know. The Information Age makes selling information a big hit!

Step 3: Review products. You at least get free products, and maybe a check!

Step 4: Host affiliate links. Email companies or join their affiliate programs. Become part of an affiliate network.

Step 5: Host ads with Google AdSense. Then sit back and watch the money pour in as people click on your ads!

Step 6: Host an online store. This is a great place to sell your products or advertise your business.

PEP TALK!

A blog is a fun and rewarding way to get your ideas out there before an audience and generate a little (or a lot!) of money on the side.

Your blog is a vehicle for publishing your ideas, promoting your views, generating business, and building a brand that people love and trust. It's also a great way to make friends and network with other people.

I can't be prouder of you! You have created a blog with meaningful posts. You have found hosting, started a site with WordPress, created some content, and started building a social media brand. As you market yourself across the web, you will see your email list grow and your readership double, triple, and so on!

Depending on your niche, blogging can be a viable way to make a living in today's era. Take advantage of this opportunity to do something both fun and impactful to earn money. The freedom and expression that a blog gives you cannot be rivaled by traditional business.

Whether you want to talk about your favorite pet or give your brick-and-mortar business a leg up, a blog is the way to do it. You will reach many people and make a name for yourself. Using the tips in this book, you will be able to launch yourself into an extraordinarily large audience.

As you can see, starting and running a blog is relatively straightforward. You don't need to be a published author, a pet expert, or a computer whiz to succeed at blogging.

With a few new skills and your passion, you can create a rock-star pet blog that garners a huge following. You can enjoy great success just by being you!

Pet lovers across the world turn to the Internet for meaningful connections, advice, and products. You can tap into a massive market of like-minded people just by offering what you are naturally good at: your own ideas!

I wish you great success and happiness on your journey in the pet writing industry. You can be successful as long as you put your mind to it. A blog is not out of reach for anyone.

> *Follow along with this book to create a riveting pet blog that people will love to read!*

Warmly,

Wendy Van de Poll

July 25, 2019

GLOSSARY

CPanel - is a web based hosting control panel provided by many hosting providers to website owners allowing them to manage their websites from a web based interface. This program gives users a graphical interface from which they can control their portion of the Unix server.

Blog - Blog posts are the fundamental of a blog. Every blog on the internet consists of different blog posts written by the blogger. ... Blogs (and blog posts) can be shared on social networks (Twitter, Facebook, Google+) and people can leave comments under the blog posts in order to start meaningful conversations.

Captcha - A CAPTCHA (a backronym for "Completely Automated Public Turing test to tell Computers and Humans Apart") is a type of challenge-response test used in computing to determine whether or not the user is human.

Hashtags - A hashtag is a label for content. It helps others who are interested in a certain topic, quickly find content on that same topic. A hashtag looks something like this: #wendy-vandepoll.com or #dogsoninstagram. Hashtags are used mostly on social media sites. They rocketed to fame on Twitter.

Internal Links - a type of hyperlink on a webpage to another page or resource, such as an image or document, on the same website or domain. Hyperlinks are considered either "external" or "internal" depending on their target or destination. Internal is a link to a page or post within your blog. External is a link out to a website other than your own.

Keyword/ Short-tailed Keyword – Short tail keywords are search phrases with only one or two words. Their length makes them less specific than searches with more words. "Pet" (one word) is an example of a short tail keyword, whereas "holistic raw cat food" (four words) is a long tail keyword.

Long-tailed Keyword/ Keyword Phrase - A keyword phrase is two or more words typed as a search query. For example, "What is the best way to feed my senior cat" is a good example of a keyword phrase.

Meta Description - The meta description is a snippet of up to about 155 characters – a tag in HTML – which summarizes a page's content. Search engines show the meta description in search results mostly when the searched-for phrase is within the description, so optimizing the meta description is crucial for on-page SEO.

Page – A WordPress Page is considered static and a type of timeless content. For example, the "About" or "Contact" pages of your website/blog do not need a published date to be displayed.

Post – A WordPress Post is a dynamic article that has a published/updated date and is displayed on the blog page. If you want to publish a blog post about anything in your niche, or an announcement, you should use a post.

SEO - SEO or Search Engine Optimization is the name given to activity that attempts to improve search engine rankings. In search results Google™ displays links to pages it considers relevant and authoritative. Authority is mostly measured by analyzing the number and quality of links from other web pages.

Server – A server is the central and usually the largest and most powerful computer in a network that houses the server software. It stores and manages the common network data and supplies it to the individual clients. It provides shared services such as access to the Internet and other networks, faxing, printing, etc. They function as file servers that receive, store, and send files, web servers that store webpages, and mail servers that receive, store, and forward emails.

SSL Certificate - An SSL Certificate (Secure Sockets Layer), also called a Digital Certificate, creates a secure link between a website and a visitor's browser. By ensuring that all data passed between the two remains private and secure, SSL encryption prevents hackers from stealing private information such as credit card numbers, names and addresses.

Website - a group of World Wide Web pages usually containing hyperlinks to each other and made available online by an individual, company, educational institution, government, or organization.

WHOIS - WHOIS (pronounced "who is") is an Internet service used to look up information about a domain name. While the term is capitalized, "WHOIS" is not an acronym. ... Whenever an individual or organization registers a new domain name, the registrar is required to make the registration information publicly available.

RESOURCES

A FREE GIFT

Create Your Winning Pet Blog Checklist
https://wendyvandepoll.com/pet-blogging-free-gift

AFFILIATE SITES**

ConvertKit - email provider
https://mbsy.co/convertkit/50525366

ProWritingAid - editing software
https://wendyvandepoll.com/pro-writing-aid

Siteground - website host
https://www.siteground.com/?referrer_id=7509454

AVADA ONLINE INSTRUCTION

Avadaphile
https://avadaphile.com

EMAIL PROVIDERS

Mailchimp
https://mailchimp.com

KEYWORD SEARCH

Ubersuggest
https://neilpatel.com/ubersuggest

Wordtracker
https://wordtracker.com

Google Keyword Planner
https://ads.google.com/home/tools/keyword-planner

MONETIZATION

Amazon Associates
https://affiliate-program.amazon.com

CJ Affiliate
https://cj.com

Clickbank
https://clickbank.com

PHOTOS

Pixabay
https://pixabay.com

Librestock

https://librestock.com

Deposit Photos
https://depositphotos.com

SERVICES

Upwork
https://upwork.com

Fiverr
http://fiverr.com

SOCIAL MEDIA ORGANIZATIONAL TOOLS

Agora Pulse
https://agorapulse.com

Buffer
https://buffer.com

Hootsuite
https://buffer.com

Later

https://later.com

ShareCount

https://sharecount.com

***The **three recommended sites** are products that I use and highly recommend. They are affiliate links which means if you purchase the product, I receive a small commission (which helps me greatly as an author.) You are not charged more because of the affiliate link.*

Pet Blogging 101:
How to Start a Riveting Pet Blog and Gain Loyal Followers

THANK YOU!

As the author of this book, I appreciate you buying and reading it. I hope you found the information useful and you now are on your way to creating a beautiful blog to share with others.

I would be grateful if you would leave a helpful book review, either with your favorite book distributor or with Amazon.

Thank you,

Wendy Van de Poll, MS, CEOL

Best-selling and Award-winning Author, Writing Coach, Speaker

www.wendyvandepoll.com

For all of Wendy Van de Poll's books, please visit:
https:amazon.com/author/wendyvandepoll

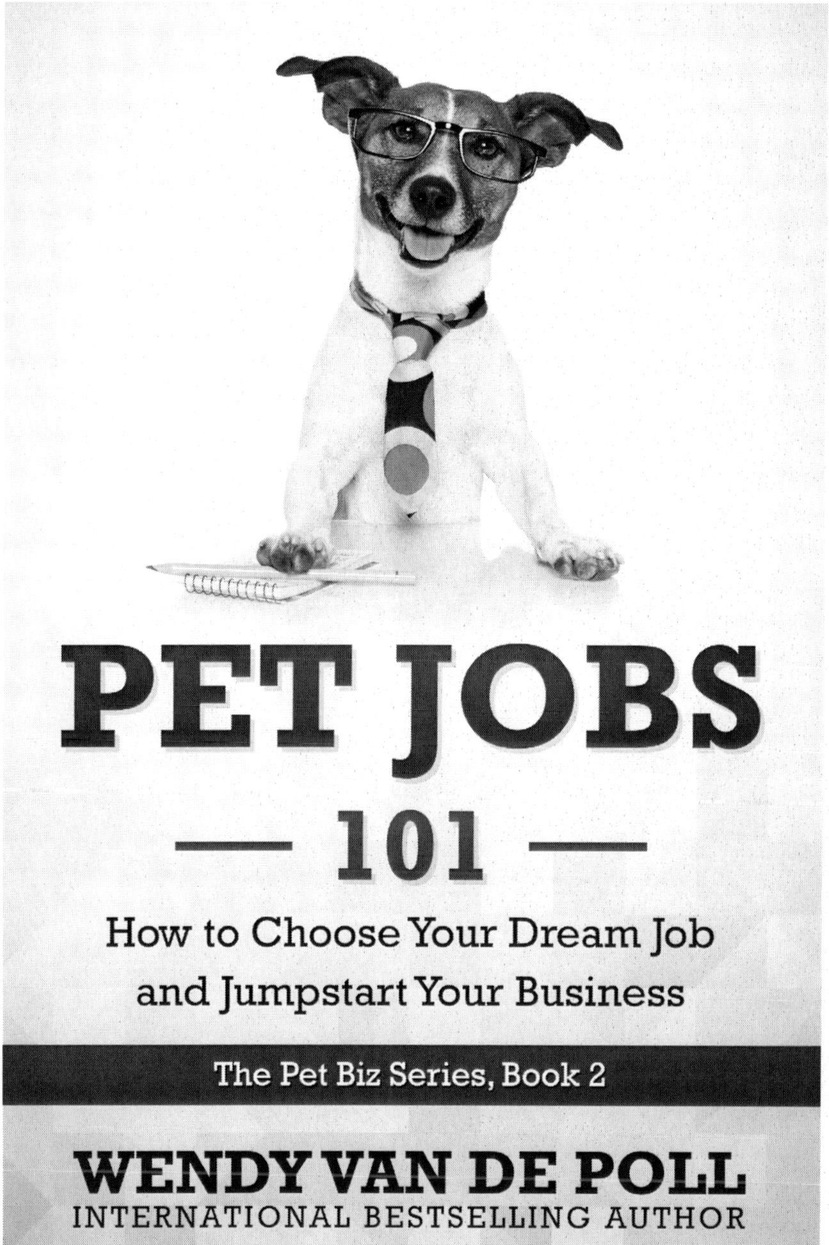

PET JOBS
— 101 —
How to Choose Your Dream Job
and Jumpstart Your Business
The Pet Biz Series, Book 2
WENDY VAN DE POLL
INTERNATIONAL BESTSELLING AUTHOR

Pet Jobs 101:
How to Choose Your Dream Job and
Jumpstart Your Business

Published by Spirit Paw Press, LLC, Concord, NH, 03303

Publisher's Cataloging-in-Publication Data
provided by Five Rainbows Cataloging Services

Names: Van de Poll, Wendy, author.
Title: Pet jobs 101 : the pet biz series / Wendy Van de Poll.
Description: Concord, NH : Spirit Paw Press, 2019. | Series: Pet biz, bk. 2. | Also available in ebook format.
Identifiers: ISBN 978-1-7324375-4-8 (paperback)
Subjects: LCSH: Pets. | Pet industry. | Pets--Services for. | Home-based businesses. | Authorship--Vocational guidance. | BISAC: PETS / General. | BUSINESS & ECONOMICS / Home-Based Businesses.
Classification: LCC SF414.7 .V36 2019 (print) | LCC SF414.7 (ebook) | DDC 636.0887/0681--dc23.

To all those who believe animals make
the world spectacular.

INTRODUCTION

Are you unhappy with your current career? Would you like to work in the pet industry but don't know where to begin? Would you love to land your dream job in the pet industry but have no idea what that is yet?

The answers to your questions are not that far away. The truth is your passion and love for animals can easily grow into a full-time job. With the help from *Pet Jobs 101: How to Choose Your Dream Job and Jumpstart Your Business*, you will get the support and guidance you need to get started.

I am living proof that you can do it. Working within the pet industry is incredibly fun and rewarding. You get to work with your favorite animals and help their people make better choices. You carve out your own place within a special community of pet lovers—united across the world by their shared devotion to the furry (or feathered or scaled) companions. When I go to bed happy at the end of a long workday, I can easily say it is the best feeling in the world. And I can't wait to share this feeling with you.

From the time I was a little girl, I knew I wanted to work with animals. I loved animals—especially dogs, cats, horses, and goats. I just couldn't imagine a different career path. As a licensed massage therapist for humans, horses, and hounds, I have over thirty years' experience working in the holistic animal field. I am the successful owner of CenterForPetLoss-Grief.com, a pet blogger, author of over twelve best-selling pet books, and an entrepreneur of a business centered around holistic healing for pets and their people. I can honestly say I have made my dreams come true.

Furthermore, the pet industry is quite lucrative and continues to grow with opportunities. It is more than possible to make a living, and, in fact, your business can flourish. Exponential projected growth in this industry will ensure that your business endures and continues to be successful for years to come.

The knowledge I am doing my part to make the world a better place for animals means so much to me. I would love for you to experience that, too. There is nothing better than to hear former clients thanking me for what I did for their beloved companions.

Because I am so confident you can make your dreams come true, I urge you to first believe in yourself. You can do it! The second part is finding out which dream job is yours, and the third is jump-starting your business.

How to Get the Most From This Book:

1. Read the entire book cover to cover. Make some brief notes of the points I raise to be successful.
2. Pick out the career or careers you are interested in. Do some research and pick one career that meets the criteria for your dream job.
3. Do the action steps for each chapter. They are designed to help you become laser focused when choosing your dream job and jump-starting your pet business.

With this book, I will show you the ins and outs of many different pet businesses and countless options to enter the pet industry. I intend to help you through the stages of opening a pet business. I will also share how to find your dream job in the pet industry and thrive.

When you read this book, you will learn various ways in which you can live your dream. Don't wait to move forward with your inspiration—especially if you love pets and want to make a difference in the world. Working in the pet industry is extremely rewarding.

Read on and make the business of your dreams come true.

It is time to make a change and...

- Be happy with your new career.
- Know exactly what goes into a pet business.
- Land your dream job with confidence!

Affiliate links are present at the end of this book. This means if you purchase the product, I receive a small commission (which helps me greatly as an author.) You are not charged more because of the affiliate link. In fact, sometimes there is even a small discount. I have personally tested all affiliate products mentioned. I would never recommend something I didn't love.

PART I
IN PERSON PET JOBS

Would you rather work with animals face-to-face? This section is all about learning how to make a career out of caring for or working with pets in person. Remember, a website and some online work is still necessary to advertise your services.

This section is for those who want to primarily do hands-on work with animals. There are many choices for in-person pet businesses. It just takes some time to figure out which one is for you.

1
PET PHOTOGRAPHER

Don't you just love pictures of adorable kittens and sweet puppies? Of course you do! That is why you can make a profitable living as a pet photographer. Not only can you be a photographer for pet peeps and take portraits of their beloved pets—you can also submit your photos for calendars, catalogs, stock photo sites, and magazines.

You can work for a company, or you can work independently. All you need is a website, professional camera, and a space for taking photos. It is also important to have the skills to work with all types of animals that have a variety of behaviors to get the perfect shot.

Start by getting a quality camera. You can browse professional photographer sites and forums to learn what you should buy. I won't discuss camera specifics here, since the camera industry is always changing. Take a few classes or skill courses to learn about lighting, pet posing, and how to use your camera. You should also get familiar with Adobe Photoshop and Illustrator, since a large part of photography entails editing pictures.

Next, practice. Do a few shoots for free to get the hang of it. You might volunteer to take photos at a shelter or have your friends bring their dogs by for photos. Try taking photos of your own pets. Use the best pictures in a portfolio that you post online and on your social media to prove your talent. Be sure to add watermarks or copyright images so that people don't copy and paste your work for free.

Create a website and business cards. You can use social media to advertise your photography. You can also hand out cards at local pet businesses and events. Be sure to include your best photo on the business card to give people a glimpse of your talent. Include your website address with your winning portfolio.

Offer your customers a few different options for print sizes. You might consider selling them engravings, T-shirts (Chapter 7), or things like mugs and calendars with their pets' photos. Have an entire catalog of products that you offer with the photos you take.

IMPORTANT CONSIDERATIONS

Pet photography is a great business, and you can make hundreds of dollars a day shooting for a few hours. However, you must get used to demanding owners and pets who won't sit still for long and/or won't look at the camera. You may also encounter nervous pets who are prone to biting or scratching in fear.

Taking and editing great photos is a skill you need if you want to be successful. Consider taking a few courses on lighting, composition, setup, and handling animals.

Always be patient with the pet you are working with. Never force a pose or behavior. Some of the best shots of pets are candid and unplanned.

It is important—and a good business practice—to explain to the client you can't guarantee the client's desired image because animals don't always cooperate. This sets reasonable expectations for the client.

Expected Salary: $36,634-plus a year

WRAP-UP

You can take beautiful or cute pictures of pets for good money! The initial investment in a camera, Photoshop, and studio space can run up to a few thousand dollars, but it is definitely worth it. As you learn how to take photos of pets and work with pets and their owners, you will get even better and develop a magnificent portfolio.

There is a learning curve with pet photography, and it isn't just about taking great photos. It is important to, first and foremost, respect the needs of the animal. Learning how to naturally work with your subject will yield beautiful photos, but patience is needed.

The action steps in this chapter outline the basics of what you need to get started. Always remember to do your research to learn as much as you can about your chosen career.

In the next chapter, I talk about becoming a pet sitter. Taking care of people's pets is a huge industry and one that can be successful. Pet sitting is a valuable service that gives owners peace of mind while they are away.

ACTION STEPS

1. Get a camera and take some courses in photography skills and pet photography.
2. Research what other pet photographers have on their websites and their specialties.
3. Practice and build a portfolio. Post your portfolio on your website.
4. Print cards with your website and best photo to distribute at stores and events.
5. Offer prints to your clients for an additional charge. Sell prints of images you own online as well.

2
PROFESSIONAL PET SITTER

Are you available on weekends and holidays when people go out of town? If so, a professional pet sitter is a great choice for a career. When people travel, they want someone they can trust to take care of their beloved non-human family members. As a pet sitter, you take on enormous responsibility. But you also make great money, have fun with pets, and give owners precious peace of mind. A rewarding career, professional pet sitting is a great way to work with animals in an unconventional setting.

Most pet sitters visit the owner's home for drop-in visits. They may stop by to take care of pets while the owner is on vacation, or they may drop in to walk dogs while the owner is at work. Others stay overnight, which is especially common for older pets or pets with special needs.

Pet sitters give animals the love, care, and attention they need while their owners are away in the comfort of their home settings. By doing drop-ins, you don't need to set up your own facility, but you do need a reliable car and phone.

Pet owners are placing a lot of trust in you by giving you a key to their homes and access to their cherished pets, so part of your job is proving that you deserve that trust.

To start, get the appropriate training and become a certified pet sitter. After your training, create a website and business cards that list your services and rates.

You can enroll on a site like Rover, which creates a profile and does some marketing for you. Advertise by leaving your cards at local pet businesses so pet peeps learn about you. If you want to provide drop-ins for busy professionals, try to approach people at business networking events and hand out business cards.

When working with a client, be sure to take lots of pictures of the pets you are caring for and send them to your client. Also be sure to learn the pet's feeding regimen and special needs—adhere to these things carefully. Let owners know what you have done with the pet after each drop-in visit with lots of photos. This reassures your client you are doing your job well and their companions are happy and safe.

Appreciative owners will likely tip you. Always urge them to leave you great reviews on Yelp, your personal website, and Rover. Good reviews will help you bring in more business. Ask the owner's permission to post photos of their pets enjoying their time with you on your site to bring in yet more trusting clients.

IMPORTANT CONSIDERATIONS

You can expect to work on holidays and weekends. You will probably get more business over the summer than the winter, since people like to take vacations during the warmer months. This means that you may have to work on holidays and limit your vacations to slow times.

While pet sitting is a lucrative business, there are going to be lulls and slower months. When gas prices rise, people travel less—and you can expect less business. Be prepared for these fluctuations.

Pet sitting is a huge responsibility, and things can go wrong. A dog may run away while you are walking. A cat may get sick. You must plan for these issues and always take great care to avoid them.

If something does happen, your best course of action is to immediately alert the owner and be honest. The owner may be able to help you figure out how to solve the problem. Always have an emergency vet's number in your phone, as well.

Expected Salary: $48,635 a year, but varies

WRAP-UP

Pet sitting is a great way to interact directly with animals and give owners peace of mind while they are away. But things can go wrong, so take extra measures to prevent problems and remain calm when problems arise.

Make sure you get the training you need to become certified from one of the organizations I recommend in the resource section of this book. There are many aspects of pet sitting that are important to learn, and by being certified, you are providing the best care for your clients.

Pet sitting is a rewarding career, but plenty of work is involved. You must be available and enjoy working on weekends and on holidays. The room for building your business potential is huge with this career.

Refer to the action steps in this chapter if you choose this career. They will help you stay focused on what is important when starting your business and gaining clientele.

In the next chapter, you will learn how to become a dog trainer! Dog training allows you to improve relationships between dogs and their people. Dog training is a rewarding career if you love to teach.

ACTION STEPS

1. Download my free gift that include websites to get you started (https://wendyvandepoll.com/pet-jobs-free-gift).
2. Choose a certification course and begin your training.
3. Create a website or Rover site and print your business cards.
4. Attend business network meetings. Leave your cards at local pet businesses.

5. As you drop in on pets, send owners updates with pictures.
6. Always adhere to a pet's feeding and medication schedule. Feed the pet food he or she is used to. You want to avoid digestive upset.
7. Have an emergency vet's number on your phone.
8. If something goes wrong, notify the owner right away.
9. Urge people to leave you good reviews. With their permission, post photos of their happy pets on your site.

3
DOG TRAINER

Do you enjoy well-behaved dogs? Training dogs is extremely rewarding. You can help people and their pets have better relationships, help rescue dogs transition into new homes, and feel as if you made a difference in someone's life.

But there is more to being a dog trainer than simply teaching a dog to sit and stay. Dog trainers provide wonderful resources for people who are frustrated with their dogs' behavior, and they help improve relationships between dogs and their people. Furthermore, a dog trainer's job may entail preparing dogs for careers, such as bomb or drug sniffing, tracking, or showing and competing.

Typically, you want to get started by choosing the field you want to train in. If you are just getting started, I would suggest basic obedience skills. However, ask yourself these questions to determine your long-term goal:

- Do you want to train dogs on basic obedience and provide people with tips on teaching a dog to be a good canine citizen?
- Do you want to teach a dog how to compete for show, agility, or some other sport?
- Do you want to train dogs for certain canine careers?
- Do you want to work with dogs used in movies?

There are many options! The one you choose depends on the difference you want to make in the dog world and your passion.

Next, you want to learn the ins and outs of dog training. Dog training is not as simple as professional trainers make it look! You have to learn how to work with dogs, read their body language, control your body language, understand animal behavior, and provide appropriate cues and rewards.

You can get training from a variety of schools. Some courses are in person, while others are online, or some combination of the two. I believe that hands-on, in-person training is ideal. The Certification Council for Professional Dog Trainers has a list of resources to help you find schools. You will find the URL when you download your free gift (https://wendyvandepoll.com/pet-jobs-free-gift).

It is often helpful to work with a mentor. Find a trainer in your desired field and work with him or her closely for at least a few months. Hands-on experience is an excellent companion to your written studies. Furthermore, you can find shelters looking for trainers or apprenticeships at training facilities. Look into dog training apprenticeships in your area or have your mentor help you find one.

Finally, you must get certified. A certification convinces pet owners that you know what you are doing, so you get more business. The Certification Council for Professional Dog Trainers is one place where you can get a trusted certification.

As you gain experience, you can start to advertise your business. Start with a website and distribute local flyers. Networking with other trainers and dog owners can help you gain loyal clients.

IMPORTANT CONSIDERATIONS

Being a dog trainer is a valuable and lucrative career that can earn you up to $150 an hour—maybe more when you specialize. However, you must uphold ethical values and please both dogs and their owners with exceptional customer service.

It is essential you stay level-headed and never get frustrated, even if a dog or owner is difficult to work with. You may encounter scared, aggressive dogs, and you must handle the dog appropriately to minimize the risk of injury to yourself. Any dog training course will offer training on how to mitigate these risks.

Certification is an absolute must in order to be considered professional and trustworthy.

Expected Salary: $30,077-plus a year

WRAP-UP

If you want to train dogs, you can make a lot of money, have a lot of fun, and provide a valuable service for animals and their people.

Becoming a dog trainer is not an overnight career choice. There is certification to consider, apprenticeship opportunities, and building your business with time-tested approaches. You must also consider what type of dog training you want to do, as I outlined in this chapter.

Next, if you like working with pets and don't mind getting a little dirty, this career may be the one for you. But first take a look at the action steps at the end of this chapter.

If you are interested in making animals look sharp, read on to learn about how to become a groomer! Groomers can make excellent money while working directly with animals.

ACTION STEPS

1. Download your free gift that includes schools and licensing bodies for dog training (https://wendyvandepoll.com/pet-jobs-free-gift).
2. Attend a certification course and get certified.
3. Find a mentor who is aligned with your principles.
4. Gain experience with this mentor and/or volunteer at shelters or rescue groups.

5. After you are certified and have established your business network, market yourself online and in person.
6. Always uphold customer service and ethical values in your training business.

4

GROOMER

Do you find satisfaction when creating something beautiful but don't mind hard work? Becoming a dog groomer may seem easy until you actually try to groom a dog! There is a large variety of cuts, hair types, and doggo dispositions that make this career interesting and unpredictable. You must learn how to groom dogs the right way, usually through a certification or apprenticeship program.

You may start by researching various certifications for dog grooming. I have a list for you when you download your free gift (https://wendyvandepoll.com/pet-jobs-free-gift). Proper certifications will expose you to a huge variety of types of dog hair and cuts, giving you valuable knowledge and experience. Plus, give you the training on how to start your business.

Another option that I don't recommend (because I'm all about certifications) is to approach a groomer in your area and express interest in training. The groomer may offer you an apprenticeship or refer you to a training program. Some groomers may hire you to wash dogs, and you can gain experience by watching how they work with and groom animals.

After your program, you can join The National Dog Groomers Association of America (Download Your Free Gift for the link), which is probably the most respected body for grooming certification. To get this certification, you must complete five tests over a five-year period and complete a course with the association.

There are a few other organizations that give certifications as well. Look into the one that fits your needs the most. You don't have to have a certification to groom animals, but it certainly helps boost your credibility, professionalism, and earning potential!

After your course, you should gain experience. Either offer services at low prices or work for a company to build a portfolio. You can also volunteer as a groomer for a shelter to gain necessary experience and help animals get adopted.

When you have some experience, glowing reviews, and a portfolio showing off at least five successful grooming jobs—create a website and start trying to draw in your own clients. You can advertise locally and online. You can also start your own shop or set up a grooming shop in your home when you believe you can get enough clients to justify the start-up costs.

IMPORTANT CONSIDERATIONS

You are likely to encounter scared animals who will bite. Then there will be those difficult clients who demand perfection. Because you will be working with animals, you will be exposed to fleas, ticks, skin conditions, and other challenging issues, including neglect.

To be successful in this profession, you must have a patient personality. Be able to soothe not only the animal but deal with challenging people. This career is a rewarding one, but it is not easy.

If you choose this profession, consider learning an energy technique (Chapter 14) or animal massage therapy (Chapter 16). They are great additions to your tool box and will help calm the animals you work on.

Also, you must keep your shop clean to not spread disease or parasites. Most groomers require proof of vaccinations before a client books with them to reduce the risk of spreading communicable diseases and parasites.

You can set your own policies if you have your own grooming business, but take as many precautions as you can. Always adhere to safe grooming and nail-trimming practices. If you do—you will succeed.

Expected Salary: $23,000-plus a year

WRAP-UP

Grooming is a fantastic way to work directly with animals. Once you are certified, you can continue with your education to include animal energy techniques, pet massage, or even specialize in cuts for show dogs.

With affordable education and start-up costs, you can have a career with a mid-range income. Certification, although not necessary—but recommended, gives you credibility, professionalism, and the business training needed to succeed.

Always take steps to keep your facility clean and free of parasites and diseases. Learn how to handle animals to prevent bites and scratches. Refer to the action steps to help guide you with this career choice.

If you are interested in making delectable treats for pets, then the next chapter is for you! Read on to learn how to start a pet bakery.

ACTION STEPS

1. Find a training course that is respected. Do your homework on this one because not all training courses are comprehensive.
2. Download your free gift for a list of schools and certifications.
3. Get certified. Although not necessary, I highly suggest this option. You will appear more

professional—which helps with business building practices.

4. Work for a company or volunteer at shelters to build a portfolio. This step is necessary when building a business.
5. Purchase equipment and a space, or set up in your home. You don't need much, but when you are starting out, you will need a few pieces. When you work from home, you can save on rent and deduct the space from your taxes.
6. Advertise your business. Even though word-of-mouth is the best advertising, you must do more. Join local business groups and network. Post your business cards around town and talk with other pet professionals to gain business.

5
PET BAKERY

As a pet lover, do you like to give your companions delicious, natural, and healthy treats? I make my own, so I know exactly what is going into what I am feeding them. If you love to bake and provide healthy treats for animals, you can make a decent living and warm many hearts by opening a pet bakery.

The great thing about opening a pet bakery is you can work out of your home or open a store. You can sell your treats online or in person. You can approach local pet businesses to carry your treats on consignment, too.

You can run your business out of your home and use something like Square and PayPal for credit card payments. Your start-up costs will only be a few hundred dollars or less for ingredients and baking supplies.

The best part is that you don't have to meet the same FDA and state standards as bakeries for humans! However, you may still need to speak to your city about applicable licenses. You may also have to register your business for tax purposes.

Anyone can create pet treats. That's why you must stand out from the competition and make owners feel that they should spend money at your bakery as opposed to buying a box of cheap pet treats made or sourced in China.

Offer something people love:

- Organic non-GMO ingredients.
- A special herbal blend that is safe for pets.
- Pet treats baked into cute shapes and frosted, as well as superior taste.

Find free recipes online and then try to make them unique, while always ensuring they are safe for the pet they are intended for!

I believe human-grade and natural ingredients should go into all pet treats and pet foods. If your human customers can eat it, then they will be more likely to feel good about feeding it to their pets. Be sure to use your packaging as advertising by sharing how you don't use preservatives, your treats are baked from the heart, you use organic ingredients, and so on.

Always advertise how your product is nutritious and healthy. This will be your main selling point. But presentation also matters, so making treats that look cute and palatable will work best for your business. Using catchy names for treats and creating holiday-themed treats and gift baskets will also boost sales.

IMPORTANT CONSIDERATIONS

Pet treats are adored by everyone, but you must market yourself by providing something better than the competition. Be sure to follow trends. Social media or trips to other successful pet bakeries can help you stay on top of trends.

A store that is dedicated solely to being a pet bakery may not thrive in a small community, so consider combining your bakery with another type of pet business if you are opening a store. While you can make a full-time career out of baking pet food and treats, this is more likely to be a successful side business.

Expected Salary: up to $40,000 a year

WRAP-UP

Since everyone loves pet treats, you can certainly make a profit. This can be a fun side business or a great full-time career depending on your business goals. Yet, you still have to treat this career as a business and do the necessary steps to be successful. The action steps in this chapter will help you.

Be sure to check with your town about regulations for having a business in your home and other possible business regulations.

If you are a creative person, you can design unique and fun treats that will delight the people that buy them and the animals who eat them. When you provide healthy and natural treats that are locally made and professionally marketed—your business will stand out.

This can be a fun career choice if you love baking and don't mind the networking needed to get your treats bought and to gain loyal customers.

Next, in Chapter 14, learn how working with animals and their energy can provide healing for a variety of physical and emotional issues. I will share how you can become an animal energy practitioner.

ACTION STEPS

1. Do your research by contacting your town offices to determine if you need licensing to open a pet bakery. Laws and restrictions will vary.
2. Choose where you will run your business—home, your own storefront, consignment space in a pet supply store.
3. This is the fun part. Research, develop, and taste your recipes before offering them for sale.
4. Make sure you purchase the supplies you need and your ingredients. Look for wholesale distributers so you can buy at a lower cost. I love Frontier Coop Wholesale (Resources).
5. Design your packaging to reflect your brand.
6. Create a beautiful and engaging website to entice your customers to buy your treats.

7. Make sure you follow trends. Offer holiday themes and gift baskets for your customers.
8. Download your free gift that has a list of contacts to start your business (Resources).

6
ANIMAL ENERGY PRACTITIONER

Are you interested in the intuitive side of life and believe in the healing power of energy? Animal energy practitioners often use Reiki (Glossary) or other energy methods to help pets heal from all types of ailments. A certification in animal Reiki or some other form of energy healing is customary.

By becoming an animal energy practitioner, you can have a rewarding and lucrative career while helping pets restore themselves from emotional and physical ailments.

As an energy practitioner, you base your work with animals on the premise that all beings have energy flowing through them. When the energy is strong, the animal is healthy, balanced, and less likely to get ill. When the energy is weak, the animal is easily affected by stress and less resistant to illness. The job of an energy practitioner is to balance these energies to provide and maintain the pet's natural state.

This type of energy work is done hands-on or from a distance. The practitioner uses his or her hands to channel the universal energy shared between the practitioner and client. Energy medicine (Glossary) is safe and works very well with conventional veterinary medicine, herbal medicine, homeopathy (Glossary), and Chinese medicine.

To become an energy practitioner, you should take a course in Reiki or some other form of energy healing before you begin promoting your business. Many practitioners like to use crystals (Glossary) and flower essences (Glossary) as part of their practice. These modalities provide more solutions for the pets you may encounter.

Once you complete a course and obtain certification, begin to practice on your pets, friends' companions, and local shelter animals to gain experience. Collect testimonials on your website.

You can then advertise online and distribute business cards promoting your healing business to local pet businesses. A woman I know who performs Reiki energy healing with animals advertises with a large magnetic sticker on her vehicle.

When you finish your training, you can open a practice where you utilize your compassion to help animals. As an animal energy practitioner, your work is to help them navigate through their life's challenges. With any professional practice, you will want to uphold your profession's code of ethics, which includes professional standard, confidentiality, education, etc.

You can work with a large number of animals, from horses to dogs to gerbils. Pet peeps want the best for their pets, and many of them are willing to try energy healing. You will find many grateful clients who are willing to pay up to $150 per hour for healing.

However, don't go into this for the money. Your heart must be in the right place to provide actual healing and comfort to animals.

IMPORTANT CONSIDERATIONS

A large part of your job entails focus and personal awareness of your abilities. This means you may take on some of the energy of suffering pets. Learning to clear your energy and maintain inner peace is essential. The certification you choose will help you with this aspect of your practice.

Another part of your work may involve assisting the animal's person with their healing. People may be troubled or feel guilty over injuries or illnesses affecting their pets. Always be professional, compassionate, and practice good listening skills.

You must be ready for all types of situations as you progress with your career. You may encounter some very painful experiences—along with the wonderful and successful. Keep in mind that compassion fatigue is prevalent in this type of work.

Expected Salary: $60,000 a year

WRAP-UP

By becoming an animal Reiki or animal energy practitioner, you are joining a field that continues to grow in popularity. Holistic medicine and alternative therapies are now considered mainstream professions. Many animal people will seek this type of treatment for their companions.

Keep in mind it is important to invest in your future by getting the appropriate credentials, joining professional organizations, and building your practice with ethics and integrity. You want to provide your clients with the best possible care.

This profession takes stamina as well. You must believe that universal energy (Glossary) is shared by all beings. If you don't believe in holistic care and its effectiveness, you will not do well with this choice.

Do your research, speak to animal practitioners, and read blogs on the subject to decide if it is for you. Take a look at the action steps in this chapter as well.

If you are interested in running a kennel, read on. Chapter 15 covers the steps required to become a professional kennel owner.

ACTION STEPS

1. Research online, speak to energy practitioners, read

blogs, and take an introductory course to determine if this field is for you.

2. Download the free gift for helpful links on schools and organizations that support pet energy practitioners (https://wendyvandepoll.com/pet-jobs-free-gift).
3. Decide if you believe in the power of energetic healing and if you have the focus that it requires.
4. Learn Reiki through a course and gain a professional certification (Download Your Free Gift for the link).
5. Practice on shelter animals and your own animals to gain experience and reviews.
6. Advertise online and in person.
7. Take care of yourself by meditating, eating healthy, and spending time doing something you love to avoid compassion fatigue.

7

KENNEL OWNER

Are you interested in boarding animals when their peeps go away? If so, you can start a kennel. You may need to rent or buy a space for a large kennel, or you can set up kennel facilities in your own home.

First, as with any business, do your research. Kennel operations require many moving parts. You must know about safety, health, behavior, and the ins and outs of the business. You will have to set up your kennel to accommodate the animals you choose to board. You will want to set up a yard, play areas, kennels, and feeding stations or food bowls.

You should also set up a station where you can bathe pets if necessary. Pet first aid kits and training are also essential. Be sure to obtain emergency vet information so that you can get help if something bad happens.

Second, set rates according to the services you offer. Market yourself online and leave flyers or business cards at local pet businesses. Attend business networking events and hand out your cards, since professionals are more likely to go out of town and require someone to board their pets.

Pet peeps will want to tour your facilities, so post pictures online and keep the facilities spotless and sterile. The better your facilities look—the more they will want to board with you. Whether you believe in vaccinations or not, it is probably a good idea to require animals to have full vaccinations.

You do want to prevent the spread of disease, as this could spoil your reputation fast. It is also best to require pets to be spayed or neutered—unless you are set up to accommodate animals in heat, etc.

When someone boards with you, be sure to learn the pet's schedule and adhere to it as much as possible. Pets are already stressed when they enter a new place; keeping their schedule can help calm them. Allow pets space to exercise and play by themselves throughout the day. Don't mix animals who don't know each other to prevent fighting.

IMPORTANT CONSIDERATIONS

You must have a set-up that allows you to care for pets in the most efficient capacity. For dogs, you must have a yard and kennels set up. Also, you must be mindful of their feeding regimens.

Another consideration is keeping up with each boarder's medication schedule. Also be mindful that not all dogs get along. Get permission from the client if it is okay for their dog to play with others.

If you are doing this by yourself, you should limit the number of dogs you keep on hand (no more than three) to ensure that you deliver high-quality care to each one.

For cats, you must have a room where they can hide and feel safe. Understand that boarding is a very stressful situation for the pet, particularly cats, and you must set the pet at ease by providing the utmost safety. Studying an energy technique (Chapter 14) is a great service to add to calm your boarders.

Owners often worry about their pets while they are away. You can set their minds at ease by sending them daily updates. Be cordial and expect to be on call almost 24/7!

The initial start-up costs can be high. Don't cut corners to minimize costs. Pet people are always in need of safe, clean facilities to keep their pets in while they are gone on business or vacation. Run your business well and you will succeed.

Expected Salary: $58,165 per year

WRAP-UP

Running a kennel is hard but lucrative work. There are many moving parts, and it is essential you know what you are doing. Make sure you are up on town restrictions and other legalities before you open your business.

Since people are going to trust you with their animals, you must provide professional, ethical, and a stellar service for their companions. A dirty, poorly run, and neglectful kennel will quickly shut down.

There are many services you can add to your kennel operation. You can offer massages (Chapter 16), grooming (Chapter 12), special walks, special diets, training, and more.

While start-up costs are high, you can expect to make an excellent salary with lots of hard work and attention to your clients. Your business will always be in demand!

Read on to the next chapter to learn how to become a pet massage therapist. Yes, pets can get massages, too! But don't forget your action steps.

ACTION STEPS

1. Decide if running a kennel is for you. Do you like to be available to work 24/7 in the beginning? You must be willing to be available at all times just in case an emergency arises.
2. If this doesn't bother you—start your research. Look into facilities, town and state regulations, health regulations, etc.
3. You can download your free gift for associations and licensing information. (https://wendyvandepoll.com/pet-jobs-free-gift).
4. Once you are done with your research, set up your

facilities with the appropriate needs for your boarders. Kennels, play areas, feeding stations, etc.

5. Start your marketing with a website, networking, open houses, etc.
6. Once you open your doors, make sure you keep your clients updated via video, texting, and/or emails.
7. Never falter from providing the best care for the animals. Their people trust you, and your success will be riding on that trust.
8. Expect to dedicate your entire life to this venture until you can hire stellar employees.

8

PET MASSAGE THERAPIST

Do you love getting massages? My animal clients love to get their sore muscles worked on, and they need massages—just like we do. While some owners just want to spoil their pets with pampering that includes massages, others actually require massage for their pets to heal chronic pain and injuries.

You can work in equine massage, feline massage, canine massage, etc. You may work independently or with a company. Some places to look for work include animal shelters and rescues, racing barns, dressage barns, pet grooming salons, pet kennels, vet clinics, and independent breeders.

Massage therapy is a serious art which has medical uses. Therefore, you must attend school and become certified in order to learn appropriate techniques. Furthermore, some states restrict pet massage to veterinarians, while others allow vets to delegate work to trusted massage therapists.

There are still some states that don't regulate pet massage therapy at all, but I still recommend certification. You want to be professional and a good business owner so potential clients trust the work you are doing is safe. Learn the laws in your state to see if this is a viable career in your area.

Look at different pet massage schools online and book appointments to visit the schools in person. You can expect to pay up to $8,000 for training. You may also consider completing a veterinary assistant program for a few thousand, as veterinary assistants are more likely to be paid well and be delegated work by veterinarians.

Build your reputation by working for a company or volunteering to massage in shelters. Using a website, you can market yourself with videos of your massages, testimonials from pet owners, and a display featuring your certification and training.

Be sure to take advantage of local businesses for referrals if you want to work independently. Your best bet to gain loyal clientele and steady work would be to work with a company or clinic.

IMPORTANT CONSIDERATIONS

Pet massage can be a very physically demanding job. You must learn appropriate techniques to avoid injury to yourself and to your animal clients. You must also learn how to read a pet's body language to gauge how the animal is feeling.

With this career, you can be self-employed or work for a groomer, veterinarian, barn, etc.

Be prepared to get the proper training. Even if you are a licensed human massage therapist, you must learn the anatomy and physiology of the animals you are treating. Our four-legged friends do not have the same muscle structure as we do.

Expected Salary: $41,240 a year

WRAP-UP

Pet massage therapy is a great way to help horses, dogs, cats, and other animals recover from injuries or congenital defects. It is also a nice way to pamper pets! As long as you are ready for a physically exerting career, you will enjoy working in pet massage. Make sure pet massage is legal for non-vets in your state before you proceed.

Pet massage certification couples nicely with energy work, veterinarian medicine, day care, pet sitting, and more as an add-on to the services you may offer.

Before you learn how to start a doggie day care—where dogs can have fun and play outside of their homes—check out the action steps for this chapter!

A doggie day care is a great way to earn some cash while enjoying time spent with four-legged friends. I can't think of a career that is more fun.

ACTION STEPS

1. Determine if you have the physical strength to give massages to animals.
2. If you do, then research laws in your state to make sure you can practice animal massage. The last thing you want to have happen is to spend a bunch of money and time to get certified and find out later you can't practice.
3. If it is legal for a non-veterinarian to carry out animal massage, get certified. Find a school where you actually have hands-on experience with animals.
4. Schools and licensing/certification/professional organizations are listed in your free gift (https://wendyvandepoll.com/pet-jobs-free-gift).
5. After certification, seek a job at local pet businesses and vet clinics to build your business.
6. Build your reputation and testimonials through volunteer work.
7. And of course, create your website and be involved on social media to build your following and client base.

9

DOGGIE DAY CARE OWNER

Would you love to operate a business where doggos get to visit you every day? Pet day care centers are places where owners can drop off their dogs for a few hours each day. People may do this to socialize their pets or to ensure their pets are cared for while they are at work.

You typically charge by the hour and spend those hours playing with and socializing pets. You can even offer massages (Chapter 16) as an additional service. It is important to know how many dogs you can handle. You must set a limit on how many pets you can care for because you want to provide quality time for each animal.

You can open a facility or run your doggie day care from your home. You must have a large space where dogs can play, as well as lots of available toys. In addition, you may need kennels so pups can have a quiet, safe space to rest.

You also should consider your energy level. It takes a lot of energy to keep up with the needs of the animals! And remember to research prices of other local pet day cares and set your own based on the industry average.

Also, set your hours based on when people are most likely to be at work, as this is when pet owners will need you the most.

While you don't need any education to become a dog day care owner, you can benefit from certifications in emergency pet care, animal behavior, or even veterinary assistance. These skills make you more marketable and give owners peace of mind.

You can give owners even more peace of mind by learning what care pet peeps expect from you. Offer to feed the food and treats their companions are used to. Finally, check with your local town ordinances to find out what sorts of permits and licenses you need for this kind of business.

Advertise at local pet stores and kennels. Mention all of the services you offer. Invite people to tour your day care and contact you for free price quotes.

When a new dog joins your day care, introduce it gradually to the other dogs to prevent fighting and injuries. If pets do get into a fight, swiftly separate them and put them in their respective kennels to "cool off."

Alternatively, if you don't want to open a dog day care of your own or you want to try the business before opening your own, you can apply to work at a local dog day care. You may earn minimum wage, but you will have a fun job with animals that you will love!

IMPORTANT CONSIDERATIONS

A doggie day care puts you in charge of the health and happiness of many pets for several hours a day. You must dedicate your full energy to the job and supervise the pets in your care. You must have the energy to play with them and keep them occupied.

A dog day care is a great way to make some cash. But you can also offer other services, such as grooming or massage, alongside the basic pet care service you are offering. Expand your services slowly as you build a clientele, gain reviews, and learn what people in your area want. Doing too much at once can raise your start-up costs and overwhelm you.

Expected Salary: $30,000 a year or more

WRAP-UP

If you want to provide pet peeps a valuable service and take care of dogs all day—running a pet day care can be a great career for you. Alternatively, you can apply to work at a local dog day care. It is a fun career, but it requires a lot of energy and responsibility.

There is a lot of responsibility that goes into a doggie day care because you are taking care of someone's beloved companion.

Be sure your facility is clean and you have the proper trainings to gain professionalism in your industry.

In Chapter 18, I talk about becoming a veterinarian. This is an amazing profession and has many specialties to choose from. Although it is a financial and educational commitment, becoming a veterinarian is a worthy aspiration. Read on to learn how to become one! But don't forget your action steps.

ACTION STEPS

1. Volunteer or work at a doggie day care center to determine if this is the type of work you want to do.
2. If so, learn about local ordinances and licenses for your type of business. You want to do this before you invest in your business.
3. Obtain certification in animal-related disciplines if desired. This is a good idea to show your people clients you are professional and their animals are safe.
4. Decide where you want to set up your facilities. Home or a separate building.
5. Research fees of your competition and then fair prices based on local pricing trends.
6. Advertise your business using a website, social media, local newspaper, etc.
7. Play with pets and care for their needs. Supervise them well.
8. Offer additional services if desired.

10
VETERINARIAN

Have you always dreamed about become a veterinarian? I know I did when I was a kid. Becoming a veterinarian is a dream for many people. While it requires a great deal of education, it can be a lucrative and rewarding career, a career where you get to work with animals and save lives every day.

To start, you must obtain a bachelor's degree in a field such as biology, zoology, chemistry, microbiology, physiology, or animal husbandry. You must earn high grades while in high school and college. Getting into a veterinarian school tends to be a very competitive process.

After you acquire your undergraduate degree, apply to a school of veterinary medicine to complete a doctorate of veterinary medicine (DVM), which can take up to four years. Veterinarian school consists of all-day classes and rigorous testing in subjects like pathophysiology and anatomy. You will have lots of studying and memorizing to do when you're not in class.

To augment your education, you should join a pre-vet club at your school and volunteer at vet clinics or animal shelters. Some veterinarians also start by working as veterinarian techs. You can expect to pay about $250,000 for your doctorate.

Once you finish school, you have to become licensed by taking the state board exam for veterinary medicine. While this exam is tough, school will prepare you for it. After you pass the exam, you can apply to work at veterinarian clinics to gain experience. Typically, you should have years of experience before starting your own clinic.

IMPORTANT CONSIDERATIONS

Working as a veterinarian is a lucrative and rewarding career. However, there are some things you need to consider first. Veterinarians need to be emotionally strong because of the wide variety of issues they may encounter in the field.

You may see some horrible things, such as chronically ill, abused, or critically injured pets. Part of your job will involve euthanizing, which can be emotionally wrenching for both the staff and pet families. While these parts of the job can be emotionally hard, they are still very important.

Veterinarians may encounter pets who are scared to be in the office. They may try to bite or scratch. Fortunately, you will learn many ways to prevent this in school as well as through experience. I also touch on how to handle difficult pets in Chapter 32.

You can make significant money as a veterinarian. However, if you are in it just for money, you are in it for the wrong reasons. A love of pets and a desire to make a positive difference in the world should be your motivation to enter this career. Since becoming a veterinarian takes a lot of schooling, you must be motivated and truly interested in the career.

It can be hard to afford school, especially since you will not have time to work throughout your training. Therefore, it may be helpful to save money, apply for grants and scholarships, take out student loans, and even enter the military for help with education costs.

Working as a veterinarian entails standing on your feet for long hours, being on call most hours of the day, and having few vacation days. You may work weekends and holidays.

Expected Salary: starting at $60,000 a year, up to $170,000 with experience

WRAP-UP

Becoming a veterinarian is a rigorous and competitive process. Working as a veterinarian entails being on call and witnessing some emotionally challenging things. You must be ready to manage your fatigue and burnout, as it is a demanding profession.

Even though school is expensive and a long process, this career can be satisfying, as you can make a huge difference in the lives of pets and their people.

After reading this chapter, do the action steps. If you decide you don't want to become a veterinarian but you want to work in animal medicine, consider becoming a veterinarian technician. The next chapter teaches you everything about how to become one!

ACTION STEPS

1. Ask a local veterinarian office if you can observe the practice for a day or couple of hours. This will give you an idea of the events that happen in a practice. Be honest with yourself and ask, "Is this for me?"
2. Complete a bachelor's in a science field, as I explained in this chapter. Strive for excellent grades, as the competition is tough to get into veterinarian school.
3. Join a pre-vet club, volunteer with animals, or work as a veterinarian technician or assistant.
4. Apply to veterinarian school and earn a DVM. Be involved with as much as you can so you get high grades and excellent experience.
5. Get licensed through your state board.
6. Work for a clinic for a while before you open your practice to gain business experience as well as practical experience.

7. Open your own practice if desired.
8. Download your free gift with helpful links (https://wendyvandepoll.com/pet-jobs-free-gift).

11
VETERINARY TECHNICIAN

Would you like to assist a veterinarian with various tasks? Veterinary technicians are to veterinarians what nurses are to doctors. You will perform a wide variety of tasks, from sanitizing equipment to providing anesthesia to clipping pets' toenails.

You are often the first person pets and their owners encounter in the veterinarian office, and you will interview owners to gather crucial information for the vet. Your place of employment will be in a veterinarian clinic, humane society, or with a mobile veterinarian.

Becoming a veterinary technician entails an associate's degree in veterinary technology, which equates to about two years of schooling. Some schools are online, such as Penn Foster and San Juan College.

Others are hands-on programs, which give you more practical skills. Even online programs require you to spend a few weeks in practical hands-on training as an intern at a veterinarian clinic. Make sure your state allows for online schooling.

Once you complete your schooling, you must become licensed with your state board by taking a veterinary technology exam. Upon passing the exam, you can apply for jobs with veterinarian clinics or other facilities. Depending on your state, you may have to take continuing education classes to keep your license current.

IMPORTANT CONSIDERATIONS

Working as a veterinary technician allows you to work directly with animals and provide life-saving support. It puts you in the forefront of veterinary medicine. You will be on your feet for long hours, and you may encounter challenging people and their animals.

While your school will train you how to handle all of these issues, you must be prepared for them as you choose to enter this career. These problems are typically far and few between; most veterinary technicians say that they love working with animals and couldn't ask for a better job!

Veterinary technicians also must practice great customer service, as they are often the face of the clinics. You must calm and comfort anxious or grieving pet owners, soothe scared pets, and address all issues for the veterinarian.

Expected Salary: $25,000–$35,000 a year

WRAP-UP

This career lets you handle animals and save lives! Becoming a veterinary technician involves some of the same aspects of working as a veterinarian for a fraction of the schooling and cost. However, it also pays significantly less.

You will be responsible for keeping the schedule moving so that the veterinarian doesn't run late, assisting the veterinarian with exams, cleaning treatment rooms, initial patient contact, and many other duties.

As you work through the action steps, do your research by asking other veterinary technicians what they love and what they find challenging in their jobs.

Would you like to work hands-on with horses specifically? In Chapter 20, you will learn about how to become a barn manager.

ACTION STEPS

1. Interview veterinary technicians about the pros and cons of their career.
2. Decide if you want to obtain an online degree, blended degree (Glossary), or face-to-face training.
3. Apply to and complete a veterinary technician degree.

4. Get your license and search for a position in a facility that meets your career goals.
5. Research educational opportunities as a licensed veterinary technician to stay current with industry standards.
6. Download your free gift that has helpful resources to get you started (https://wendyvandepoll.com/pet-jobs-free-gift).

12
BARN MANAGER

Do you want to combine your love for horses with business? As a barn manager, you are the one in charge of feeding and grooming, exercise schedules, turnout schedules, transportation, showing schedules, brand inspections, and veterinarian and farrier appointments.

You must order necessary supplies, direct employees, handle payroll, and fix emergency situations. You also must ensure the barn is kept clean, manage the prevention of diseases, and have strict precautions against injuries.

The smooth operation of a horse barn is your job! You will be in charge of horses and people alike.

There are different kinds of barns that you can work in. Some are for horses that race or show in dressage, etc. Others are for boarding horses for people that cannot have a horse on their own property. There are also barns in need of a manager where they rescue unwanted animals. Your tasks will be influenced by the type of barn you work in.

The main component of being a barn manager is developing extensive equine knowledge and experience. If you grew up around horses, you have a head start, but you can also gain experience by working in a horse barn. Taking courses in equine medicine, massage (Chapter 16), energy healing (Chapter 14), and pet care can also help you get the expertise you need.

Learn about payroll and other skills useful for a barn. You can find cheap or free classes online for these things. Furthermore, you should possess basic computer and filing skills. Most community colleges offer classes on computer skills and business administration for low prices.

When you find an opening for a position as a barn manager, you want to prove that you have what it takes. Be prepared to show off your office skills and your equine knowledge. You will probably be asked to handle a horse as well.

If you want to open your own barn, you must invest money in purchasing or building a facility and obtaining all the necessary supplies, equipment, horses, and employees. Create a business plan and formulate a solid idea of how you will manage your barn.

Barn management can be an extremely lucrative career, and there are colleges now that offer associate's and bachelor's degrees in equine studies.

IMPORTANT CONSIDERATIONS

Barn managers have very important jobs, and they have a lot of responsibility. Expect long hours and lots of work. Also, expect to be on call even at night and on holidays should anything go wrong in the barn.

To excel at this career, you must love working with horses and people. You must not be above office work or outside work that gets you dirty. You will have to be flexible and take on a wide variety of tasks and duties.

The entire barn operation relies on you, so you will have pressure to perform exceptionally well. You will also have immense control over the barn and the ability to make decisions.

Expected Salary: $67,950

WRAP-UP

Barn managers do so many things and become the entire foundation of a successful barn operation. As a barn manager, you will work with people and horses every day. This career can be stressful, but fun and rewarding as well. If you love horses, this is an excellent career to get started in.

Before you jump into becoming a barn manager, go over the action steps in this chapter. They will help you streamline the process.

To augment the work of veterinarians, you can become a veterinary acupuncturist or chiropractor. The next two chapters detail how you can enter these rewarding careers in animal medicine and care.

ACTION STEPS

1. Research colleges to obtain an associate's or bachelor's degree in equine studies.
2. Become skilled in working with and around horses if you don't have the experience.
3. Decide if you can manage many tasks at one time. Being a barn manager requires organization, knowledge, and careful planning.
4. Work at an established barn for a while to gain experience before you invest in schooling.
5. Graduate from the college of your choice. Then consider opening your own barn. Obtain a space and acquire appropriate licenses. Create a business plan for success. Then stock and staff the barn.

13
VETERINARY ACUPUNCTURIST

Are you holistically minded, and do you want to be a veterinarian? Then consider acupuncture once you become a DVM. Although in some states it is legal to become an acupuncturist without a DVM, do your research before you start your training.

Acupuncture is the ancient Chinese art of using needles to relieve pressure at certain points throughout the body to treat maladies. In recent years, Western medicine has realized the high success rates of acupuncture, and the military even offers acupuncture to their members now. Animal medicine is no different. You can find a lucrative career in the animal medicine industry with veterinary acupuncture.

Veterinary acupuncture treats many things:

- Injuries

- Chronic pain
- Digestive issues
- Infertility
- Anxiety
- And more

If a pet has an issue, stimulating certain points on his or her body can bring about the results a pet's person desires. This service oftentimes offers a solution or critical piece of the pet healthcare puzzle.

To offer this service, you must attend an acupuncture training program. You can find a program on the website for the American Board of Animal Acupuncture or a Google search. This program will probably take about two years, depending on your rate of completion.

The American Board of Animal Acupuncture offers certification. This certification is legally required in most states (as is veterinarian licensure). The test is mostly written. After getting certified, you will have to attend continuing education every year through the American Board of Animal Acupuncture to keep your certification current.

You can add acupuncture to your current practice or travel to barns, breeding facilities, farms, other veterinary clinics, show rings, racetracks, kennels, zoos, etc. This career can be exciting and lucrative if you love helping animals and feel a pull toward Chinese and alternative medicine.

IMPORTANT CONSIDERATIONS

Acupuncture is an amazing way to help facilitate health and healing in pets. Do your research to be sure you can be a practicing veterinary acupuncturist without being a licensed DVM.

Honestly, I wouldn't recommend this field without becoming a veterinarian first. In most states and countries, acupuncture is considered to be a surgical procedure.

Animals have many differences in anatomy. There is also a potential to do harm if your treatments are done incorrectly. A DVM has extensive training with disease, anatomy and physiology, structural issues, etc. Without this degree, you risk not being able to treat an animal correctly. That said, if it is legal in your state, you can work under a veterinarian with the proper certification.

Expected Salary: $49,000 a year, considerably more if you are a DVM

WRAP-UP

Acupuncture is becoming more and more accepted in Western medicine as a viable means of promoting and maintaining healing and health. You can practice it on animals with stunning results. Work alongside veterinarians or independently to help animals.

The more you know about traditional Chinese medicine and philosophies and the Western scientific background, the more you can treat the animals under your care properly.

In the next chapter, you will learn more about becoming a veterinary chiropractor. But first, take a look at the action steps in this chapter to determine if acupuncture is for you.

While becoming an animal chiropractor is perhaps even more challenging than becoming a veterinarian, animal chiropractors have rewarding jobs with high pay.

ACTION STEPS

1. Ask a local veterinary acupuncturist or human acupuncturist if you can observe the practice for a day or a couple of hours. This will give you an idea if you are ready to commit to hard work.
2. Research your state's laws about practicing without a veterinarian license. Obviously, if it is not legal, you don't want to spent the time and money to get a degree you can't use.
3. Apply to veterinarian school and earn a DVM if acupuncture without a license is not legal.
4. Get licensed through your state board and continue your education.
5. Work for a clinic for a while before you open your practice to gain business experience as well as practical experience.

6. Open your own practice if desired.
7. Download your free gift for veterinary acupuncture organizations (https://wendyvandepoll.com/pet-jobs-free-gift).

14
VETERINARIAN CHIROPRACTOR

Have you ever thought it was possible that animals could benefit from chiropractic care? Just like humans who need their necks adjusted or their backs manipulated into place, so do animals.

Dogs, cats, horses, and all other types of vertebrates sometimes need alignments. Pets in special need of chiropractic services include animals...

- Who have been injured.
- With congenital deformities.
- Who work hard, such as racehorses, police dogs, or service animals.

As an animal chiropractor, you will work closely with veterinarians to provide much-needed skeletal alignment services to animals.

Most veterinarian chiropractors are DVMs, or doctors of veterinary medicine, themselves. If you become a veterinarian (Chapter 18), you may choose to specialize in chiropractic medicine. If you choose this specialty, you will attend additional clinics and training in chiropractic skills, usually for seventy-five to one hundred hours.

The American Veterinary Medical Association lists various schools that offer this training on their website (Resources). These are postgraduate programs for licensed veterinarians; you must have a license to register for them. The costs vary for these programs.

When you complete your hours in the course, you will sit for the Animal Chiropractic Certification Commission Exam, which contains practical and written portions to ensure you have the necessary knowledge to practice. You cannot work in this field without this certification.

With the certification in hand, you can work in a variety of settings. You can start a traveling practice that visits animal in their homes or other settings. It will be important to promote yourself online and at animal-related events. You can also work for a barn or numerous veterinarian clinics as a traveling chiropractor.

Once you graduate and are certified, you must complete up to thirty hours of continuing education training each year to keep your certification current. You will learn new skills and advancements in animal medicine.

IMPORTANT CONSIDERATIONS

Animal chiropractors go through extensive education, but that education is certainly worthwhile. You will earn an excellent salary, provide helpful pain relief to animals, and facilitate healing in sick and injured animals. You have a lot of choices when it comes to where you work.

This job is very physical and requires long hours on your feet. You must have the strength to perform the duties, which can become more strenuous depending on the type of animal you choose to work with. For instance, equine chiropractors must have intense upper body strength; a dog chiropractor may not need as much upper body strength. You will often work on weekends and even holidays, and you may be on call.

Expected Salary: $62,424 a year

WRAP-UP

Working as a veterinary chiropractor allows you to treat joint conditions and injuries in animals. You can work in a huge variety of settings on all types of animals. Your job is highly specialized, and, if you develop your business properly, your services can be of high demand.

Once you graduate and are licensed as a veterinarian, there are various programs for animal chiropractic medicine you can apply to. This is a rewarding career that can offer many possibilities for growth and continued education.

So far, you have explored many options for careers and businesses in the pet industry. We talked about working with animals, both in person and online. Now let's get into how to volunteer with animals.

Volunteering means you work with animals for little or no pay, but it can add significant meaning and contentment to your life. Get involved in your animal community today by starting the next section of this book.

But first, to get a quick overview as to what is involved with becoming a successful animal chiropractor, go to the action steps for this chapter.

ACTION STEPS

1. Determine where you want to go to veterinarian school. After you have your DVM, research animal chiropractic certification trainings.
2. Download your free gift for veterinary chiropractic organizations (https://wendyvandepoll.com/pet-jobs-free-gift).
3. Chiropractor certification programs are approximately seventy-five to one hundred hours in length. Decide on the program you want to attend.
4. After you receive your certification, determine if you want to be a traveling chiropractor or work in your office. Also decide which type of animal you want to work with.

5. Be sure to keep up with your required thirty hours of continuing education a year.

PART II
VOLUNTEER

Is it your goal to do good for the animals of the world regardless if you are paid or not?

Volunteering would be the perfect choice. In this section, I will cover a variety of volunteer positions you can explore. Some of the career choices I cover can actually be paid positions as well. I included them in this section because I wanted to give you the chance to choose the right one according to your goals.

VOLUNTEERING IS WONDERFUL

1. You get the needed experience as you prepare for other careers mentioned in this book.
2. You can do what you love in your spare time.

3. You will make a tremendous difference for many animals and pet families.

15
HUMANE SOCIETY/RESCUE VOLUNTEER

Do you want to save pets from abandonment, abuse, or neglect? If you answered yes, you can become a rescue worker. Rescue workers save the lives of animals and keep them out of kill shelters—where they are euthanized if they are not adopted quickly enough.

Often, this job does not pay anything, but you can obtain many government grants and individual donations to cover expenses. You can also rely on volunteers for labor.

You may volunteer at a rescue or open one of your own. To start volunteering, visit local rescues and ask if they need help. Your hours will be flexible, so you can put in as much time as you want. Your duties will involve:

- Walking
- Bathing
- Cleaning up after animals

- Going along on rescues
- Attending community outreach events, like adoption events
- Feeding
- Socializing

To open your own rescue, it is best to have a large facility with lots of room for animals to be safe and comfortable. You may be able to get a federal or state grant for all your equipment and start-up costs.

Before you apply for grants, come up with a mission statement that summarizes your interest in helping animals and the needs you plan to serve in your community. You will also need to draft a business plan to show where any money you receive will go.

There are different types of shelters. For a no-kill shelter, you accept potentially adoptable pets and never euthanize them, except for incurable illness or injury. Sanctuaries are lifelong habitats for animals where they are never euthanized unless necessary. All of these rescues entail caring for animals and attempting to get them adopted. Decide which one you want to operate.

It is best to forge partnerships with local veterinarians, pet food suppliers, and other local shelters so that you can get supplies and resources at a low cost. Be sure to post ads soliciting the community for donations to help animals in need.

You want to assemble a team of volunteer and/or paid workers, depending on your budget. Seek out people who are true animal lovers and who have prior shelter or rescue experience.

You can take on rescue pets from high-kill and/or no-kill shelters. You can also acquire them through other rescue organizations. Contact local rescue organizations and the ASPCA to find out how to get started. You may also contact Animal Control and let them know that you will take on some of the animals that they rescue. Getting involved in the community is probably the most crucial part of becoming a rescue founder.

Your opening day should be a big event with lots of press and advertising. Host monthly adoption events to further spread awareness about your organization, recruit volunteers, and get animals adopted out. You can also put up flyers and cards to raise awareness. Many rescues also participate in spay and neuter clinics. These clinics prevent overpopulation of pets.

IMPORTANT CONSIDERATIONS

As a rescue worker, you will work long hours for little or no money. You will encounter many difficult situations, including severely sick and abused animals. This can be emotionally difficult, so make sure you are prepared for compassion fatigue, which could lead to burnout. I cover this in my book, *The Pet Professional's Guide to Pet Loss Grief: How to Prevent Burnout, Support Clients, and Manage the Business of Grief.*

Despite the difficulties and hardship that go along with this position, always remember you are saving many lives and serving one of your community's biggest needs.

WRAP-UP

The life of a rescue worker can be exhausting and thankless. But when you look into the eyes of every animal you rescue, you will realize why you are doing this.

Getting started can be challenging, but once you become a part of your local rescue community, you will enjoy much success.

To learn how to help people in need and work with animals, read the next chapter about becoming a service animal trainer, but first, check out your action steps.

ACTION STEPS

1. Download your free gift for a list of humane society, rescue associations and rescue organizations (https://wendyvandepoll.com/pet-jobs-free-gift).
2. Volunteer at a local rescue to determine if you want to do this type of work.
3. Get a business plan and mission statement together if you decide you have the stamina to witness neglect, abuse, and other unpleasant events regarding animals.
4. Obtain the funding you need to open your rescue.

5. Set up your facilities so the animals are safe and comfortable.
6. Get a good team together. It can be difficult to do this work by yourself. When you have a great team with designated jobs, the process can go much smoother.
7. Spread the word through lots of events and advertising. Participate in community education about responsible spaying and neutering.

16
SERVICE ANIMAL TRAINER

Have you seen the service animals in their black or bright orange uniforms guiding people through their daily activities and reacted with a smile? These animals offer companionship and help to their person. The following are a few types of service animals. This is not a full list. You can do a Google search to find out more.

Here are some examples of service dogs:

- Seeing eye dogs for people with vision impairment
- Scent dogs who can alert their owners to oncoming diabetic or epileptic crises
- Guide dogs for the hearing impaired or wheelchair bound

These dogs work hard and faithfully to help their companions through everyday life. Companions and service animals often become extremely close and attached to one another, forming an unbreakable partnership.

Service animal trainers typically work on a volunteer basis for organizations or individually, though some are paid. To get started, you should start by gaining experience working with dogs. You may become a certified dog trainer or simply have dogs of your own. Volunteering at a dog shelter is another way to get comfortable with dogs and make a great, memorable difference in the world.

Once you have some dog experience, you must enroll in a program. There are many programs out there that teach basic techniques. While these programs can get you familiar with the training methods used, they are not sufficient to become a certified service animal trainer.

Reputable programs offered through universities or specific dog training schools take two to three years and require a three-year apprenticeship. Costs will vary but can reach the tens of thousands. The free gift that goes with this book has the two associations that recommend legitimate trainings (Resources).

Before you enter school, it is best to contact other service animal trainers and gain an apprenticeship. Getting into service training schools is a competitive process, so having an apprenticeship and some experience will give you a leg up. Work hard alongside your mentor and pay attention. You won't be paid, but the education and hands-on practice you get will be priceless.

After three hundred hours of training, completion of a course, and three references in the training field, you can sit for an exam with the Certification Council for Professional Dog Trainers (Resources). If you pass, you will have a certificate. This certificate is not mandatory by law, but most organizations won't hire you unless you possess it. A few states do require a special license as well, which your school will inform you about and prepare you for.

Begin volunteering with an organization or offering training on an individual basis. You may also want to volunteer in a prison dog program and teach prisoners how to train service animals, which I cover in more detail in Chapter 25. As you gain experience, you can post testimonials, videos of you training, and videos of your trained dogs working as service animals as a sort of portfolio on your website.

The best places to advertise include rescue organizations, agility organizations, pet stores, doctors' offices, and disability offices. You should also consider reaching out to places like schools for the visually impaired or schools for the hearing impaired. By networking with other animal professionals, you can make your business known so that they can refer people who need service animal training to you.

Definitely consider working with shelter dogs. If you can train viable shelter dogs to become service animals, they instantly become much more adoptable. You give them a new lease on life and help out people with disabilities who need a canine companion.

Consider offering service animal training alongside other forms of dog training, such as obedience or agility training. You can make more money and attract more clients if you expand your training services.

IMPORTANT CONSIDERATIONS

Service animal training requires education and time. While it does not pay well, if at all, it is a highly lucrative career in terms of making a difference in the world.

You will have the opportunity to work with animals and help people with challenges as you show them how to work with their new service animal.

This is a job you will need to train for. There is a lot that goes into the position—education, experience, patience, and compassion are necessary.

Expected Salary: $34,000 a year or volunteer basis

WRAP-UP

Service animal training is a lovely way to make a difference in the lives of both animals and humans. After completing your education, you can work in a variety of settings and help many individuals gain security and independence with the help of animals.

Your skills will always be in high demand, so you will likely find business anywhere you live. To make extra money, you can offer service animal training along with other forms of dog training.

I mentioned prison dog programs earlier. Now, you might be wondering how to get involved. You may be wondering what prison dog programs are. In the next chapter, I will show you how to get involved in these super helpful rehabilitative programs!

Here are your action steps for this chapter. Training dogs for service is a great choice if you want to help people become more independent and train dogs to assist.

ACTION STEPS

1. Gain experience with training dogs first and become a certified dog trainer (Chapter 11). This will give you training skills as well as an additional career to add to your service dog training ventures.
2. Attend an educational program for service dog training. Download your free gift for the associations that list legitimate trainings (Resources).
3. Sit for certification and any legally required licensing in your state.
4. Work with an organization, such as a shelter or prison dog program.
5. Market yourself in places where people who are looking for service animal training are likely to go.
6. Combine service animal training with other training services to secure a viable income.

17
PRISON DOG TRAINER/HANDLER

Would you like to be involved with a community service program that helps prisoners and shelter dogs? This is a wonderful community outreach program. Statistics show that hundreds of dogs that were taken out of shelters and then handled and trained by prisoners became more adoptable.

This program not only saves animals, but it enriches the lives of prisoners and helps with their rehabilitation. These programs have had such a positive impact on communities. A study shows that prisoners are much less likely to return to prison if they worked in a dog training program.

Some prisons work exclusively with dogs, but some, like Ohio Reformatory for Women, also involve wildlife rehabilitation and other types of animals. The prisoners will keep the animals in their cells and provide for their care around the clock. They will socialize, groom, and care for them. In addition, the prisoners are also involved in training.

Prisoners often have more time on their hands than other people, making them excellent volunteers. They have more proven success than other types of volunteers in training service dogs for this very reason. You can help rehabilitate prisoners, train service animals, and make shelter dogs more adoptable by volunteering in one of these programs.

To get involved in this program, look up "local prison dog programs." If there is one in your area, you can contact them to find out how to get involved. You will need to pass a background check and prove that you have experience in dog training.

IMPORTANT CONSIDERATIONS

Prisoners are screened before becoming dog handlers and earn the privilege of working with dogs. Don't worry—animal abusers are not going to be in the program! Most of the people in the program may have criminal history, but they love animals and genuinely want to do their part to help the world.

You can meet many wonderful people and make a huge difference by volunteering with them. Often, the only thing these prisoners have to look forward to is their time with their dogs.

You won't make any money doing this, but the rewards are so much greater than the money! Many prisoners in the program have helped produce over four hundred adoptable dogs or service animals. In addition, many of these animals were on death row in shelters and now have a new lease on life.

WRAP-UP

Prison dog programs are effective programs changing the lives of animals and prisoners for the better. Animals with nowhere to go and criminals with no hope are able to find love and happiness with each other. The program benefits prisoners, who often learn important life skills and don't return to prison later on after release.

You and the prisoner assigned to you will share custody of the dog while in training. It is important for the dog to have experience with living in someone's home prior to adoption.

There aren't many action steps for this volunteer position, but they will help you stay focused if you want to get involved with this great community project.

Now, if you are interested in opening your home to pets waiting to be adopted, then read on to learn how to become a pet foster parent. This volunteer opportunity requires a big heart, an open home, and some pet food!

ACTION STEPS

1. Learn about local prison dog programs. Search Google as a start to see if there are any in your area.
2. Download your free gift for suggested programs (https://wendyvandepoll.com/pet-jobs-free-gift).

3. Sign up to volunteer. If they don't have any open positions for working with prisoners, consider volunteering in the office, etc. This will get you known within the organization.
4. Keep in mind you are providing an excellent service. You are helping to save the lives of unwanted dogs as well as giving an inmate the opportunity to be successful.

18

FOSTER PARENT

Would you love to open your home to animals who are in need of a temporary home before they get adopted? Becoming a foster parent has many benefits. You can choose:

- How many animals you will foster
- When you want to foster
- What type of animal you would like to help

I never fostered an animal, but all my rescue dogs who lived in a foster home prior to adoption have been wonderful. They have been socialized and some even trained.

My friend, Robin, fostered a dog that I will never forget. This little guy was a poodle cross. Freddy had been found wandering the street—abandoned. No one knew his history. Robin took him into her home, groomed his scraggly tangled hair, and fed him.

Freddy looked at Robin with so much adoration in his eyes—I could tell he was truly grateful. After a few weeks, a rescue group for poodles was ready for Freddy, and he left. Robin and I cried, but we both were happy. I received an update one week later—Freddy had been adopted by a lovely couple! The rescue sent Robin a picture of them holding him. We didn't even recognize him with his new haircut.

Fostering gives a pet who is up for adoption a temporary place to stay out of the shelter. You are not only freeing up space in shelters, but you are also socializing and handling these animals to make them more adoptable. You may keep a pet for a few days to a few months, but your role in his or her life is very important.

Some organizations may let you adopt the pets you foster and grow attached to. Others won't. However, you still get to spend time working hands-on with a pet and getting him or her ready for a forever home.

Contact your local rescues and shelters to learn about local foster programs. They will tell you who to contact to get started. You will probably have to fill out an application and possibly even pass a background check, which is more concerned with crimes against animals or abuse than anything else.

The person in charge of the program will probably visit your home to ensure that you will be able to care for the pet. Once you are approved, you may get a new foster pet the same day, or you may have to wait a while before a pet is ready to enter your home.

If your community doesn't have a foster program, you can start one by volunteering to take in animals at local crowded humane society shelters. By volunteering at a humane society shelter, you can also learn a lot about rescue work and perform many of the same functions as a foster parent. The shelter may let you take animals home, especially if it is near capacity.

IMPORTANT CONSIDERATIONS

You may fall in love with your new friend, and then you will have to send him or her on to his or her new home. This could be difficult. Always remember you touched his or her life in a way he or she will never forget. You helped this animal get one step closer to a sanctuary or forever home.

Let this thought help you through the sense of loss you may feel. In time, you will get used to seeing pets come and go from your home, so you will be able to avoid becoming attached to every cute dog or cat you take in.

Some pets will be absolutely wonderful. Others will be more difficult. Part of your job as a foster pet parent is socializing the animal and getting him or her used to humans so that he or she becomes more adoptable.

Furthermore, you have to get the foster pet used to your pets through gradual introduction and supervised play time. Socializing the foster pet with your pets will be another important step in getting him or her ready for a forever home.

You will be responsible for a pet's veterinary care, grooming, food, and other supplies while he or she is in your care. While some organizations will help offset these costs, some won't be able to. The cost of fostering a pet is small compared to the rewards you gain, however.

WRAP-UP

If you are not ready to adopt a pet, but you want to make a difference in the animal community of your area, then please consider becoming a foster pet parent. While the work is not always easy, it is certainly impactful for you and for the pet. Your lives will be forever changed for the better, and you will have beautiful memories of so many animals you have helped.

You have the choice of when you want to take animals in, the type of animal you are willing to share your home with, and the number. In fact, if you want to take a break from this position, you can just alert the organization you volunteer for that you will be taking a vacation, need to be out of town, or you just need your home to care for your own animals.

The action steps in this chapter will provide you with the top tasks you need to carry out in order to get started.

Working with wildlife is an interesting and challenging form of volunteer work that you can get involved in. The next chapter will show you how!

ACTION STEPS

1. Sign up for a local foster organization. Contact shelters, search for rescue groups, and ask breeders for leads on how to become a foster parent.
2. Pass a background check and home inspection. This is necessary for the animal's safety. The last thing that needs to happen is for an animal to be placed in a foster home of an abuser.
3. Love the pets you foster, socialize them, and handle them in various situations and environments.
4. Be ready to pay for their care as a foster parent. Always ask the agency you volunteer for if any fees are covered.
5. When the pet is ready to go to a sanctuary or get adopted, you may be responsible to transport it or bring it to a place for transport.
6. If there is no foster program in your area, you can start one by volunteering to foster at your local humane society.

19

WILDLIFE REHABILITATOR

Do you love nature and wild animals? If you do, you will thrive as a wildlife rehabilitator. Wildlife rehabilitators are the responders who help clean up animals impacted by oil spills. This can be a paid as well as a volunteer position.

A wildlife rehabilitator rescues and rehabilitates injured wildlife and then releases them back into the wild. They also play an integral role in educating the public about wildlife to prevent some of the mistakes people make. Plus, they spend many hours raising money to support their mission.

Most rehabilitators have degrees in biology or zoology, but you don't have to have a degree to enter the field. It is best to contact your local U.S. Fish and Wildlife Service and local state Fish and Game to learn about permits in your area before you even get started, as a permit may be required to even volunteer with an established wildlife agency or individual organization.

Working with an established wildlife rehabilitator is a great way to get started and gain the experience necessary. You will learn how to handle and care for sick and injured wildlife, plus how to release animals safely back into the wild, raise funds, and manage a business.

When you are ready, you can obtain your permit and open a rehabilitation facility of your own. It is important to get proper training and experience. As a part of this job, you will encounter countless types of wildlife with unique and varied care needs. This is one job you cannot skimp on in regards to education.

Advertise your skills and services statewide. Wildlife rehabilitators often serve large areas because they are few and far between. By having a website and regularly posting in Facebook wildlife groups, you let people know who you are. Contact veterinarian offices. Oftentimes, people call the local veterinarian when finding injured wildlife.

Once you get a permit, you will be listed with Fish and Game in your state, so people can get your contact information from them when in need of your services.

There are many national organizations that you can volunteer with, as well. As you volunteer with an organization working with disasters, you may encounter various dangers, including hazardous materials. However, the organization will provide you with training before you begin.

IMPORTANT CONSIDERATIONS

Wildlife may try to bite you because they terrified. They may also carry diseases and parasites. You must work in wildlife rehabilitation and gain experience to learn how to handle animals correctly and safely.

There are special techniques for handling all animals, from rabbits to birds to snakes. Never make the mistake and assume an animal is harmless! While animals don't mean harm, they instinctively act in self-defense, especially when they are hurt and afraid for their lives.

You cannot get personally attached to these animals. They are not meant to be pets. When they recover from an illness or injury, you will be releasing them back into the wild (if possible). This can be emotionally difficult for some people, but it is the ethical thing to do.

WRAP-UP

Working with wildlife is a unique experience and a way to make a positive difference in your environment and ecosystems. With many animals sick or injured, largely from human activities, your job will play a crucial role in helping these animals return to their habitats healthy again.

You will work closely with your community and state Fish and Game and/or U.S. Fish and Wildlife department to rescue and heal sick and injured birds, mammals, reptiles, amphibians, and more.

Now that you have read about various volunteer opportunities as well as in-person and online pet businesses you can start, you must learn how to handle the most important part of your business—your clients.

Your clients will be both animal and human, so you must learn special skills for handling each. While pet businesses are fun and heartwarming for everyone involved, you may still encounter difficult clients of all species.

If you know how to handle them properly, you will get many happy repeat clients and great reviews that promote your business better than any other form of advertising.

However, before you move into the next section, go through the action steps to determine if a career (volunteer or paid) as a wildlife rehabilitator is for you.

ACTION STEPS

1. Download your free gift. It contains links for schools and associations to get you started (Resources).
2. Do a search for local wildlife rehabilitators in your general area. Be prepared to drive, as many are located rurally.
3. When you find one that you feel is up to standards and meets your career goals, spend some time volunteering to determine if you enjoy this type of work and to learn the trade.
4. Consider taking courses that would increase your knowledge and efficiency.

5. Determine if you need to be licensed or certified to practice in your state.
6. Research appropriate licensing and permits needed to be a career rehabilitator or volunteer by reaching out to your state Fish and Game department or U.S. Fish and Wildlife.
7. List your information with Fish and Game, local veterinarians, and emergency veterinarian clinics.
8. Reach out to organizations that need wildlife rehabilitator volunteers if volunteering is your interest rather than a career.

PART III
JUMPSTART YOUR PET BUSINESS

Are you excited to get started? I am so excited for you! Starting a pet business is the key to making money doing something you love and enriching the lives of pets and their people alike.

In this section, I am going to cover ways to decide on your career by asking you to explore some important considerations. I am also going to help you get started with suggestions on business plans and financing.

Then there is creating your website and your brand. When you are in business, you must have a social presence so people can find and hire you. Without one, it could be nearly impossible to succeed.

Please read on to gain the knowledge necessary to start your own pet business.

20

DECIDING WHAT YOU WANT TO DO

Have you decided what you want to do yet? Before you start your own pet business, you have to decide what kind of business to start. There are so many options in the pet industry, and this book is not able to cover all of them, though I do cover the most common ones and some uncommon choices.

Whether one of the job choices covered already speaks to you or you're still figuring that part out, you can benefit from considering business practices that will best fit your needs.

Let's get started!

IDEAS

First of all, do you have an amazing idea for a business that I haven't covered? If you have a unique idea, then you already have an edge on your competition. You can corner the market and start a trend.

But not everyone has a fantastic, original idea for a pet business. That is still okay. You can enter an established line of work in the pet industry and still stand out. If you have a unique idea, however, you must market it because you are adding something to the world that no one has ever seen before.

COURAGE, GUTS, AND STRENGTH

One thing all business owners in the world share is courage. It takes a lot of guts to try something despite the risks of failure. And it takes a lot of strength to leave behind a career you may already have to make your dreams come true.

But all business owners can agree—mustering the courage and opening your dream business is one hundred percent worth it. If your heart is in this, then you absolutely can do it. The fear that holds you back is not as important as the wonderful return you can get from a career you love.

LOVE FOR ANIMALS

Have you ever taken your pet to a veterinarian or pet store where people clearly didn't like animals? You probably never went back! Yet, it warms your heart when you go into a place and the staff ooos and ahhs at your pet—telling her how cute she is.

To thrive in the pet industry, you must have a deep love of animals. Why go into an industry if you don't love it? That love will motivate you even when the going gets tough. You will actually want to go to work each morning—can you imagine that?

SUPPORT

Without a doubt, opening your own business is hard. You may have poor sales at first, or you may struggle with the start-up process. Having someone to support you is so important.

A partner or team in your business is always an amazing source of support. Having people you can trust to run your business with you is quite helpful and takes a load off of your shoulders.

At the very least, have someone who you can talk to about your trials and tribulations. A friend who listens can do you a world of good. You may also want to get to know other people in the pet industry who can give you advice.

ONLINE OR IN PERSON

Do you want to work from home in your pajamas or handle pets in person? Some pet businesses, such as massage therapy (Chapter 16), are incompatible with the online format. Other ideas, like blogging (Chapter 1), can't be done in person. You have to choose whether you want to work from the computer or in a brick-and-mortar business.

Of course, many businesses can be split between online and in person. It is more than possible to run a small pet supply store and have an online store as well. You could be a veterinarian (Chapter 18) and write books (Check out my book, *Pet Authorpreneur 101: How to Become a Successful Pet Author and Grow Your Business* on Amazon) from home for pet people who care about the health of their beloved animals.

TIME

Time is always a consideration. You must consider how much time you want to spend opening your business and how much time you want to spend working in your new pet career.

Many businesses take time to get started. Look at when you want to open the business. Then learn more about the time it takes to start to adjust your expectations realistically. If something takes too much time for you, you may want to consider a different business type.

How much do you want to work? Are you looking for a full-time business or a side gig? Some businesses are more than full time. As a veterinarian, you may be on call all of the time; as a store or kennel owner (Chapter 15), you may even have to work on days when you are closed, and you may not have much time for vacations.

Other businesses, such as pet writing, blogging, and animal communication (Chapter 3), are side gigs that you can do on top of other jobs or in retirement.

EDUCATION

Some of these careers require going back to school. To become a veterinarian, you need an advanced professional degree and up to four years of veterinarian school, on top of three to four years in undergraduate school. If you already have a degree in biology, zoology, or a similar field, you already have the undergraduate covered, but you are still looking at years of school and tuition. Don't let that discourage you—just consider it.

Veterinary technician (Chapter 19) often only requires an associate's, which usually takes two years full-time. Other careers covered here may also require some schooling, such as massage therapy (Chapter 16) and energy healing (Chapter 14).

If you don't want to go back to school, that is okay. There are many options that don't require a special education. But going back to school to make your dream come true is always worthwhile. Don't let time or money discourage you from creating an amazing career.

INITIAL INVESTMENT

Another important consideration is your initial investment when starting your business. Like all businesses, you have to spend some money to make money. Consider your budget and what you can spend to launch a pet career.

Some businesses have start-up costs that are much higher than others when you consider tuition, licensing, inventory, etc.

Other careers, such as pet blogging (Chapter 1), only cost as much as your website and your time. Depending on the hosting service you pick and the theme you use, your start-up costs can be quite small, less than a thousand per year.

CREATE A TO-DO LIST

The actual first step is creating a to-do list. It is going to be quite long at first, but as you check items off, your confidence and sense of accomplishment will soar. Begin to read the section of this book that applies to your chosen job and then add each action item to a to-do list. Check it off once it is accomplished.

Here are a few items that will be on your to-do list. I will cover them in more detail in the next chapter:

- Research
- Develop a business plan
- Procure funding if you don't have enough money to start the business
- Find a space
- Start a website
- Fund advertising

WRAP-UP

In this chapter, you have learned that starting a career in the pet industry can be very rewarding. You also learned how important it is to follow your heart and nurture your love of animals to create a dream job.

There are a number of factors that you must consider to find the business that best fits your needs. Starting any kind of business or new job takes time, money, and effort. Be sure to use your inspiration to fuel your motivation.

Use the action steps at the end of this chapter to get you started with finding your direction and being honest with all the considerations this book has presented to you.

Now, read on to learn more about the steps to launching your own business. In Chapter 29, I will cover developing your business plan, marketing and sales, funding, finding a space, developing your brand, creating a website, and more.

ACTION STEPS

1. Make a list of all the considerations outlined in this chapter.
2. Under each consideration, add your thoughts, feelings, and inspirations as it pertains to your life and goals.
3. Start writing a preliminary to-do list to make your dream happen.

4. Stay focused, believe in yourself, and know you can excel with your dream job.

21
GETTING STARTED

Do you have a specific niche in the pet industry in mind, and are you are ready to get started? You just need to start researching your niche and figuring out what to do first.

Using this book, you can learn everything you need to get started. But you may also have to look into your local prices, business licensing practices, and labor laws to start your business—especially if you are opening a storefront business. You may also have to research funding sources.

START YOUR RESEARCH

The first place to start is online. Look at other businesses in your area if you are starting a storefront business. If you are starting an online business, research your competitors and influencers.

Look at their business practices, prices, and even statistics from the Department of Labor (storefront). All of this can be useful for learning about the industry and what you can expect in your area.

You can also visit your library. You can learn about real estate rates, the history of businesses, and other such information there. View public records to see how pet businesses in your area are faring.

Contact your local chamber of commerce to learn about how to proceed with legally opening a storefront business. You want to find out about any necessary licenses and permits. You also want to learn about applicable taxes.

Get the appropriate paperwork to begin the process of opening a legal business. Add any costs you learn about to your budget. With an online business, you don't need to do this step.

If you are entering a career that calls for schooling, research schools. Contact admissions for information about how to get started, estimated costs of attendance, and the time needed to complete a degree. You may want to go on college tours to find out where you want to attend. Visiting a campus in person lets you get a much better feel for its culture and whether or not it is right for you.

Talk to pet business owners, both online and storefront. Some of these owners may not be willing to talk to future competition, but some are more than amicable to the idea of helping others and expanding the pet industry.

You may even meet people interested in hiring you, working for you, supporting your business, entering an affiliate partnership with you, or going into business with you somehow. Networking is key to business because you never know what opportunities other people have for you.

Reach out to pet business owners in your niche and politely introduce yourself. Disclose why you are contacting them and ask, "Would you be willing to help me?" Then ask them how they started the business, how they fare in different economic times, and other such questions.

DEVELOP A BUSINESS PLAN

Whether you are starting an online or storefront business—and before you procure a loan or get a business license—you must have a business plan in place. If this part is overwhelming for you, consider hiring someone to help you. SCORE (Resources) is a free resource. You can find them by going to score.org.

Your business plan has to reflect what your business is, what your business provides, how much your start-up costs are expected to be, and what you plan to do with all funding.

It should also reflect what you expect to make. While you may not know exactly what these figures are, you can find a projected estimate of profits by researching similar businesses in your area or online. If there are few businesses like yours in your area, you may still thrive, but you look like a risk to potential investors.

Using the information from your research, start to devise a plan. To learn about business structure, you can download free business plan templates online or get help from SCORE.

A BUSINESS PLAN MUST INCLUDE:

EXECUTIVE SUMMARY

The executive summary is quite simple—it describes the information covered under the headings mentioned in this chapter in one paragraph. This is a succinct way to break down the information of your business plan for any person who will be reading it. You place the executive summary on top of your document.

There is no need for flowery words and long sentences. Someone who is not interested in your business will not waste any more time on the plan after reading the summary; someone who is interested will be intrigued enough to read on.

Next, you want to provide more detail with each of the headings mentioned in this chapter. This information will be presented under the executive summary.

COMPANY PROFILE

First, describe your company. Talk about:

- what kind of business you are opening

- the products/services you are offering
- your mission to make a difference in your community or the world
- the history of your company
- any resources you have
- the types of animals and people you will serve
- what makes your business unique from others

This part needs to be clear. But it also can be a bit more detailed than your executive summary. Basically, you want to give someone a very good feel for the company you are founding. Once you write this profile, you can reuse it on your "About" pages online.

MARKET ANALYSIS

This is where your research comes in handy. You want to show that you know your market well. Show the statistics for your type of business, the gains and losses you anticipate, and the way you have licensed or will license your business. Describe your location and how it will serve your business. Document your anticipated cash flow and expenses based on what other businesses in your niche make.

BUSINESS STRUCTURE

First, what will your role in the business be? Do you have any partners? Will you have employees? Describe how the business will be run and how you will hire employees. Describe the roles and ranks of these employees.

You also want to describe how you plan to run this business. For instance, if you're running a kennel, will you be boarding the dogs in your home? Do you have a big yard?

SERVICES AND PRODUCTS

This part is easy enough. All you have to do is list the kinds of services and products you are going to sell. Describe each in brief detail and add how much you plan to charge. Also, describe the ingredients of the products and how they are unique from what other people offer.

MARKETING AND SALES

Describe how you plan to sell your products or services. In detail, go into the kinds of advertising and marketing you will use. Discuss how you plan to reach people. You may also mention things like sales or specials you will use to boost sales. The point here is to prove how you plan to make money.

You want to go into a lot of detail here. Don't just say, "I will host spring sales." Instead, describe how you will bundle products, offer up to fifty percent off, and other such deals in spring every year.

FUNDING REQUEST

When obtaining a loan or investment, you want to include a formal request for the money you need. You want to describe how much money you need, where that money will go, and how you will benefit from it. You also want to describe the sort of return the bank or investor can expect.

This request can be tailored to each person. Write it as if you are addressing the person you give your business plan to personally. You may even write it as a letter, starting with "Dear [reader's name]" and ending with "Sincerely, [your name]." Include formal language and ask, "Please consider providing funding to this venture."

FINANCIAL PROJECTIONS

To get any sort of investment or loan, you have to prove that your business will return the money others have given you. You want to use your marketing analysis to predict how much money you will make. Then describe how you can pay off loans or return investments with this profit. This part will read similar to a college dissertation.

I highly recommend hiring an accountant if you need help with this part. Determining investments and loans can be extremely intimidating if you are not good with numbers. If you cannot afford an accountant, SCORE will offer help with this. Or you can maybe barter with an accountant with services from your new business!

PROCURE FUNDING

If you have enough money to launch your business, that is awesome! You can dip into savings or use a second job to help fund a business. But if you don't have the money, don't despair. There are ways you can procure funding from other sources.

The first way is to obtain a loan from a family member or friend. If you can get someone to lend you the money, you may be able to avoid the high interest rates some banks may have. If no one can give you a personal loan, you can approach banks for a small business loan. Show the bank your business plan and your plan to pay the loan back.

You may approach investors. Investors are people who will give you money and expect some sort of financial return. They may buy a percentage of your company, for example. Approach businesspeople in your area and ask if they are interested in investing. Pitch your company and how it will make them money, and show them your business plan. The point here is to prove to investors how they will benefit.

You may also get someone to go into business with you. You will have to share a part of your company with this person and give this person certain responsibilities and privileges. However, this person can provide you with financial and business support. A good partner would be someone who has already worked in the pet industry and has some know-how.

FIND A SPACE

If you are running a business that is in person (See Section II), then you will need a space. You may rent a commercial space, or you may run the business out of your home. You must obtain appropriate permits for either, and then you must rent or buy the space, set up the space with appropriate equipment, and pass inspection in most states.

Start by visiting your local chamber of commerce and learning what you must do to get a space approved within your city and state. Adjust your business plan accordingly. Some cities have ordinances that don't allow you to operate businesses from inside your residence—for instance, if your business plan involves starting a home-based business, you may have to edit that.

Next, contact real estate offices in your area to find a commercial real estate agent. Discuss your budget and needs with the agent and tour some available commercial spaces. Lease or purchase the one you like the most.

Once your space passes state inspection, you can start to set it up according to your needs. Get the equipment you need. Install any special plumbing or wiring necessary. For a grooming business, for example, you may want to install special sinks and floor drains. For a pet bakery, you will need to install display cases and ovens. For a store, you need racks and display cases and a counter for a cash register.

Keep in mind, for an online business, you do not need to do this. What you do need to consider is your home workspace. Do you have a place in your home to set up your computer? Is it large enough for your needs? Do you have appropriate Internet service to handle your work?

BUILD A WEB PRESENCE

In this modern age, you cannot have a business without a website. You must have a web presence, whether your business is online or not. Fortunately, a website is fairly cheap. Please see Chapter 30 for how to build one.

Also create social media accounts separate from personal accounts for your business. You want to feature yourself on Instagram, Facebook, Twitter, LinkedIn, and other popular social media sites that may arise with the times.

On these accounts, feature a profile describing your business, mission, and vision.

- Have your logo or a cute picture representing your business as your profile picture.
- Feature pictures of your products and services; for example, as a dog groomer, you want a portfolio of some of your best grooming jobs.
- Also feature a link to your website.
- Post business hours in your about me section.
- Make it easy for people to access your online store and contact you.

For a small fee, you can purchase Facebook advertising, which will get you more followers. You can also get followers by posting frequently in groups related to your business.

Frequently post on your accounts about new products, specials, or jobs to engage with followers. Always answer messages as soon as you can. I recommend setting aside a certain amount of time each day to answer correspondence from social media and your website.

Finally, post a listing on Yelp, among other local business sites, if you are opening a storefront. You can register on these sites for free at Yelp.com. This lets potential customers find you online if they search for your type of business. You want to post your hours, your location, your phone number, and your website.

Also, post a picture of your business and use your logo for your profile picture. The registration is free, but you can also purchase advertising for a small fee that lets the site you are registered on put you in front of more customers.

ADVERTISE

You can run the best business in the world, but you won't get any customers if they don't know you exist! You have to put yourself out there. That's why you should budget a few hundred to a few thousand a year for advertising, or at least seven percent of your revenue. It will be worth it!

GET BUSINESS CARDS

The first thing you should do is order business cards. Vistaprint (Resources) and Shutterfly (Resources) are great places to get affordable, professional-looking business cards. Make the cards simple—your business name, hours, website, phone number, email, and logo.

On the back, you can write something personal, such as "Can't wait to meet you and your beloved companion!" This is a nice touch that makes an even better impression on potential customers. I have found that bright colors and cute logos of pets are often more attractive to customers in the pet industry.

You can also use Vistaprint or Shutterfly to print T-shirts, flyers, and signs for your business. Also, look into local businesses to do your printing and build your network of supporters. If you are running your business out of your home, consider a sign to put on your lawn to advertise what you offer.

CREATE A LOGO

You might be wondering how to create a logo. Fortunately, you don't need to be an artist to accomplish that. Simply visit PicMonkey (Resources), a graphic design site. There, you can use the tools to create a logo.

You can also search on Fiverr.com (Resources) to find logo makers and graphic designers. Freelance sites like Guru.com and Upwork.com (Resources) often have many graphic designers looking for jobs. Hire someone whose portfolio matches what you are looking for. Make your specifications clear.

Your logo doesn't have to be fancy. My logo for CenterForPetLossGrief.com is a classic example of a simple logo that is instantly recognizable. Have your logo feature a pet that your business serves or a group of animals. Use bright colors to attract people's attention if appropriate for you niche. If you can, incorporate the name. When you don't have any ideas for how to do this, just hire someone and have them propose a few different logo ideas.

Once you have your logo, you have a symbol that makes your business instantly recognizable. You can post it on your website, your social media accounts, and your business advertising. Be sure to include it on your business cards.

ADVERTISING OPTIONS

You can start by using online advertising. Facebook, Instagram, and Yelp all have great advertising options that cost very little. You can explore other online options as well. Promote your web presence, especially if you are an online business.

You should also consider a radio ad. Radio ads are fairly expensive, but they bring in twice as much traffic! Contact your local radio station to find out rates. Often, they will help you record your ad. Then they will play it as often as your package specifies. TV ads are also an option, but they can run very high costs.

Your local newspaper is a great place to post a weekly classified ad for your business if you are locally based. Contact local papers and find out their rates. Create a small ad featuring your business name, logo, and slogan, and run it every week.

Ask your local chamber of commerce about places to post signs for your business. Often, the chamber of commerce itself will have a board where you can pin your sign or business card. That's free advertising right there.

You can also advertise at other related businesses. For instance, if you are a pet groomer or photographer, you can post a sign at your local shelters, pet stores, and boarding kennels (with the owners' permission, of course). Or if you run a boarding kennel, post a sign or offer a stack of cards at all local groomers, shelters, and pet stores. Don't try to advertise at a competitor's business, as that usually won't go over well!

Sometimes, you have to advertise in person. I know a woman who runs an at-home doggie day care. She likes to stand at local festivals and events and hand out her business cards. She gets a lot of business this way. By being present at events and handing out cards or hosting a booth, you get to interact with people and make a great impression that sticks with them.

Finally, be sure to utilize signage. If you are opening a brick-and-mortar business, post your name as soon as you have your space. Place a banner advertising your business and announcing when you will open in the window or over the door.

On the first week of business, have a large "Grand Opening" sign. Signage attracts lots of vehicle and foot traffic. Of course, this does not apply to strictly online businesses.

WRAP-UP

You have learned how to hone in on the development, purpose, and future of your new business. Your to-do list may seem long at first, but as you tackle each item, you will feel more and more invigorated!

Making your dream business or career happen is no easy feat, but it is completely worth it. Take some time to start research and draft your business plan, if necessary. Research and visit schools if you want to go back to school. Then, read on to learn how to create a website and go into your desired field.

Use the action steps at the end of this chapter to help you do the necessary research and development. This step is necessary whether you are starting an online or storefront business.

In Chapter 30, you will learn about creating your website, which is imperative for every kind of business. Your website lets you define who you are. It also is a form of affordable advertising.

ACTION STEPS

1. If you are opening a storefront business, reach out to five local businesses and introduce yourself and your new business. If you are starting an online business, reach out to five influencers in your niche.
2. Create a business plan. Tailor it for each person who will see it.

3. Get funding through partnerships, investors, and loans.
4. If you are starting an in-person business, rent or buy a space.
5. Develop your web presence. You want to create a website and social media accounts, even if your business is not online.
6. Advertise!! You want to let people know that you exist. Do it online and in person. Use a logo. Print business cards.
7. If any of these steps are overwhelming, get help from SCORE or business owners that would be willing to give you advice.

22
CREATING YOUR WEBSITE

Would you like to get away with not having a website for your business? Well, I hate to disappoint you...but you absolutely must have a website to go with your business.

If the idea of starting a website makes you shudder in horror, never fear! You can either hire a great web designer to create one for you or you can read my book, *Pet Blogging 101: How to Start a Riveting Pet Blog and Gain Loyal Followers* and find out how to create one yourself for very little money.

In this chapter, I am going to cover what goes into creating your website to gain loyal followers and customers. Please read on to learn why a website is important and what content you should include.

PEOPLE FIND YOU WITH A WEBSITE

First, a website is important because it helps people find you. Say you own a grooming shop. Someone just moved to your area, and they don't know where to go for their grooming needs.

Because most folks rely heavily on the Internet, this person will probably look up grooming shops in the area and find your site. When they call you and visit your shop, you potentially earned a new customer! If you are not online, however, this new customer will go to a competitor who is. You just missed out.

Having a web presence lets people know who you are, what you offer, and where you are located. Since people often use iPads and smartphones to find local businesses or order products, you should have a website they can easily find on all devices—not just on a computer.

Consider having listings with Yelp and Google so people can find out about your business when they are looking for local places. Make it easy for people to contact you by including links to your website, phone number, address, and hours.

With a website, you can advertise yourself fairly cheaply. You can pay for advertising in a variety of places so your website and business are placed in front of people. This is cheaper than most other forms of advertising, and it reaches more people, since people are often online.

Furthermore, if you are an online business, no one will find you unless you rank highly in searches and have ads. You need to have a website so people can access your products or services. You also need to optimize (Glossary) your website. When people search for their pet needs, your site pops up and provides what they are looking for.

A WEBSITE DEFINES YOUR BUSINESS

A website lets you express yourself and show people who you are as a business. Someone may drive by your grooming shop or boarding kennel and think, "I want to check that place out!" They do an online search and find out about your history, your deep love of pets, and how you like to do business. They see testimonials and reviews attesting to how awesome you are. So... they are inclined to do business with you! See why this is so important?

Now imagine the opposite scenario. Have you ever driven past a place and want to find out more about it, yet when you search online, you find no website and a disconnected phone number on the Yelp listing? This has happened to me before, and I lost interest in the place of business as a result. You don't want to lose customers just because you're not accessible online.

With your website, you can show people what you are about and what you do—your brand. You can showcase your skills or products and reviews. Then, people feel like they know you and want to take a chance on you. They know what to expect when they walk into your place of business or click through your site. A sense of trust is forged long before they even meet you.

Realize that entering your business or calling you personally takes a time investment for people. They won't do it if they don't already have an idea that they want to do business with you. Your website helps you prove your business is worth the time investment.

WRAP-UP

A professional website is a necessary business choice when you want to stay in communication with your customers and clients. Whether you have a storefront or online business, creating your website allows you to build a following of loyal customers and alert them with important updates and announcements.

The action steps at the end of this chapter will help you begin thinking about your website. This step is necessary whether you are starting an online or storefront business.

In Chapter 31, you will learn the steps needed to create your website.

ACTION STEPS

1. Make a list of why you think your business needs a website. Try to think of different ideas than the ones already discussed in this chapter.
2. Create another list that includes five needs your

customers may have. Interview friends, family, current clients, and potential clients.

3. Complete the list you made for number two by adding to your list the solutions you have for your customers. You want to have solutions for their five needs that you will provide for them.
4. With each solution, write a short three- to four-line paragraph on how you are going to solve their issue

23

DEVELOPING YOUR WEBSITE

Are you feeling overwhelmed with the idea of creating a website? No worries...I am going to teach you what goes into a website so your business can thrive.

I can't stress enough how important it is to spend time developing your brand (Glossary) and website. If you rush through this step, your website will not accurately reflect the business you do. Business is then lost.

In this chapter, you will learn how to organize and develop the content that goes into your site. Developing and creating a website is a fun project. In fact, it is one of my favorite tasks when helping people create a pet business. Take the time to make your business personable and stand out to gain those loyal customers who keep coming back for more.

What Your Website Should Include:

COMPANY PROFILE

First and foremost, your website must include a company profile. This is a page where you talk about you and your staff. You mention the things your business sells and how you help animals and their people. You also talk a bit about your history and your inspiration for creating the business.

The company profile is essential because it lets people know if their values align with yours and if your business can meet their needs. You want to be very clear with the services and products you offer to help your customers solve their needs—remember the work you did in Chapters 28, 29, and 30?

When you make it easy for your website visitors to understand what you do to help them, you have easily gained a new customer or client. However, if you are vague and not sure exactly what you offer, it becomes confusing for them, and they won't go past the first page.

CONTACT PAGE

Always have a page with a contact form. Once someone submits the form, you should receive it through your contact form widget (Glossary). The contact form should include a way to get back to the person as well as the subject and message of their trouble or question.

In addition to this form, you should post your business hours, address, and phone. That way people can reach you in a variety of ways. Also offer your social media links.

STORE

It's always a good idea to offer a store on your website showing what products you carry. Even if you don't want to sell things online, having an online showcase of what your storefront business offers can help people see if you carry what they are looking for before they come by your place of business. Include descriptions and photos of the products you carry.

That said, I would strongly consider supporting online ordering. People are relying more on this method to obtain the products they need more than ever before.

SERVICES

If you are in a service industry, include a page outlining the different services you offer. You want to include as many details as possible so people have fewer questions.

In Chapter 30, you outlined the needs of your clients and the solutions you offer to help them. This page is a perfect place to state those needs and solutions again to remind your potential new client.

Offer a contact form at the bottom of the page so that people can conveniently reach you with questions or a place for people to book a service with you. These little thoughtful things make people like your business more and thus encourage them to seek your business out when they need help!

PORTFOLIO

Show off your artwork, grooming, photography, or T-shirt designs with a portfolio. Showcase your best work to prove to people that they should hire you. Let people get a sense of your style so that they know what to expect and if you are the right fit for their wants.

Your portfolio must include photos that are high resolution, well lit, and flattering. A grainy, dim photo can't show off your work. Be sure to crop the photos or take them against a white or black background so there is no clutter or distractions in them. Also be sure to include the entire item, not just a small part. A watermark can help you prevent image theft.

QUOTES AND A BOOKING SERVICE

A lot of people love the convenience of getting a price quote and booking a service online. If you are in any sort of pet service industry, make it easy and convenient by offering a booking button under each listed service and a form for requesting or generating quotes. Make sure you also offer a contact form on this page so that you can get back to a customer with a quote.

REVIEWS/TESTIMONIALS

The only way potential customers know to trust your business is by reading the experiences of other people. By providing a page for reviews and real testimonials, you make it easy for word-of-mouth advertising. Dedicate a page to reviews and have a form so people can post them. Encourage customers to leave you reviews and tell them how much it will help you out!

Ask permission from your reviewers to use their picture and full name. This way the testimonial looks professional, credible, and personal.

On Facebook, Google, and Yelp, people can also leave reviews after they visit your business. Customize these listings with your hours and contact information and link to your website. That way, people can easily find you and your reviews in one place when they look up local businesses. To reach more people, expand the area your listing serves to include nearby towns.

BLOG

Even if you don't want to make money as a pet blogger, hosting a blog on your site can be very helpful to your business. To get started, my book, *Pet Blogging 101: How to Start a Riveting Pet Blog and Gain Loyal Followers,* will help you every step of the way.

A blog can help you teach people information about your products, or share valuable insights with pet owners, or simply make pet lovers smile as you share cute stories and photos of your own beloved animals.

A blog gives you a medium to communicate with your customers. It lets you express who you are and who your company is. Finally, it creates discussion and interaction with your customers and readers. People will get a good feel for you through your blog.

SOCIAL MEDIA LINKS

You must create accounts on all of the popular social media sites for your business. Then, post links to each in the form of handy buttons on the bottom of each page of your site. That way, people can easily follow you and stay in touch with you.

Social media helps visitors learn about new posts, new services, new products, and other news through your social media posts. It can be a lot easier to reach people through social media posts than email lists that may go to spam or posts on your site that people may not see.

Once you are present on social media, be sure to stay active—post regularly. Some software plug-ins make posts on a schedule for you. The more you post, the more people feel engaged with you. You will attract and keep followers. You can post things that talk about your business or illustrate your opinions so that people know more about your business.

Also, take advantage of the ad programs offered on some sites like Facebook and Instagram. The ad programs can be profitable. However, there is a learning curve to ads.

Finally, when people comment on your social media posts or contact you—be sure to answer them. This helps with your reputation as a trusted pet business owner.

COLLECT EMAILS

When people visit your website, have a place allowing them to sign up for your email list. Include a sign-up link on every page.

You can send people on your email list newsletters that talk about your business, advertise new products, or alert people to important information they should know about. This keeps people aware of your business and helps you stay relevant to their needs.

WRAP-UP

A website is imperative for any kind of business. Not only does it define your business, but it lets people know who you are. For online businesses, your website is the epicenter of your business. Websites are a place for you to advertise and promote yourself—they give you the means to connect with people worldwide.

In today's Internet Age, you can make a lot of money working online from the comfort of your home. In fact, you may do even better than brick-and-mortar businesses. You can also cut down on overhead costs like space rental with an online business. The Internet has many opportunities, so be sure to take advantage of it!

After you complete your action steps for this chapter, read on to learn about some important customer service tips in Section V. I have been in business for a long time and can share countless stories. My goal in the next chapter is to prepare you so that you may avoid some unnecessary issues.

ACTION STEPS

1. Start brainstorming your website with the components I listed above. Not all of them will be appropriate for your business, but many of them will.
2. Learn how to build your website with my first book, *Pet Blogging 101: How to Start a Riveting Pet Blog and Gain Loyal Followers.*
3. Hire someone if you don't want to do it yourself. Websites can be tricky, so if you are hesitant to try, just find someone that has experience.
4. Remember to post your company profile.
5. Include an easy way to contact you.
6. Showcase your items or services or art.
7. Post all reviews and make it possible for people to add reviews.
8. Write a blog so you can be found by the search engines (Glossary).
9. Collect emails and send newsletters to people on your email list.
10. Include social media links. Always have social media accounts and update regularly.

PART IV
CUSTOMER SERVICE TIPS

Are you a people pleaser? And are you wondering why I didn't ask if you were an animal pleaser?

Well...you probably already love animals. And you know how to do great things for them. However, their sometimes not-so-cute owners can be extremely challenging. Plus, sometimes those cute animals are scared—they can, and will, bite!

How can you handle difficult customers and clients plus still have passion for what you do?

IN THIS SECTION, I AM GOING TO COVER HOW TO:

1. Handle animals that are fearful, stressed out, and possibly aggressive.

2. Handle people that are rude, nasty, and a pain in the $*#! with grace.
3. Get your clients to keep coming back for your services and more!

24
HANDLING AGGRESSIVE AND DIFFICULT ANIMALS

Do you know why an animal is being aggressive or difficult? Probably because he or she is scared. Some dogs (and other animals) may not be socialized well and are terrified when handled by someone other than their people. They can lash out by biting in self-defense.

Cats and birds are particularly known for becoming scared and agitated when they are taken out of their element. Depending on your pet career, you may encounter animals who are petrified, freaked out, and feel trapped.

Furthermore, you may not have an animal's full history. Some pets may have been traumatized. You may have a dog become afraid of you if you wear a hat. Someone who always wore a hat may have abused this dog.

You also don't know how a pet has been trained or socialized. Some animals have not been raised to be friendly to others, and thus they pose significant challenges to pet industry workers who handle them.

The first step is to watch any animal you work with closely. Even a friendly, likeable pet may become scared at any moment. Maybe you are a groomer and you approach an area of a dog's body that he doesn't want you to touch. That sweet dog will turn into a snapping wild animal in a matter of milliseconds. Be on your guard at all times.

Once when I was giving a massage to a quarter horse, I touched a sore point on his back. He almost kicked me in the head. It was a good thing I was paying attention because I was able to jump out of the way just in time.

Animals give clues to their emotional state with their body language. A cat might pin its ears back and switch its tail in short, rapid strokes. A dog might pin its ears back or point them sharply forward, lower its head, and show its gums. Learn the warning signs for different kinds of animals.

Never trust an owner who insists, "He's friendly." Or, "She won't bite." Even if you have worked with the animal before—or the owner says he or she is nice—you never know what may send him into scared mode. Be equally cautious with all animals you work with.

HERE ARE SOME GENERAL POINTS TO FOLLOW:

- Have a firm but gentle and calm approach.

- Try to keep their person around if they are calm. If not, ask them to leave the room.
- Encourage the person to hold the pet as you introduce yourself to him or her, if appropriate. This can make an animal either more nervous or can let the animal know the owner thinks you are okay. Hopefully, this will set him or her at ease.
- Talk to the pet and let him or her smell you, if applicable.
- Spend a few minutes getting to know each other.
- Move around him or her firmly and deliberately—talk to him or her the entire time.
- When you touch him or her, start slowly and gently.
- Don't try and trick any nervous pet, as he or she can sense your behavior. I promise you it will make him or her more nervous.

Many veterinarians report they like to tell the pet what they are going to do. The veterinarian's confidence and reassuring tone helps set the pet's nerves at ease. Try this approach and talk to the pet you are handling.

If the owner is okay with it, you can offer their companion a treat. This further lets him or her know you don't mean harm. When a pet associates you with food, he or she may not fall in love with you, but he or she will think, "This person is safe and will not harm me."

Don't be afraid to employ restraint systems or muzzles if need be. If the owner does not like it, show him or her how the system is not meant to hurt animals and explain why you use it.

Groomers and veterinarians will sometimes use a humane restraint system that keeps an animal from biting—if needed. Also, protect yourself from bites, scratches, and diseases with gloves and protective clothing appropriate to your profession.

WRAP-UP

We all love animals. But sometimes our favorite animal clients can become difficult when they become afraid or sense they are being threatened. Since your profession may expose a pet to a new environment and new people, the pet's sense of nervousness will be heightened. You can take steps to minimize bad experiences for the animals you work with.

Our animal clients are not always our most difficult. Sometimes, people can prove to be much more troublesome. Read on to learn how to mitigate problems with your human clients after you do the action steps for this chapter.

ACTION STEPS

1. Watch a pet closely for signs of potential stress, fear, etc.
2. Be gentle but firm—move with confidence.
3. Tell pets what you are going to do with a calm voice. They find your voice soothing.
4. Appease the pet and provide treats. Have the owner

calm the pet, if possible—and only if they are not making the animal more uncomfortable. If they are, ask them kindly to leave the room for the animal's safety.

5. Use safety measures like restraint systems and gloves, if needed. Introduce them to the animal slowly.

25
HANDLING DIFFICULT PEOPLE

Are you worried about handling demanding people? I must say that pet owners are wonderful people. But anyone who has worked in any kind of customer service (which is what any pet business involves) can tell you some people are just difficult.

The human component of the pet industry is definitely something you have to contend with. The pets may be great, but the owners, not so much.

HERE ARE A FEW THINGS TO CONSIDER:

1. Pet people have high expectations, and you must be willing to meet them.
2. You must treat your customers well or they will feel unappreciated and refuse to use your business in the future.

3. If they are not happy with your service, they will leave bad reviews and tell other people not to use your services or products. That can majorly hurt your bottom line.
4. Even reasonable and levelheaded people can become belligerent and overprotective out of sheer worry for their pets' safety.
5. You must brush up on your customer service skills even if you prefer animals over people.

CALMING ANGRY CLIENTS

When someone is berating you, it is easy to begin crying or yelling, depending on your temperament. You must keep a smile on your face, and you must speak clearly, gently, and politely at all times. There is no room for sarcasm, yelling, or other such behavior when you are a business owner—even if some clients deserve it!

It is only human to react when someone is being difficult. Becoming defensive is natural to any person. But you must train yourself to ignore the impulse to become defensive when someone attacks you as a business owner.

Arguing will only provoke the angry person. Instead, smile, listen, and then ask what you can do to help. And *never* tell a client he or she is wrong—even if he or she is—because that will only infuriate the client more.

In some cases, it is necessary to apologize. Only apologize when you have actually done something wrong, like send the wrong product or charge a customer incorrectly. Say, "I'm so sorry. How can I resolve this issue for you and make things right?" Let the customer come up with a solution. This will start to defuse the customer's anger and let him or her feel as if you are actively trying to solve the problem at hand. It also makes the customer feel valued.

Listen to what your customer wants. By calmly asking questions about the issue, you can get a better picture of the problem and how to handle it. You also force the customer to calm down as he or she has to answer questions and provide information. Using "we" terms, invite collaboration with the customer:

"I am sorry this happened. We can certainly make this problem right. How do you feel about an exchange?" is an example of doing this. Or you could say, "Can we come up with a solution together that will make this right?" You can even say, "I want to make this right. How can we do that?"

However, if you have done nothing wrong, don't say sorry. Simply stand by your company's policies and say, "Unfortunately, this is the policy, and you can see it on our website. How can we meet your expectations?"

The customer may have a lot of unreasonable suggestions that you simply can't do. Smile, listen, and then state why you can't meet the customer's expectations. Offer some other solution that is reasonable. It is up to the customer at this point to take your solution or get angry and give up.

Some customers and clients are totally unreasonable. An example that comes to mind includes a friend of mine, who is a dog groomer. A client dropped off a terrier and requested a Schnauzer cut. My friend performed this cut. When the client returned, she was livid and screamed, "My dog looks horrible! I wanted this and this." She went on to describe a cut that was not a Schnauzer cut at all.

My groomer friend simply had to smile as the client berated her and repeat, "I'm sorry. This is the cut you requested. I will happily groom him differently." The client was not having it, however, and demanded her money back. She insisted that she would go to another groomer who performed better work. In the end, my friend was forced to give the client a refund, and the client still left her a terrible review on Yelp.

The only way my friend was able to mitigate this problem was by replying to the client's review. She apologized again and politely described her side of what happened. Her explanation seemed to do the trick because she didn't lose any business.

The lesson here is that if you try your best to please a client and you can't please him or her, you just have to take the hit. Try to do some sort of damage control, such as replying politely to a bad review. Other people know that some customers are unreasonable and not every negative review on your business is legitimate.

It is also possible to get people to retract bad reviews. You may reach out to a customer and offer to send him or her a free product if he or she removes the review. You can also ask clients to rethink their reviews by offering your side of the situation.

In some cases, such as on your personal website, you can remove bad reviews yourself. Doing this can make you appear dishonest, however, so be careful. Yelp and Google will remove reviews that violate their policies or that come from people who did not actually use your business.

SETTING REASONABLE EXPECTATIONS

Every once in a while, you will get clients who demand the world and the moon, as well. You can't please them because they just want more. Some of these clients are not willing to pay for all that they demand, either. While these customers are rare, they do appear now and then—you have to know how to handle them.

I have found absolute transparency is imperative in any industry. By making your business policies and all the things that your services or products include clearly visible to customers, you avoid miscommunication.

When a demanding client wants more than what you can offer for a certain price, you can point out that your prices and services are clearly listed. If they want added services, they must pay for them.

Furthermore, find out exactly what your client wants before providing services. For example, my groomer friend in the above example may have benefited from asking the client for a picture of the cut she wanted before grooming the dog.

Don't assume customers know what they are asking for. Always clarify before performing any service. Ask for details and pictures, if applicable. That way, you can meet the client's expectations or let the client know you can't do something.

Never promise a client more than what you can deliver. Always set reasonable expectations. "This is what I can do." Make it clear. Then, any issues that arise are out of your hands.

WRAP-UP

Our human clients can be quite difficult. Remember—they just want what is best for their beloved pets. Approach them clearly and fairly and you will be able to defuse most ugly situations. Customer service skills are key to running any business.

The clearer you are with what your business provides in regards to policies, services, etc., the easier it will be to avoid issues with clients.

In the next chapter, I will show you how to get repeat business and promote excellent word-of-mouth referrals. But I would suggest putting the following action steps on a postcard and keeping it handy for when you may need it.

ACTION STEPS

1. Never yell or raise your voice. Never tell a client he or she is wrong.
2. If you are wrong, apologize and ask how you can fix the situation.
3. If you are not wrong, don't apologize and stand firm by your policies.
4. Listen well to figure out how to best handle the situation. Propose reasonable solutions in a calm voice. Invite clients to propose solutions as well and work together.
5. Ask lots of questions to cool clients off and get a full picture of the problem.
6. Try to keep clients from leaving bad reviews.
7. Set reasonable expectations with your clients by being clear and transparent.

26

BUILDING CUSTOMER LOYALTY

Do you like to do business by making a good first impression? When it comes to working in any industry, you want to make such a good impression that people come back and use your services again.

Furthermore, you want people to spread the news—your business is great. Word-of-mouth positive reviews work much better than any other form of advertising for your business. Even if you spend thousands on fancy advertising, you will still get more business from client referrals and reviews.

But how do you get people to come back time and time again? How do you get those positive reviews? Providing the excellent services and customer service your business promises is the first step.

But there are many additional things you can do to make people feel confident about using your business in the future.

Certain little things mean a lot to people and make clients happy.

FREE GIFTS

Free gifts attract clients and also make them want to come back. To get people to use your services or products, offer some type of free gift as an incentive. This brings the rule of reciprocity into play: Once you give a free gift, at least a few people will feel obligated to purchase something from you.

Just make sure the free gifts won't break your bank! Find something small that you can offer people at little cost to you. Make it something fun or interesting.

HERE ARE SOME IDEAS:

- Free nail clippings with first grooming appointment.
- Free one-week trial for a subscription service or information service.
- Access to a free sample of a course or book to get customers to buy the rest. In this case, you want to use a teaser. Offer about twenty percent of the information included in your course, the basic stuff. Then promise they can learn so much more if they purchase the other eighty percent.
- Free sample of pet shampoo with any purchase. If they like it, they will purchase the full-size bottle!
- Free night of boarding if first-time customers book

more than five nights or some other number of nights you feel is fair.

- Free bag of dog cookies with purchase of a full-size bag of food.
- Free ten-minute medium or animal communication session for first-time clients.
- Free pamphlet about pet grief, urging customers to sign up for a course or purchase a book to learn more.
- Free fifteen-minute training session for new customers to see if they like your methods.

DISCOUNT PROGRAMS

My favorite coffeehouse has a program where I get a punch on a card every time I buy a cup of coffee at any of their locations. When I collect ten punches, I get a free cup. Now, this isn't a huge discount, and it probably costs their business a few cents. Yet, it makes me feel as if my patronage is rewarded.

By offering an affordable discount program at your business, you make your clients feel rewarded as well. This encourages repeat business. People will keep coming back to collect the points necessary for that free reward or that percentage discount you promise.

HERE ARE A FEW EXAMPLES OF HOW YOU CAN APPLY DISCOUNTS TO YOUR BUSINESS:

- A rewards program that gives customers points for every item purchased. After a hundred (or some other arbitrary number you set) points, the customer gets one free bag of food or some other product.
- A referral system where a customer gets a free item for every person referred with a special code.
- A punch card for veterinarian visits. After so many visits, a client can get ten percent off his next visit.
- A free acupuncture or massage treatment after referring someone else or spending X-amount of dollars at your business.
- Ten percent off of a second T-shirt or portrait.
- Buy-one-get-one-free deal for your products.
- Twenty percent off customer's first stay in a boarding kennel or first pet walking/drop-in visit.
- Discount codes and coupons for using affiliate links on your blog.
- Free product or visit as a reward for using your company for a year, six months, or some other dedicated amount of time.

CUSTOMER SHOUT-OUTS AND ENGAGEMENT

Social media is a great place to engage with clients and customers. It is ideal to be present with your clients so that you form professional relationships with them. Let them know that you care and that you are a real person. It also makes clients and customers feel as if you actually care, so they remember your business with a smile and pass on recommendations.

When people comment on your blog or social media posts, be sure to reply to them. When people ask questions, be sure to answer in a friendly manner. Even when people have negative things to say, be sure to acknowledge their comments and ask how you can help. Spend some time each day online looking at and responding to customer feedback.

Shout-outs make loyal customers feel honored. Say someone just buys a ton of one of your products for use in her animal rescue. You can then run a banner on your website or feature her rescue for a month on the front page of your website and mention her in social media posts.

You can also use a system that identifies people who have been loyal to your blog or business for a long period of time, and either post a shout-out to the person on social media, or at the very least, send the person a thank you email.

If you are running a blog, consider engaging with people by running information sessions and live chats. This is where you can answer questions people have. Post that you will be holding a Facebook live on all social media sites and your business site and then attend the live event and chat with your clients, letting them see your face. Bonus points if you show them your own pets!

You can also personally reply to emails and answer questions and concerns people have. By being present and helpful, you make your customers feel as if they are engaging with a real person, not some anonymous Internet robot. This makes them remember you fondly and recommend you to others.

It is not always possible to address every email, so set automatic replies on your email server to acknowledge everyone who emails you. A simple acknowledgement and a promise to reply later is better than silence. As long as you make an effort to reply later when you have the time, your client will appreciate your customer service.

HANDWRITTEN THANK YOU NOTES

When someone orders something from you or comes by your business and uses one of your services, always try to send a handwritten thank you note. In your note, always include the client's name and the pet's name.

THERE ARE TWO REASONS FOR DOING THIS:

1. Saying thank you makes customers and clients feel validated.

- Do you enjoy it when a business owner you spend money with thanks you? Absolutely! I know I sure do. Let clients know how much their business means to you and they will want to come back.

1. A handwritten note with the client's and pet's names shows you took time and effort to thank them.

- It means so much more than some automated email or some mass-produced note. To save time, you can mass-produce notes and then sign them personally with the names of your client and his or her pet and then sign with your name. Just adding a touch of personal writing will make the note so much more meaningful.

One of my favorite drop shipping companies will always enclose a handwritten note with a bag of dog cookies taped to it. They pick out the cutest stationery. This free product and handwritten note are probably why I have used them for years.

GO ABOVE AND BEYOND

If you are running a boarding kennel, your job is pretty straightforward—as long as no issues arise. You board the pet, feed, and exercise. You look after his or her safety. Doing your job without issue will get you at least four stars in a review.

But what gets you five stars is when you go above and beyond.

FOR EXAMPLE:

1. Give them an extra walk or two.
2. Send unexpected cute pictures of his or her experience at your boarding kennel.

3. Give a massage as a treat.
4. Send them home with a bag of homemade and healthy dog treats.

Find some way to exceed a customer's expectations. Do something a little extra for them. You will make them smile, and they may leave you a better review as a result.

WRAP-UP

There are many wonderful and fun things you can provide your customers. Always keep in mind you want clients and customers to come back. You never want to give them a reason not to return.

The best way to increase your odds of getting repeat business is with the tips and tricks in this chapter. I have used most of them and am always thinking of new and creative ways to say thank you. Check out the action steps below to get you started.

I love giving back to my clients and customers. They appreciate the extra care and thoughtfulness. In turn, I get loyalty, great reviews, and lots of recommendations.

ACTION STEPS

1. Implement some of the free gifts suggested in this chapter—if they are appropriate for your business.

2. Come up with some of your own unique ideas that your customers or clients would love.
3. Consider offering a discount or rewards program—if appropriate with your business brand.
4. Post about great clients on social media or in a newsletter.
5. Always do special things for your clients and customers. Go above and beyond—it always pays off with reviews and loyalty.
6. Send handwritten thank you notes with purchases. People love handwritten notes even in the digital age.

PEP TALK!

Are you beyond excited to begin your chosen pet career? Have you done the action steps to organize your goals, educational plan, and business ideas? Are you ready to finally do something you love every single day?

If you love pets, you will love working with them and for them. The pet industry is a multibillion-dollar industry that shows even more expansion in upcoming years. You deserve to be happy with what you do, but you must also make enough to survive! Fortunately, the pet industry has a special place for you.

Working with animals is fun and rewarding, but it does come with some challenges. Your new career is just beginning, but always remember the possibilities are endless. If you feel like you are going to give up...don't. Instead, be creative. Think of a new service you could offer. Get more education. Get involved locally for animals in need.

There are endless opportunities when choosing a pet career. Depending on your choice, you can create a viable way to make a living for yourself. The other benefit is you will be part of the pet industry—helping to make the world a better place for animals and their people.

Your work is a vehicle for new ideas, promoting your views, generating business, and building a brand that your clients will love and trust. Never forget this.

- Start making your dream career come true with this book.
- This is the starting point.
- The next step is up to you.

If you have the desire to work with animals, then you should absolutely make it happen! You won't regret it. I know I never regretted chasing my dreams to work with animals—*never*!

> *I am so proud of you for taking the steps to fill your life with animals. I wish you great success and happiness on your journey. You will be successful as long as you put your mind to it and don't let anything stop you!*

Warmly,

Wendy Van de Poll

October, 2019

ALL BOOKS IN THE PET BIZ SERIES

- Pet Blogging 101: How to Start a Riveting Pet Blog and Gain Loyal Followers, (Book 1)
- Pet Jobs 101: How to Choose your Dream Job and Jumpstart Your Business. (Book 2)
- Pet Authorpreneur 101: How to Become a Successful Pet Author and Grow Your Business, (Book 3)

GLOSSARY

Affiliate Links – Or affiliate marketing is a type of marketing in which one business rewards another business (affiliate) for each visitor and/or purchase by that visitor. It is up to the affiliate to market. A special link is provided by the company the affiliate is promoting.

Amazon Algorithms – A complicated system by Amazon. Their layers of algorithms determine how books are ranked in the best-seller charts, popularity list, which books appear in the keyword search and the order in which they appear.

Animal Mediumship – Is another term for "animal communicator"; a person who has the ability to speak to animals that have died. Some animal communicators may speak to animals in spirit but not all. Many animal communicators offer both or specialize.

Blended Degree – A hybrid course designed to provide students with instruction through classroom sessions as well as online. Blended courses/degrees give you control over the place, time and pace of classes.

Blog - Blog posts are the fundamental of a blog. Every blog on the internet consists of different blog posts written by the blogger. ... Blogs (and blog posts) can be shared on social networks (Twitter, Facebook, etc.) and people can leave comments under the blog posts in order to start meaningful conversations.

Branding – The marketing practice of creating a name and logo that identifies your product from others. A great brand strategy gives your business a major edge in competitive market. It is your promise to your customers' needs.

Contact Widget – A contact widget is basically an add-on in your WordPress site. It allows your visitors to communicate with you via email when it is filled out.

Crystal Healing – When holding crystals or placing them on various parts of the body they promote physical, emotional, and spiritual healing. They do this by positively interacting with your body's energy field.

Energy Medicine – Is defined as any energetic or informational interaction with a biological system to bring back balance in the body. For example: Crystal Healing, Reiki, and Flower Essences.

Flower Essences – Liquid extracts used to address issues of emotional, physical, and spiritual well-being. They are part of energy medicine which includes: homeopathy, acupuncture, color therapy, crystal healing, Reiki, etc.

Google Keyword Planner – A tool that provides keyword ideas and traffic estimates to help you build traffic to your website.

Hashtags - A hashtag is a label for content. It helps others who are interested in a certain topic find content on that same topic. A hashtag looks something like this: #wendyvandepoll or #dogsoninstagram. Hashtags are used mostly on social media sites. They rocketed to fame on Twitter.

Homeopathy – The practice of holistic energy medicine. It is a natural approach to treatment of physical ailments, as well as, emotional and spiritual. Created in 1796 by Samuel Hahnemann. It is based on his doctrine of like cures all disease or a substance that causes the symptoms of a disease in a healthy person would cure similar symptoms in sick people.

Hosting Ads – The practice of promoting an affiliate product on your website. You join another company's affiliate program. You place a banner on your website to sell these products. You can either post for free or charge the company. It depends on the affiliate contract.

Keyword/ Short-tailed Keyword – Short tail keywords are search phrases with only one or two words. Their length makes them less specific than searches with more words. "Pet" (one word) is an example of a short tail keyword, whereas "holistic raw cat food" (four words) is a long tail keyword.

Long-tailed Keyword/ Keyword Phrase - A keyword phrase is two or more words typed as a search query. For example, "What is the best way to feed my senior cat" is a good example of a keyword phrase.

Optimize – On your website you add relevant keywords and phrases, meta tags, image tags, and other components to ensure it is accessible to a search engine and improves the over chances your website will be indexed by search engines.

Reiki – An energy medicine healing technique based on the principle that the therapist can channel energy into the client by means of touch. This will activate the natural healing process of the client's body, mind, and spirit.

SEO - SEO or Search Engine Optimization is the name given to activity that attempts to improve search engine rankings. In search results Google™ displays links to pages it considers optimal according to your keywords.

Search Engine – A program that searches for and identifies items in a data base that correspond to keywords or characters specified by the user, used especially for finding particular sites on the World Wide Web.

Universal Energy – Is the basis of our entire existence. It is the energy that sustains life and provides vital energy to all living systems.

Website - a group of World Wide Web pages usually containing hyperlinks to each other and made available online by an individual, company, educational institution, government, or organization.

RESOURCES

A FREE GIFT

A Complete List of over 150 Animal Resource Sites including but not limited to:

Animal Training
Grooming
Veterinary and Veterinary Technician
Wildlife Rehabilitator
Animal Reiki
Animal Massage
And MORE!

Here is your link to download:
https://wendyvandepoll.com/pet-jobs-free-gift

****You can also get the following links in your free gift that you downloaded above.****

BOOKS IN THE PET BIZ SERIES

Pet Blogging 101: How to Start a Riveting Pet Blog and Gain Loyal Followers https://amazon.com/dp/B07XWRS95W

Pet Jobs 101: How to Choose your Dream Job and Jumpstart Your Business
https://amazon.com/dp/B08478KMYD

Pet Authorpreneur 101: How to Become a Successful Pet Author and Grow Your Business
https://amazon.com/dp/B0852QD6DH

AFFILIATE SITES

ConvertKit - email provider
https://wendyvandepoll.com/convert-kit

ProWritingAid - editing software
https://wendyvandepoll.com/pro-writing-aid

Self-Publishing School – self-publish your book platform
https://wendyvandepoll.com/self-publishing-school

Siteground - website host
https://wendyvandepoll.com/siteground

Teachable – course host
https://wendyvandepoll.com/teachable

DROP SHIPPING MARKET PLACE

Aliexpress
https://azliexpress.com

Spocket
https://spocket.co

Printful
https://printful.com

Doba
https://www.inventorysource.com

Oberlo
https://oberlo.com

GRAPHIC DESIGN SITES

Canva
https://canva.com

PicMonkey
https://picmonkey.com

MULTI-LEVEL MARKETING

Life Abundance
https://lifesabundance.com

pawTree

https://www.pawtree.com

Nevetica
https://nevetica.com

HB Naturals
https://hbnaturals.com

PHOTOS

Pixabay
https://pixabay.com

Librestock
https://librestock.com

Deposit Photos
https://depositphotos.com

SERVICES

Guru
https://guru.com

Upwork
https://upwork.com

Fiverr
http://fiverr.com

SCORE
https://score.org

Smashwords
https://smashwords.com

Vistaprint
https://vistaprint.com

SHOPS TO HOST YOUR PRODUCTS

Amazon
https://services.amazon.com

Rush Order Tees
https://rushordertees.com

Shutterfly
https://shutterfly.com

Stitchfix
https://stitchfix.com

SOCIAL MEDIA ORGANIZATIONAL TOOLS

Agora Pulse
https://agorapulse.com

Buffer

https://buffer.com

Hootsuite
https://hootsuite.com

Later
https://later.com

ShareCount
https://www.sharedcount.com

SUPPLIES

Frontier Coop Wholesale
https://wholesale.frontiercoop.com

OTHER

Spirit Paw Academy
https://spiritpawacademy.teachable.com

If you would like even more links!
Please download my free list of over 150 links to pet careers, pet-related job, organizations, and much more.
https://wendyvandepoll.com/pet-jobs-free-gift

The* ***recommended sites *are products that I use and highly recommend. They are affiliate links which means if you purchase the product, I receive a small commission (which helps me greatly as an author.) You are not charged more because of the affiliate link.*

Pet Jobs 101
How to Choose Your Dream Job and Jumpstart Your Business

THANK YOU!

As the author of this book, I appreciate you buying and reading it. I hope you found the information useful and are on your way to choosing your dream job and starting your business.

I would be grateful if you would leave a helpful book review, either with your favorite book distributor or with Amazon.

Thank you,

Wendy Van de Poll, MS, CEOL

Best-selling and Award-winning Author, Writing Coach, Animal Advocate

www.wendyvandepoll.com

For all of Wendy Van de Poll's books, please visit:
https:amazon.com/author/wendyvandepoll

Check out my Free Gift that Goes with This Book
https://wendyvandepoll.com/pet-jobs-free-gift

PET
AUTHORPRENEUR
— 101 —
How to Become a Successful Pet Author
and Grow Your Business
The Pet Biz Series, Book 3
WENDY VAN DE POLL
INTERNATIONAL BESTSELLING AUTHOR

Pet Authorpreneur 101:
How to Become a Successful Pet Author and
Grow Your Business

Published by Spirit Paw Press, LLC

Publisher's Cataloging-in-Publication Data
provided by Five Rainbows Cataloging Services

Names: Van de Poll, Wendy, author.
Title: Pet authorpreneur 101 : how to become a successful pet author and grow your business / Wendy Van de Poll.
Description: Concord, NH : Spirit Paw Press, 2020. | Series: Pet biz, bk. 3. | Also available in ebook format.
Identifiers: ISBN 978-1-7324375-5-5 (paperback)
Subjects: LCSH: Pets. | Self-publishing. | Authorship--Handbooks, manuals, etc. | Authorship--Vocational guidance. | Authorship--Marketing. | BISAC: LANGUAGE ARTS & DISCIPLINES / Writing / Authorship. | PETS / General.
Classification: LCC PN161 .V36 2020 (print) | LCC PN161 (ebook) | DDC 808.02--dc23.

THANK YOU

A Free Gift

Thank you for purchasing *Pet Authorpreneur 101: How to Become a Successful Pet Author and Grow Your Business.* To show my appreciation, I am offering a free gift to help you as a new or experienced pet author.

A Winning Checklist
~ Become a Successful Pet Author and
Grow Your Business ~

Your Link to receive your Free Gift!

https://wendyvandepoll.com/pet-authorpreneur-free-checklist

To the animals that enrich my life
with their words.

PART I
GET READY TO WRITE

Are you wondering where to begin? Before starting a book, there are some preparations you need to make.

This section is about how you determine the purpose for your book, create your avatar, and mind map your ideas. It is both for the newbie and seasoned author.

I will:

- Help you get organized to begin and improve your project
- Show you the preliminary steps to take before you even type that first letter

If you are nervous about writing, please take a deep breath. This section is about preparation, the preliminary period before writing a book. It will get you into the right frame of mind to apply yourself and create an amazing manuscript.

Please know you have everything it takes to create a great book—even if you have never written one before, you do not have an English degree, or if your grammar made your English teachers wince in school (mine did).

You do not need to be an expert to write a book for pet lovers and/or professionals. All you need is a deep love of animals, a desire to share your thoughts and stories with other people, plus some great people on your team (Section III).

The second thing is to lower your expectations of yourself. Perfectionism is a sure way to kill your inspiration and develop writer's block. The first draft of your book does not have to be the world's most stunning dissertation.

In fact, it is guaranteed to be a bit messy and rough. The important thing is to believe in yourself and get your ideas down. From there, you will be able to smooth out your manuscript (Glossary) and utilize an excellent team of editors, proofreaders, cover designers, and the like to help your book reach its full potential.

Last but not least, find your inspiration. Your inspiration is your heart's passion and the message you want to share with your readers. This will be your biggest motivator. It will also help you overcome fear and apply yourself to the task of writing. Even on days when you want to give up or you start thinking that writing is not for you, your inspiration will whisper in your ear, "You have to get your idea out into the world!"

1

WHAT DO YOU WANT TO WRITE ABOUT?

People say, 'What advice do you have for people who want to be writers?' I say, they do not really need advice, they know they want to be writers, and they are gonna do it. Those people who know that they really want to do this and are cut out for it, they know it.

— R.L. Stine

What do you want to write? This question may seem absurdly simple, but it is critical to ask yourself before you even begin.

Maybe you already roughly know what you want to write, but now is the time to solidify your desire into a true topic (non-fiction) and/or plot (fiction) for your book. Once you know what you want to write, you can begin to develop and map your ideas into a cohesive whole that takes shape into a great book.

FIND YOUR PURPOSE

To begin, you will need to determine: Why is the topic you want to write about important? How is it going to help or entertain your reader, and/or solve a problem they may have? Think about the purpose before you even open up your word processor or put pen to paper.

The thing is, a book has to have a purpose. Otherwise, you won't be able to attract readers. Having a clear purpose:

- Guides you through the writing process
- Keeps you on task with your writing
- Motivates and inspires you
- Attracts readers and holds their attention
- Makes marketing a snap

When you begin writing, you can start the process by carefully selecting a topic aligned with your purpose and then outline what you plan to address about the topic.

Before you start your manuscript, be clear with what you want to share with your readers. You can cover many topics related to your purpose in your book, but the topics should all be linked in some way.

Having a book about many unrelated subjects is too scattered; if you have two drastically different topics, consider separating them into two different books. Let me phrase this in another way: Select one topic for your book and then cover all of the related subtopics that you want within its pages.

ARE YOU READY?

It is time to delve into your soul and locate your purpose for writing. Ask yourself if your book is going to be:

- A passion project, where you share stories or aid a cause
- An educational book to help pet owners
- A collection of true stories, or completely fictional
- Something to go along with your business (nonfiction) or something you want to create because you have a story in your heart (fiction)

There are many different topics to write about regarding animals. You can write fiction stories about adorable talking cats or true stories about your amazing seeing-eye companion. You can write informational guides to help pet owners provide the best care to their beloved friends. Or you can write books centered around causes, such as raising awareness about common training and care practices that harm horses.

There are two main things to consider—are you passionate about this topic, and do you have your purpose? Writing a book is an arduous task, so you should not write about things that you care little about.

If you don't care about your topic, you will probably lose motivation long before you complete Chapter 1. But when you have passion to drive you, you will be willing and able to do what is needed and have fun while writing. You will be able to find the motivation to complete your book, and readers will be able to feel your enthusiasm through your written words.

I am sure, as an animal lover and/or professional, you have many pet topics you are passionate about. If you run a pet business, that is a good clue about the part of the pet industry you care deeply about.

Look at what drives you and what you want to share, then write about that. Ask your clients—if you have a business—if they have a burning issue they cannot solve. You can also do research on Amazon to determine what fiction and nonfiction animal books are bestsellers.

Your book should center around a story. This could be:

- A story you made up for fiction
- A story from your own life or one you heard while working in the pet industry
- A common story about pets that everyone could relate to
- A story about how to care for pets to avoid ill health, injury, abuse, neglect, and other tragedies
- A story that is personal or general

Ask yourself, "What story do I want to tell? Why do I want to tell it?" That story must have some sort of message that changes readers' lives or entertains in some way.

Remember how the best books you have read touched your heart and soul? And you think of them long after you reach the final period and set them down. You might even reread books because you love the message so much.

To write a great book that people love, you must deliver a message they will remember after they finish reading. Even heartwarming pet fiction has a deeper message. Ask yourself:

- What message you want to impart to other people
- How you want your readers to feel and do after setting your book down
- What you want people to learn from your book

EXAMPLE

Charlotte's Web is an example of how a story delivers a powerful message. If you are like me, then you shed more than a few tears over that book. I am not saying your book must become a tear-jerking, award-winning saga that becomes a staple of children's reading experience. I am saying your book's purpose must somehow affect readers in a way to match your desired intent.

My pet loss grief books (https://amazon.com/author/wendy-vandepoll) support people all over the world when going through the loss of a pet. I get beautiful and heartfelt messages in my inbox on a daily basis telling me how my books have helped my readers.

A book is a powerful thing. You can change lives with it as you educate other people about your thoughts. It is a way to express yourself and leave a lasting imprint on the world.

If you want to write and publish a book you can be proud of and feel good about, find your heart's passion. It is the best way to accomplish this goal.

DARE TO BE UNIQUE

There is no right or wrong topic when writing about animals! The fact you want to write a book to begin with is commendable. Lots of people want to write a book—but you are actually taking action! You are accomplishing something amazing. This book will be your baby—create it the way you want.

This means you should not focus on what you think people want or what the current trends are—unless you have an interest in writing about those things. It really depends on your goals for self-publishing.

Find your own unique voice and story, then offer the world something they cannot get from any other book. You must share something that matters to you because chances are it will matter to other people.

When I first started my site, centerforpetlossgrief.com, I knew I wanted to help people recover from the heartbreak of losing a beloved family pet. This issue is a major one for animal lovers and professionals, yet it is seldom addressed in the pet industry. I knew I would find readers who were looking for heartfelt, compassionate help while navigating grief. People wanted someone who understood and acknowledged their pain. Instead of looking at precedented businesses, I created something totally original and offered people a service they could not find many other places.

My books center around the topic of pet loss grief and enable my clients to mourn their deceased animal companions. Thus, I managed to find a unique purpose for my writing. I am confident that you have something unique to offer the world, too.

BOOKS FOR YOUR BUSINESS

If you are running a pet business, a book can be a great way to both market yourself and also offer clients additional products. It can raise awareness about your brand and products or services. Finally, it can become a product in and of itself that you can offer customers.

As a result of writing for my pet loss grief center, I now have a huge following. I have helped many people around the world. My books are unique and a direct byproduct of the business I created.

ASK YOURSELF:

- What your type of business is
- What topic within that business you want to address with your book
- How you can spin the book to market your business

If you sell homemade and organic pet treats, for instance, write a book about pet nutrition, why brand name treats may not be the best for our beloved companions, and how your treats are ideal for pet health and owner convenience. This offers customers something tangible—a book full of useful information—and also markets your treat products, all in one.

PASSION PROJECT

A passion project is a book that centers around a passion you have, not a business you run. For example, my passions are animals and writing, so I wrote an entire series of books about pet blogging, pet jobs, and pet authorpreneurship that you can find on Amazon (Resources).

I also write children's picture books called *The Adventures of Ms. Addie Pants* (https://amazon.com/author/wendyvandepoll). These books pay tribute to my rescue dog and the lessons she learned as she grew up. My premise for the Ms. Addie Pants series was to teach children they can believe in themselves with unaltering love, friends, and family.

In addition, I have a pen name, W. Van de Poll, for fiction, under which I write a series of cozy mysteries (https://amazon.com/author/wvandepoll). This series has a talking dog named Addie and a budding witch with animal-communicating abilities named Sarah. Both of them save the town of Witchland from environmental destruction. Writing cozy mysteries has always been a passion for me.

Does it come easy for me to write fiction? *No*. But since I am passionate about the premise behind my characters and message, I am having fun.

Your passions are areas of life you undoubtedly know a lot about and also care about. Passions in life are great sources for stories and messages that you can share with your readers.

You may also want to use your book as a way to connect with other people who share your passion. For instance, if you are a passionate dressage champion with a wall of awards, you will be able to connect with other dressage riders. Your book won't appeal to anyone outside of the dressage world, and that is okay. Your purpose here is connecting with dressage riders and imparting a message that will make a difference in their lives and competitions.

The important thing is you are writing from your heart and sharing your deep enthusiasm for animals. This alone will excite readers and influence their lives. When you write about your passion, you instill the same in others.

Your book can raise awareness about some pet-related cause, inspire people to take action, and/or help people enter a pet-related hobby of choice. Whether you are attempting to educate readers or inspire them, your book will offer them something useful that they can utilize in their own lives.

FICTION OR NONFICTION?

Will your book be fiction—a story you came up with? Or will it be nonfiction—based on facts and information? Or will it even be a hybrid of the two—such as a fictional children's book that shows children how to actually take care of dogs? Your book is your creation; determine what direction you want to take with it.

Nonfiction is based on facts and information, but that does not mean it has to be a boring, dry textbook. You can offer personal anecdotes, client examples, memorable quotes, and even jokes as part of your nonfiction writing. Have fun with it. If you can present facts in an interesting way, your readers will love you all the more for it.

Fiction, similarly, does not have to be lighthearted stories about cute kittens—though we all love those, too! You can impart a powerful message through your fiction writing. By using fictional stories to relate to readers and stimulate their emotions, you create a stunning platform for delivering a realistic message. A fiction story about shelter animals can inspire readers to adopt instead of shop and to spay or neuter their pets to keep shelter populations down, for instance.

Do not let genre labels and previous books create a box that limits your creativity. If you have a unique idea that bends genres and combines fiction and nonfiction—go for it!

WRAP-UP

In this chapter, you learned how to decide what you want to write about. The action steps at the end of this chapter will also help you laser focus your project.

I presented ways to:

- Find your purpose and topic
- Discover if your book is a passion or business project
- Decide if you want to write fiction or nonfiction
- Be unique and follow your passion

Keep in mind your book has to be about something. Find out what that something is and split your ideas into groups to ensure that they are related. When you have a cluster of related ideas, you are able to find the true topic of your book and related subtopics to include. I will cover this in more detail in Chapter 3.

Find the story you want to tell. Then identify the message you want to leave with readers after they read your story. Your book can be nonfiction or fiction, a passion project or a business-related book, but it still has to have a story and message under the book's overarching topic.

In Chapter 2, you are going to learn about creating your avatar (Glossary). But before you read on, take some time with the action steps. They will help you tremendously, whether you are a first-time writer or a seasoned author who wants better results.

ACTION STEPS

Ask yourself the questions listed in this section and write them down. If there is no answer, move to the next. Then use these notes to help shape your ideas as you continue reading this book. Remember, do not let genres or rules limit your creativity.

1. Why do I want to write a book?
2. What is my purpose?
3. What is my vision?
4. What issues do my readers have?
5. How do I want to solve those issues?
6. Is it a passion project?
7. Do I want to write fiction or nonfiction? Why?
8. Will my book serve the purpose of supporting my business?
9. Do I want my book to be purely educational?
10. Will my book change lives?

2
CREATE YOUR AVATAR

If the book is true, it will find an audience that is meant to read it.
— Wally Lamb

Are you clear about who you are writing your nonfiction or fiction book for? In my experience, if I am not clear about my audience, my writing is all over the place, self-editing is not fun, and my editor gets her red pen out with a vengeance.

It is important to create an avatar (Glossary) before you begin to write. This is a detailed description of one person who will love your book. Your avatar is like a real person—they have a name and family status. They live in a particular place and have hopes and dreams like any one of us. You write the book for them.

I promise you, this step will make your job easier when you are brainstorming, writing, and marketing your book.

Creating an avatar will:

- Help you write your book with focus and direction
- Give you a clear picture as to who you are writing for—an audience
- Direct you to appropriate marketing venues
- Laser focus your target audience—those who will buy and read your book

Keep in mind, people seek books that match the topic they are looking for and that speak to them. Particularly in the pet genres. Animal lovers will spend hours searching for the perfect book to meet their needs. When you are clear about who you are writing for, it will be easier for your potential reader to decide if your book is for them. The result—better reviews for you.

This means your book is not going to appeal to just anyone—it will appeal to a specific type of person. Thus, you must find ways to reach that particular person and convince him or her to give your book a try.

When it comes to creating an avatar, you do not need to expend too much effort thinking of every possible reader. That is too mind-boggling and confusing. Instead, develop a picture of one single person who will love your book. Give this person an identity, complete with:

- Name
- Social class
- Place to live

- Family status
- Interests
- And more

Should you ever describe your avatar to someone, he or she will be able to picture the person perfectly because you have specific details. Creating an avatar is fun and inspiring. You will be making up the perfect fictional character who absolutely loves your book.

CREATE YOUR AVATAR

Start with asking yourself, "Who do I really think would love my book?"

In my case, my reader avatar was a middle-aged, educated woman who had lost her beloved dog and/or cat. Of course, in time, my avatar expanded as I did my research and developed a more concrete method for how to create my avatar. I wanted my book to appeal to someone who felt lonely after losing a close animal companion and who had little human support. I knew that type of person was out there and she would love my books.

For niche-specific books like mine, your avatar should be fairly easy and straightforward. If you are teaching people about snake handling, for instance, you know your readers will be people interested in snakes. But who is interested in snakes? "A lot of people" is the short answer. The long answer would be people who are typically daredevils, non-conformists, animal lovers, geeky types, etc.

You can make some educated guesses and then perform some research to back up your ideas. Who seems to be into snakes? Look up snake groups on Facebook and look at the profiles of members. Visit local reptile shops and get a feel for the crowd.

WHAT ABOUT FICTION?

For fiction books, the reader avatar may seem a bit trickier. You can employ your imagination here. Who would like a horse book, for instance? Probably a pre-teenage girl or a woman who owns horses. Who would love a Christmas cat cozy? Probably a middle-aged woman who likes romance but does not read violent mysteries and who needs a cute, heart-warming distraction from the stressors of daily life.

Forming your avatar does not require exact science. You do not have to be spot-on. You are creating a "person" to appeal to for your marketing. You are developing your voice as well when you consider how to write for this person.

WHY IS THIS IMPORTANT?

Creating a reader avatar is actually quite important.

For one thing, when you first get the idea for a book, you may not know how to write it. Technical, formal language may appeal to certain people, while a friendly, informal tone would appeal to others. By determining the type of person who would love your book, you can determine the type of style you should write in.

I know my readers would come from many different demographics, but I also know they are looking for compassion, support, and love—not a scientific dissertation. That helped me find a voice to match their expectations.

For my readers, if I wrote in a silly tone, I would alienate them in their moments of grief, when they needed my books the most. But if I wrote in a scientific, formal tone, I would also alienate them because they were not looking for a lecture. I had to find a voice that was compatible with their needs to make them want to keep reading.

This is going to be your first mission when creating a reader avatar. How do you write to make someone love your book? You now know your topic from Chapter 1, but you also need to find your voice and tone. It helps guide your writing and prevents you from rewriting the book later. Ask yourself, "What would this character (my reader avatar) want from this book?"

NEXT

A reader avatar helps you figure out how to market your book. Once the writing is done, you have to engage with readers and post on social media relating to your book. You also have to create marketing emails, a book description, and other such content that convinces people to buy the book.

The only way to get people to read the book is by making them feel the book is right for their needs. By knowing your reader avatar, you can target people with marketing that makes them think, "Yes! This is what I want!"

The reader avatar helps shape everything—the book cover design, description, and the marketing. You have to know this avatar well to both write and market. But your launch team (Chapter 13) will also have to know who your avatar is. This will help them review your book. In short, you reader avatar will drive sales.

FINALLY

What if you are hiring a ghostwriter to write the book for you? A ghostwriter is a viable option if you do not have the time or skills to write a book on your own. After hiring a ghostwriter, you have to ensure this writer can create the book you truly want. You have to be clear and specific in your instructions. The only way to do this is to provide the writer with an avatar that he or she can clearly understand and base the book on.

LET'S BUILD YOUR AVATAR

DEMOGRAPHICS

The first half of your avatar is built upon the demographics of your reader, or the basic facts about his or her existence. You can start by determining these details:

- Gender

- Age
- Family status
- Marital status
- Income
- Career
- Amount of spare time
- Where he or she lives
- Whether he or she lives in an apartment or house

PSYCHOGRAPHICS

The second half relates to psychographics, or your reader's interests, values, and needs. This is the psychology of your reader that drives him or her to buy your book. Ask yourself these things:

1. What does my reader value?
2. What does my reader like?
3. What does he or she dislike?
4. What is he or she looking for in a book?
5. What is his or her biggest fear?
6. Favorite book, music, and movie?
7. What are his or her hobbies?
8. What pet does he or she share life with?
9. What does he or she want for this pet?
10. How does this person want to feel?
11. How would this person describe himself/herself?
12. What are his or her dreams and aspirations?
13. What are some of his or her habits?
14. How does this person feel about spending money on

books? (This is important for setting a price and convincing the reader that the price on the book is worthwhile.)

15. How often does he or she read? (This helps you determine the length of the book and tone.)

NEXT

As you build your avatar, ask the above questions and jot down short, simple answers. Maybe find a picture online of some person who matches this avatar. As you answer the questions, you start to build a robust picture in your mind. To ensure you do not lose this picture, be sure to write it down and create at least five paragraphs describing this fictitious person.

Once you have built an avatar from these answers, read it to somcone. See if the person can picture your reader based on this avatar. If someone else can picture a person based on your avatar, then you know that you have a strong one that you can reliably build a book around. You want to make sure other people can picture this avatar simply because you will be sharing your avatar with your launch team later on.

SAMPLE AVATAR

Here is a sample avatar for a snake handling book.

Ethan is a thirty-seven-year-old motorcycle mechanic and detailer. He owns his own business and is married with no children. He is heavily tattooed and has a free spirit.

He lives in a rented house with his wife and two dogs. He drives a standard truck that he fixed up himself and also has two motorcycles. He spends his weekends riding, taking long trips with his wife, and taking his dogs on long walks. His family often hosts large barbecues where lots of friends get together on weekends, listen to rock, drink beer, and let their dogs play together. While he is not rich, he is also sure to designate money for the things he enjoys.

People think he is tough, but he is a teddy bear at heart. Animals are his main love in life, and he will do anything for his dogs. His greatest fear is doing something wrong as a pet lover. To rectify this fear, he likes to be informed and spend money on books that educate him. He prefers an informal tone he can relate to, but he also appreciates clear, concise, accurate information.

Now Ethan wants to make his dream of owning a snake come true. He is ready to get a snake and everything he needs for the reptile to be happy, but he wants to learn about caring for snakes first. He is looking for a solid guide to inform him.

Ethan is interested in getting an ebook he can read on his phone before bed because he is too busy to read at any other time. He is willing to spend a decent amount of money on an ebook, but he has to be sure the ebook he gets will deliver all of the information that he needs. He will be comparing a few in order to select the best one. His wife will want to read the book, too, because she shares his desire to get a snake and provide the best care for it.

You want to write a book that Ethan would like. Full of useful information, loving and compassionate toward animals, informal and relatable, perhaps some humor and a laid-back vibe. You want to offer a decent price (no more than $5.99) and stand out from the competition by offering more or better information than other books on the same topic. Your love of snakes will make Ethan like your book more because he will feel like he can relate to you.

DEAR AVATAR

In Chapter 8, I am going to share with you in more detail the different ways in which to write a rough draft. However, before I share those methods with you, keep in mind this exercise.

I use this exercise for every chapter in my books. I start by writing the chapter as a letter to my avatar. First, I pose a question according to my avatar profile, mind mapping, and outline. Then I write my letter to my avatar in a way that will answer that question and continue with the chapter from there. When I get to the self-editing phase (Chapter 9) I clean up the draft by removing their name and any reference that would confuse my readers.

My writing clients love this exercise, whether they are writing nonfiction or fiction pet books. It can make your writing journey personal, fun, and productive. Here are some examples:

NONFICTION

Chapter 1: What is Normal Grief?

Dear Sally (my avatar for my pet loss grief nonfiction),

Are people telling you that your feelings are crazy? Sally, I have heard comments from people who do not understand the emotions of pet loss grief that are hurtful. Let me help you by outlining the normal feelings of grief.

Chapter 1: Courage and Inspiration (*Pet Blogging 101*)

Dear Laura (my avatar for The Pet Biz Series),

So you want to start a pet blog? Do you know where to begin? Do not worry, Laura, if you are nervous about this venture. I was, too, when I first started writing blog articles. It takes courage to put yourself out there, but the rewards are phenomenal!

FICTION

Chapter 1:

Dear Tina (my avatar for The Spellbound Paranormal Cozy Mystery Witch Series),

Would you like to meet Sarah and Addie? Would you like to know what they are getting themselves into? Please let me introduce Sarah Spellwood and her dog, Addie. The thing is —whenever people heard her last name, Sarah would almost instantly raise her hand and say that, yes, she was related to that famous witch, Lativia Spellwood. But despite her last name, she did not believe in witches—or faerie folk, for that matter.

WRAP-UP

An avatar is a crucial piece of information about how to shape your book and market it. Your book can appeal to many people, but base it on one person who could really use the information or enjoy your story. Your tone should match what this person would appreciate. You can perform research to help you find your reader avatar.

Keep in mind, no one will bother to buy it unless they get a good sense it will satisfy their needs. This is why creating your pet-loving avatar will help you write a great book and help you with marketing later (Chapter 15 and 16).

Please do not be concerned if you know nothing about marketing. I will teach you about the basics on how to market your book and find a knowledgeable team in Section III. All you have to do now is develop your reader avatar. This exercise helps you match your book to the ideal person who will buy your book.

Before you go to Chapter 3, where you will learn about taking your ideas and putting them down on paper, check out the action steps for this chapter. Then proceed to discover how mind mapping is a great way to get your ideas down and organized.

ACTION STEPS

1. Answer the demographic questions in this chapter.
2. The psychographic questions in this chapter are also important—do not skip.
3. Write the avatar's characteristics down in detail.
4. Research if necessary. Social media groups, local pet clubs, and/or shops are great for this!
5. Get a picture of the person who would like your book in your mind.
6. If you have clients, consider doing some polls to get an idea of their needs.
7. Get to know your avatar well—you will be "talking to them" in the next two sections in this book.
8. Read your creation to a friend. Can he or she picture this person?
9. Overall, figure out what this person wants and consider this with your mind mapping efforts.

3

MIND MAPPING TECHNIQUES

'Let's put on our thinking caps and see if we cannot have an idea,' said Cricket, passing the caps around.
— Anna Rose Wright, Whirligig House

Do you have a ton of ideas in your head, and are you having difficulty putting your first word on paper? My solution—stop trying to write your book, now! Instead, consider a mind map.

Mind mapping (Glossary) is the process of getting your mind's thoughts onto paper and organizing them. Then you can use the mind maps to outline (Chapter 4) your manuscript. When you have a ton of ideas in your head, they can seem convoluted, messy, and disjointed. But when you create a graphical representation of these ideas, they start to make sense.

The great thing about mind maps is you can figure out how to develop, manipulate, pattern, and order your ideas. This will help you when you are outlining and writing your first draft for your avatar (Chapter 2).

While reading is a visual activity, your brain processes the written word quite differently from a picture. It is harder to organize blocks of text or sentence fragments into a cohesive whole when they are not down on paper. That is why you use a mind map to make your ideas visual.

There are many different forms of mind maps. You can certainly find one that works for you. I use different techniques—depending on the book. For example: I use different mind maps for fiction and nonfiction. And I have different techniques for my pet loss books and for this series (The Pet Biz Series).

The one aspect they all share is how they make complicated ideas simple. They quiet and organize the convolution of ideas in your head. And they present information in an accessible manner.

Let's take a look at some of the different mind mapping options you have to help you create a stellar book for pet lovers and/or professionals.

WHEN TO USE A MIND MAP

You will want to use a mind map for a variety of tasks within the process of writing your nonfiction and/or fiction manuscript. For example:

1. Creating a character for fiction: You want to figure out who the character is, details of the character's life, things that will happen to the character in the story, and how the character relates to other characters. This helps you remember details, since consistency is key in any book.

2. Organizing your plot for fiction: You have a rough idea of where you want the book to go, but you need to connect the dots and determine everything that happens. As you get ideas for the plot, you can sort them into beginning, ending, and middle. You can also keep track of events and maintain consistency if you are using an alternate timeline—something other than chronological where keeping track of events can be difficult.

3. Summarizing all crucial information for nonfiction: You want to be sure to cover many useful topics in your nonfiction pet book, but what if you forget one or two ideas while you are writing? It is known to happen! Also, what if you cannot figure out where to place a point or subtopic in the overall scheme of the book? A mind map can help you figure out how ideas relate and where each idea fits in the book.

4. Getting ideas down: You have tons of ideas—you want to get them down before you forget any of them. You will want to make sense of these ideas and remove the ones that do not fit into the manuscript. A mind map will help you find how ideas relate to each other in order to organize them into a book form.

5. Working out a problem: You want to show readers how to do something or you want something to happen in your fiction plot, but you cannot figure out how to present your story. A mind map can help you brainstorm a variety of ideas and test them. Then you can narrow your options down to the best one.

6. Organizing research: As you research a topic, you find new things to include in your manuscript. You want to save those facts for later when you are ready to write about them.

TYPES OF MIND MAPS

A Tree Map

These are more useful for mapping out nonfiction.

Step One: With a tree map, you want to start with a piece of blank paper and at least three colored pens. The trunk of the tree is your basic idea, or the main subject of the book.

Start by writing your basic idea vertically down the center of the paper and draw some lines around it to form a tree trunk. You can use one color for your core subject. For instance, my book might be about overcoming grief after pet loss—that is my trunk. I write it vertically, and it forms a tree trunk in red pen.

Step Two: Start writing your main ideas that connect to your overall basic idea as the branches in the second color.

These are the points you will touch on within your book—no exceptions.

I generally draw a thick, curvy line to represent each branch and then write the idea in black pen. Generally, I let each connecting idea represent one chapter. My branches might include how children grieve, how to have a pet funeral, how to memorialize your pet, normal aspects of the grieving process, etc. A chapter will center around each branch.

Step 3: For each connecting idea or branch, you want to write down different subtopics. Such as how you plan to present the idea or related smaller subtopics that you plan to write about. These will be in the third color.

Under the branch on how children grieve, I would draw several tinier branches shooting off the big one in blue, including subtopics like "Explaining Death to a Child," "Emotional Support," and "Activities Your Child Can Do." Often, these become subchapters or separate sections within the book, or I may work them all together underneath the same chapter. As long as I get my ideas down and they are directed toward the needs of my avatar (Chapter 2), I am content—because I know I'm not missing anything.

Example

A book about house-training a puppy would have *house-training puppies* as the trunk. Then each branch would be a *chapter,* and each offshoot from the branch is a *subtopic within the chapter*. For example:

- Branch 1 or Chapter 1 - House-Training Methods
- Branch 2 or Chapter 2 - Rewards and Positive Reinforcement
- Branch 3 or Chapter 3 - How to Avoid Negative Reinforcement
- Branch 4 or Chapter 4 - Reading Your Puppy's Cues, etc.

Off of each branch are offshoots with *subtopics*, such as:

- Offshoot for Branch 1 or subtopic - Types of Training Tools
- Offshoot for Branch 2 or subtopic - Types of Treats to Give a Puppy for Going Outside
- Offshoot for Branch 3 or subtopic - What Words to Choose for Training
- Offshoot for Branch 4 or subtopic - Body Language, Tail Positioning, Facial Expressions

As you get new ideas, find the branches and offshoots (subtopics) where you can add them. When you do this exercise, you will never forget an idea, and you can organize the information for nonfiction in a useful way. If words do not work for you, you can use images to make the mind map even more visual and striking.

Your tree map can get quite huge as you develop ideas. You can prune it at any time to get rid of ideas that do not fit into the book or offer much significance to your topic or avatar.

Maybe, as you write and research, you realize some ideas are beyond the scope of your book and need to be pruned. Be flexible and open to cutting out ideas to keep your book reasonable and on topic.

Thought Bubbles and Flow Charts

These can be used for both fiction and nonfiction.

When I have tons of ideas, I like to write them down as they come to me. Thought bubbles and flow charts can be helpful when you want to get your ideas or plot points down fast.

When this happens, I write my idea in different colored markers on a whiteboard in my writing space. The different colors help me tell them apart. When my ideas are all down on the whiteboard, I'm ready to get organized.

Then: I draw circles around each idea, plot point, or chapter to create a bubble and use lines to connect bubbles that relate to each other. In time, I can keep drawing lines to create a sort of flow chart, where one idea flows into the next or one events flows into the next to create a sequence.

Next: When I have my flow chart, I then take that information and enter it into an outline format. I can now see the placement and relation of ideas or plot points so I know where to stick them in the outline.

Example - Nonfiction

Let's go back to the example of my pet loss grief book. I might have a dozen ideas about how to help children grieve pet loss. I write them all down where they fit on the board. Then I see how important it is to explain how children grieve and express their grief. I choose this to be the central idea that needs to be explained before I write anything else. I circle the central idea and start the entire flow chart from that point.

From there, I draw a line to the next subtopic, how to talk to children about grief and explain death. Then I draw another line connecting to activities children can do to mourn and grieve pet loss.

Now, in my outline, I can start the chapter on children and pet grief with the subtopic about how children perceive loss and express grief. The next section is about talking to children about death and grief. After that, I place the subtopic about activities. And now I have an outline for the whole chapter.

Example – Fiction

A fiction example is a bit more difficult to give because as writers we all have different preferences and personalities. However, when you have a flow chart or your road map calculated it can make your job so much easier. Here is a condensed example of my flow chart for my cozy mystery fiction series.

1. Ordinary world: Sarah Spellwood is a former attorney from New York City finding herself in a small New England town full of paranormal people and a talking dog.

2. Inciting incident: Sarah's mentor is killed and it completely changes her life.

3. Setting: Witchland, New Hampshire.

4. Identify main character's greatest fear: Sarah is afraid of the paranormal.

5. Identify main character's happiest moment: Sarah gets to see Michael again.

6. Main character's external goal: To save the town of Witchland and all it's inhabitants.

7. Main character's internal goal: To figure out her purpose.

8. Obstacles– what or who gets in the way of her achieving her goal: The bad guys and Madras.

9. What will happen if the main character doesn't get what she wants: Witchland, New Hampshire will be destroyed.

10. The quest. The journey your character takes to find her new ordinary world: Sarah turns to learning environmental and paranormal law. She also learns about her spirit animals that help save Witchland.

11. The fork in the road. Your character has to choose which way to go. Each path/decision has consequences: Sarah has to make a choice whether to believe in her abilities as an animal communicator, witch, and psychic.

12. The black moment. This is when everything that can go wrong does. The character's worst fear happens: Witchland is on the verge of complete destruction.

13. The climax. The ultimate point of tension in the story: The real killer is revealed.

14. The aha moment. That moment when your character discovers something internal about himself. Or when he realizes the lie he thought was the truth, was really a lie: When Sarah is comfortable with her new changes and sees the utility in them for her to forge on.

15. The happily-ever-after–or not: Sarah gets closer to becoming content with her new life on many levels.

This is a brief example of what I do for my entire book as a whole and for each chapter. When I have this flow chart completed my mind map can easily be made into an outline (Chapter 4).

Post-It Notes

These can be used for both fiction and nonfiction.

Another mind mapping technique is to purchase a large poster board and a collection of differently colored Post-it notes. Or find a large wall in your home or writing space.

Example - Nonfiction

1. Write your central idea on one note and stick it in the center of the board.

2. You can start working outward with other notes containing other ideas.

3. When you have an idea, jot it down on a note and stick it to the board in the appropriate place.

4. I usually like to color-code my notes. Connecting ideas or sub-plots to the central idea will be green, while ideas I will write about under each connecting idea are pink.

5. Sometimes you won't know if an idea is worthy of its own chapter or simply a subtopic, so do not worry too much about color-coding in the beginning. You can always rewrite the notes in the proper color when you get organized later on.

6. When you have your ideas down, you can then rearrange the Post-it notes in order of importance. Change the colors if you must.

With Post-it notes, the central idea stays in the center and is surrounded by important supporting ideas worthy of their own chapters or at least some emphasis. Further out are the supporting ideas that go into each chapter. You can use strings and thumbtacks to link ideas with lines.

Example – Fiction

Again, either get a large board or designate a few walls in your writing studio to create your mind map. I have a few fiction walls going at once because I have so many ideas going for my series.

1. Write your main idea or working title (Glossary) down on a Post-it and stick it in the center of the board.

2. As you work outward you will have each chapter noted.

3. Under each chapter you will have the main scene for each chapter.

4. Under each main scene you could note a particular incident.

5. I find it equally as helpful to include a Post-it for each character I am including in my story and their point-of-view.

Using Post-it notes for fictions can be as creative as you want. I gave you a condensed example of what I do to get me going. I branch off from this basic idea as my story develops.

Computer Software

Nonfiction books are usually not terribly complicated to mind map and outline. I love to make my maps messy and organize them once my thoughts are documented. The act of using my hands and creating a beautiful mind map satisfies my creative personality.

But fiction novels can get quite complex, and you have a lot to keep track of. The more convoluted your plot is, the more you should consider using a computer software to mind map your ideas.

There are several software options for brainstorming and mind mapping. Scapple (Resources) is one of them. Personally, I still love the activity of using Post-its, markers, and the creative wall in my writing studio. But for those of you who rather use computer software, many of my authorpreneur friends love Scapple for fiction.

WRAP-UP

Mind mapping is a critical step to getting organized and making your ideas clear. Once you organize your ideas, it will be easy to form an outline (Chapter 4). By using one of the mind mapping techniques I presented, you will never forget an idea, and you will stop feeling lost about how to get started with your writing.

Consider mind mapping to be part of the creative process—instead of a dreaded exercise. It takes patience to write a book, and the more time you spend with preparation, the better your rough draft (Chapter 8) will be.

In the next chapter, you will learn how to outline your manuscript from your mind map. It is a short chapter, but necessary if you are writing your first book. Remember to do all the action steps before you go on so outlining is less of a challenge.

ACTION STEPS

1. Have the idea for your topic well established (Chapter 1).
2. Develop your avatar from Chapter 2 before you get started with mind mapping.
3. Purchase the necessary supplies. Markers, paper, Post-its, etc.
4. Establish a place in your writing studio, home, etc., where your mind map is a "permanent fixture" (i.e.,

you do not have to move it until you are done with your writing).

5. Play with the methods presented in this chapter and find one that works for you.
6. Choose the best method of mind mapping for your needs.
7. Start mind mapping your ideas with your chosen method or a mixture of methods.
8. Have fun—this is part of the creativity of writing a book.

4

OUTLINING YOUR MANUSCRIPT

The work is always accomplished one word at a time.
—Stephen King

What is an outline, and why do you need one? Before you get started writing, it is important to organize the information in your visual mind map into a usable written outline. Your outline is the basic plan and flow of your topic and/or story. It is a skeleton of your manuscript and your blueprint to finally use when you start writing.

I like to think of my nonfiction outlines as a journey to create a comprehensive guide for my avatar. And in fiction, my outlines are adventures to deepen my creative outlet to entertain my avatar.

NONFICTION

My outlines for nonfiction are not too fancy. Mainly, I want to get my mind map organized in chapters that focus on the needs of my avatar. Here is what I include:

1. I start with my title—what I call a "Working Title" (Glossary)—because often a great title does not come to me until I have finished the book. A working title is the basic name of your book that sums up the book's theme and central idea. It can be boring and clunky—what matters is it states what the book is about. Do not worry about it for now.

2. Next, I always write "introduction," since every book needs an introduction. Here you may also want to include additional things such as forewords or notes.

3. After that, I write each chapter number and the basic topic of the chapter. Again, I do not stress about catchy names unless I have one in mind already. Make sure the topic of the chapter is clear by the name.

4. I also include a conclusion or afterword at the end. Every book needs to be concluded nicely—with its points summarized for the reader. Of course, I should add, a conclusion and an introduction are not always necessary in fiction books.

5. When I have my chapters down, I go back to Chapter 1 and start outlining the information and ideas I want to include in that chapter. Looking at my mind map, I know what will go into Chapter 1—I write those ideas down. I bold the ones that will become subheadings, or separate sections. I

leave the supporting ideas under these subheadings alone for now until I know what precisely to do with them later.

This is a basic outline. I now have a clear guideline for writing my book. I start at the beginning and work my way through, completing subsections as I go. I always save my introduction and conclusion for last.

FICTION

When I outline fiction, I go into great detail and describe what happens in each chapter. An outline in fiction can take me at least three to six weeks. You do not have to do an outline if your mind does not work in this way, but I have found creating a detailed outline for fiction helps me when the actual writing takes place. Writer's block (Glossary) isn't something I have to deal with because I spent time organizing and fleshing out my ideas and plot points.

Outlining for fiction is very detailed and beyond the scope of this book, but here is a list of what I include in my fiction outlines. My goal for this chapter is to give you an idea of what goes into a basic outline.

STEP 1: SETTING THE STAGE

The first step is to come up with your premise (Glossary). Your premise is where you answer the questions, *What if? What is expected? What is unexpected?* Write your premise in two sentences.

For example: (Your character) must (do something) to (story goal) or else (reason why your avatar should be concerned).

Character Profiles: I will cover this more in Chapter 5. But right now, you should have a clear idea of who all your characters are before you start outlining your fiction manuscript. Basically, understand his or her motives, relationships, desires, traits, etc.

Think About the Big Picture: How is your story going to begin and end? What is the central conflict and the major turning point? What happens between these points?

For example, consider the:

- Beginning of your story
- First inciting incident
- Rising action
- Falling action
- Resolution

STEP 2: ORGANIZE YOUR SCENES

These are the questions you can ask as you create the scenes in your manuscript:

Decide how you will:

- Organize the scenes so they flow and build upon your premise

- Introduce your characters
- Connect the scenes to the big picture of your story (See Setting the Stage)

STEP 3: TROUBLESHOOTING ISSUES

When writing fiction, your first draft with your outline isn't going to be perfect, but its purpose is to prevent you from running into issues while you are writing.

Some common examples:

- A scene has an undeveloped idea
- There is no connection between two scenes
- A particular scene makes no sense and does not fit
- A plot hole (Glossary) is revealed

WRAP-UP

Whether you are writing nonfiction or fiction animal books, outlines are a great way to keep your thoughts organized. When you spend time with an outline, you will avoid future issues with your manuscript.

Creating an outline happens directly after mind mapping. This is a simple step, crucial for guiding your writing because you know what to write about and when. You can build your writing schedule, covered in Chapter 6, around this outline.

Always consider your avatar and mind map when creating your outline. This consideration will help you with your writing later on. Although you might want to skip this part—please do not. Honestly, like everything else I presented to you so far, outlining will help you with writing your rough draft.

As promised, in the next chapter, I am going to help you develop your character profiles. When you know your characters well, you will have solutions if an issue arises. Before you go to Chapter 5, please check out the action steps for this chapter.

ACTION STEPS

1. Have your avatar created and mind map completed.
2. Do additional research for outlining your nonfiction or fiction book.
3. For nonfiction and fiction, set a working title for your manuscript.
4. If you are writing nonfiction, consider the topic and subtopic for all chapters.
5. Do not forget to set the stage, organize your scenes, and troubleshoot your outline with fiction.
6. When writing fiction, have a well-thought-out outline—beginning, first inciting incident, rising action, falling action, and resolution.

5

CHARACTER PROFILES FOR FICTION

Character is like a tree, and reputation is like its shadow. The shadow is what we think of it;
the tree is the real thing.
—Abraham Lincoln

Do you know the characters in your story? When writing fiction, you must know your characters well. Character development is an enjoyable step in the writing process. Why? Because you can create any personality you want. When creating a character profile (Glossary), you need to understand his or her motives, relationships, and traits as they fit into your story.

For each character:

- Outline who the character is
- What he or she does in the book

- How he or she relates to other characters

Always save these profiles in case you need them later. Do not be afraid to edit them as needed. When I create character profiles, I keep them all handy while writing. This way, I can refer to them throughout the writing process and change them if necessary. When I get new ideas, I can add them to a particular character's profile. Like real people, characters grow and evolve.

I write each character profile in a separate document and save them under the same file titled "Characters for [enter name of story]." If you organize yourself in this way, you can easily retrieve the information when you need it.

Furthermore, you can save each profile and use characters later on for other stories. Maybe you create a great character, but she does not fit into the story you are writing now. You can save her for a later story where she is better suited. Or maybe you want to write a sequel or prequel and you need to read a character's profile to get reacquainted. Never get rid of character profiles!

STEPS TO CREATE YOUR CHARACTER PROFILE

First: I always start with the bare bones. I make up a name, age, and a brief description of the character's appearance. I'm not much of an artist, so I usually write the description, but if you feel like drawing the character or even using a photo of someone who resembles the character, go for it!

The more visual the better. You want to be able to picture your character perfectly in your mind's eye. But I also describe the character's basic personality for a guide on how to shape dialogue and make the character react to the other characters.

Second: I list how the character relates to everyone. Is he or she cousins with someone in the story? Who is he or she dating? How does he or she know the main character? Sometimes, it is helpful to create family trees or flow charts showing how the character relates to the other characters.

Third: I create a backstory (Glossary). The backstory does not have to be long or detailed, but it needs to explain why a character does what he or she does, and it needs to provide relevant information to the story. A backstory might include how the character's father left when he was young, creating self-esteem issues and trust issues for the character.

Fourth: I determine the character's place in the story and ask:

Is he or she the main character, a supporting character, an antagonist (a villain), or the protagonist (the hero)? You will also want to determine how much importance the character has to the overall story and how much you should focus on him or her.

I summarize this information briefly. Remember, this profile is flexible, and the character's relevance in the story can change. Sometimes I come up with awesome characters who do not fit into the story. I have to cut them out, as much as I hate doing so. Other times, insignificant characters suddenly have great uses in the story—I then make them more important.

Finally: Last but not least, I figure out a rough outline of what happens to the character throughout the story. From beginning to end, I show how the character plays into the overall story. I want to summarize what the character does, feels, and says. Then I want to show how the character is affected by the whole story.

EXAMPLE

Let's say you have a character named Susie. She is short, about thirty-five, with short brown hair and two Afghan hounds. Susie is jealous, competitive, and domineering, but she also loves to help, and she has a special place in her heart for animals.

Susie can be rude and abrasive, but her occasional acts of kindness betray she is a good person at heart.

Now I create her backstory. Susie grew up with a critical mother, which is why she is competitive and always has to win. There is a strong rivalry between her and the main character, as they both compete with their dogs. Susie envies the main character's trophies.

Susie is officially the antagonist to the main character, and she is going to be the villain of the story, but you also want to make people sympathize with her because she's not an evil person at heart. She is a cousin to the main character, and they have been in competition since they were kids.

Susie's role in the plot is to sabotage the main character's dog show so she will win. The main character has to find out what Susie did, confront her, and somehow resolve the conflict.

You could write down things like:

- What Susie does throughout the story
- Some flashbacks and dialogue to show how the main character and Susie have been competing with each other for years
- A few acts of kindness on Susie's part
- Some scenes with vulnerability where Susie cries about her critical mother's cruel words to make readers sympathize with her more
- A happy ending where Susie finds peace with herself and makes up with the main character

Now you have a completed character profile for Susie.

WRAP-UP

Your characters are a vital piece to writing your fiction book. They can make your book exciting or boring. It is crucial to have a clear idea of who they are before you start outlining—how they got to a certain point in their life, how they think, their desires, goals, and wishes.

A character profile gives you a focal point for writing. They can help you get your creativity flowing. You can test them out in different scenes to determine if they are influential and/or necessary. You can even *talk* to them and find out their secrets to make your story more interesting.

There is a lot to consider when developing your characters. Interview them by asking pertinent questions about who they are, what they like, life experiences, political views, etc. Give your imagination the freedom to write down every idea your character wants you to know.

You have now completed Section I: Get Ready to Write. You figured out what you want to write about, created your avatar, designed your mind map, outlined your manuscript, and created character profiles for writing fiction (if that is your choice).

After you do the action steps for this chapter, go to Section II: Ready. Set. Write. I will show you how to allocate time for your writing, ways to stay motivated, how to write your rough draft, and more.

ACTION STEPS

1. Make a list of all your characters.
2. Give each character a separate file or piece of paper.
3. Ask them as many questions as you can possibly think of: name, age, job, salary, enemies, lives with, fights with, outlook on life, do they like themselves, personal demons, etc.

4. Figure out how your character relates to others.
5. Determine where your character fits into the story.
6. Always figure out and document the backstory of your character.
7. Establish what happens to your character in the story.

PART II
READY. SET. WRITE.

Are you ready to get writing? Do you have your avatar, mind map, and outline done? Let's get started with your writing journey!

Maybe writing isn't fun for you yet, but it is really enjoyable once you get down to it. Whether you are a seasoned writer or a newbie, writing is a mentally complex, enriching, and entertaining experience.

There will be times where you:

- Feel stuck or cannot concentrate
- Cannot think of the right word and want to hurl your computer across the room
- Want to be doing something else instead of writing
- Cannot sleep because the ideas keep running through your head

You will find certain parts of writing you despise and parts you want to ignore. But overall, I hope you will love your writing journey just like I, and many of my clients, do.

If you are like some writers, procrastination is the worst part of writing. However, once you actually sit down to write, it can come easily. I have many useful tips in this section to help you with your writing goals.

When you accomplish your writing goals, your sense of pride and accomplishment will astound you. In this section, I will show you how to overcome procrastination, gain inspiration, work through the hard parts, and get your book ready for editing.

Are you ready? Do not put it off any longer. It is time you get your thoughts out into the world. Ready. Set. Write.

6

MAKE TIME FOR WRITING EVERY DAY

The way to write a book is the application of the seat of one's pants to the seat of one's chair.
—J.B. Priestley

Do you have a bunch of excuses to keep you from writing? Probably one of the biggest impediments you will face as a writer is getting over the excuses that keep you from being productive.

Your intentions are probably good. You plan on writing every morning, but sometimes life takes over. Before you know it, it's bedtime. You say you will start writing tomorrow. Tomorrow comes, and you have to do your grocery shopping. Pretty soon, six months have passed, and you only have a few sentences done.

The truth is—writing does not happen by itself. I know this seems obvious now, but trust me, the longer you put off writing, the longer it will take you to self-publish. If you are not careful, you will miss a deadline—or worse, give up on writing your book altogether. To actually finish your book, you absolutely must work on it every day and have a plan you follow.

That does not mean you have to finish a chapter a day. You do not even need to finish a whole page. As long as you work on the book a bit each day, you will see the bits add up until the book is complete.

THE BENEFIT

This also keeps your ideas fresh in your mind. You get more inspired as you write—a process called momentum. Momentum comes from the work you have done thus far. It then builds upon itself and propels you forward. Your manuscript starts to come together, and before you know it, your rough draft is complete (Chapter 8).

As you get started, plan and pick a time each day to write. It could be ten minutes before your shift or your yoga class. It could be twenty minutes before you go to bed. As long as you work each day, you will get the book done!

WHERE WILL YOU FIND THE TIME?

With twenty-four hours in a day and a lot of those hours spent asleep, at work, fixing dinner, playing with your pets, and spending time with family—you may wonder how you can possibly make time for writing. After all, writing takes concentration, and it is quite time-consuming. You cannot exactly multitask while writing your book.

But I assure you—you do have time in the day. You have to look at how you divvy up your activities. How many hours you actually spend in front of the television, scrolling through Facebook, or any other activity that isn't actually important.

One time, I actually measured myself and realized I was wasting a good hour and a half a day—time I could have been using to write! When I started setting aside an hour and a half a day to write thereafter, I found I did not feel the time crunch. I did not miss idly wasting my time, either.

Who knew I was wasting time—I never checked myself before. My first piece of advice is to look at how much time each day you spend on Facebook, playing solitaire, and/or searching the Internet for *nothing*. You may be surprised to see you actually do have time to write every day.

WHAT I TELL MY CLIENTS

- Set a timer on your phone and measure yourself as you engage in different activities, like social media or napping
- Multiply the hours of your favorite television shows by how many times you watch them each week
- List the things you do every day, then weed out the things you do not actually enjoy or gain any benefit from

You will quickly find you do many things you do not need to do—thus wasting time where you could be writing.

When it comes to writing a book, you have to budget your time a bit differently. Do not worry—this does not have to be permanent. You can get back to binging on your favorite shows in a few months. For now, you are committing to a worthwhile pursuit, making a dream come true. It is worth the new time budget.

FINDING THE RIGHT TIME FOR YOU TO WRITE

Most writers I have worked with have different times of day when they write best. Some people write late into the night—gaining inspiration by the solitude of darkness. Others wake up early, and their first task is to write. Yet others can write indiscriminately at any time of day.

To get a sense for when you write best, think of when you tend to have the most energy to tackle projects. Do you stay up till 2:00 a.m. making crafts? Then you might be a night owl writer. Do you wake up early feeling refreshed and energized? Then you might be a morning writer.

But if you have never written before, then you cannot know for sure when you write best until you actually try it.

A WRITING SCHEDULE FOR CHAMPIONS

I prefer to assess what I must do for a book and then break up tasks and schedule them over time. When I plan in this way, I feel less overwhelmed and more eager to work. I also cannot put off the parts of the book I dislike doing—I have a schedule I cannot stray from. This enables me to meet deadlines and get things done. I urge you to try a schedule, too.

MY SCHEDULE FOR THIS BOOK

This is the process I have followed for most of my books. Your schedule can change depending if you are writing nonfiction, fiction, children's books, etc. Take my suggestions and figure out what works for you.

1. I knew I wanted to write sixteen chapters.
2. I gave myself three days for each chapter.
3. One day was for research, and two days were for writing without editing.
4. After my first draft was done, I started self editing.
5. After four self-edits, I sent it to my editor.
6. When it came back, I made the changes and sent it to my proofreader.
7. When she finished, my beta readers (Glossary) read and critiqued it.
8. I then went to the next steps, which I will share with you in Section III.

As I suggested in Chapter 2, start by developing your avatar after you know your topic (Chapter 1), then start mind mapping (Chapter 3) and building a basic outline (Chapters 4 and 5). Then break it into chapters and determine their approximate length from your mind mapping. Guestimate how much time each chapter will take.

Make sure you set a date when you plan to finish your first draft. Some plan on three months or less. I did less than three months for most of my nonfiction books. For my fiction, it takes me longer.

DEADLINES

You do not have to meet these deadlines exactly, but now you have incentive and guidance for getting the rough draft finished. As you get a sense for how fast you write, you can then adjust your timelines to be more realistic.

Please do not beat yourself up for not meeting a deadline—but also take the deadlines seriously and try to meet them to motivate yourself, which I will talk about more in the next chapter.

A NOTE ABOUT RESEARCH

Researching your material is a good thing, but I have found with my clients, research can easily become an excuse not to write. This is why I only allow myself one day for researching each chapter for my first draft. If I find I need more, I make a note to myself to continue research during my self-editing period.

Be honest with yourself when conducting your research. Do you really need a week of research before you start a new chapter or section? Or do you find you write better by doing all the research before you start work?

Whether you are writing nonfiction or fiction, figure out the way you want to research and how to do it. You might need more time and flexibility if you are interviewing people or traveling for research, for example. Be open to last-minute changes and take your time. This research process should not be overly stressful, or you will not want to do it.

Remember to catch yourself if your research is a form of procrastination.

SELF-EDITING BEFORE YOU ARE FINISHED

One of the best pieces of advice I got from Chandler Bolt, founder of the Self-Publishing School (Resources), was to *not* edit as I write. Prior to learning this, I wasn't getting my manuscript done—because I edited each sentence after I wrote it. And of course, I hated it.

When I changed my habit and wrote without reading or editing a word until I was done with my rough draft (Chapter 9), it was then I became a successful best-selling author.

Some people do prefer to self-edit at the end of each writing session, some at the end of each chapter, others at the end of each sentence or paragraph. If this is your preference, and it works for you, then do it. But always adhere to a schedule as best you can, and do not use self-editing as a method of procrastination or not getting your book done.

Your set schedule is your guide to the successful end of writing your manuscript. It helps you create a flow that writers must enter to create unimpeded. However, be flexible and change the schedule as you must. Things can, and do, happen. Please do not stress out about missing a deadline or changing the order of your writing process.

KEEP A STRONG WRITING SCHEDULE

Now you know why it is important to set aside time each day to write—with no exceptions. This schedule will help you complete each step of the writing process. But how do you create the discipline necessary to make yourself adhere to these habits? Not everyone has a natural ability to write in this regimented fashion.

In this regard, I compare writing to exercising. Once you get in the habit, you find it easy to write every day and follow your schedule. It becomes a reliable part of your routine you do without question. But until you have this habit and routine, you will have to force yourself to write each day. This can be particularly challenging when you struggle with procrastination.

Here are some tips to help develop discipline for writing and make your writing schedule a habit:

1. Get enough sleep. When you are well rested, your mind is sharper. That is obviously helpful for this intellectual pursuit.
2. Reading is crucial for any writer. Reading teaches

you how to write, how to express ideas, how to get imagery across. You may also need to read for research. Set aside time to read each day. It does not matter what you read—just read something!

3. After reading, do your writing. Does not matter for how long, as long as you write each day.
4. Wake up, go to bed, and eat at the same times—develop a solid routine for your day. Consistency helps you develop a practice where you can fit your writing time in neatly.
5. Make your life more about writing. This means you create an immersive experience for yourself. Read blogs and articles about writing, join writer's clubs and social media groups, take writing challenges, and attend seminars or courses on writing. Writer's retreats are also great for getting away from the demands of daily life. I even participate in a daily email word challenge called "Word of the Day" (Resources). All of these activities motivate you, remind you to write, and make you think about writing.
6. Reward yourself when you finish writing each day. Most people never even sit down and write. Take some time to pamper yourself or reward yourself in some manner. You certainly deserve it!
7. Do not worry about being perfect (Chapter 8). Focusing on fixing every little typo while you write is aggravating and distracting from your actual inspiration and content. You can forget great ideas for how to phrase something or what to write next if

you go back to fix a small detail. Save all of that for self-editing, your editor, and professional proofreader. I always say just write—even if it is an incoherent mess!

8. Do not worry about readers. Worrying about how you will get five hundred readers or whether or not people will like your book is a surefire way to deaden your inspiration and confidence. You really cannot know if your book will be received well. The suspense and insecurity about readership is an inevitable facet of being a writer. Focus on writing for now and worry about readers later. Do not let insecurity kill your creativity and stall your progress. And do not worry about something you cannot know for certain or control.
9. Set a daily word count when you get familiar with your writing speed and ability. Aim for a thousand words, for example. If you can comfortably write five hundred per day, set that as your minimum—but challenge yourself by trying to hit one thousand on weekends when you are off work.
10. Stay comfortable while you write. A comfortable chair, an ergonomic keyboard, sweatpants that are not too tight—these are important. I also love setting myself up with some herbal tea, my water bottle, and healthy snacks. This way, I do not have to get up if I get hungry or thirsty. I set the temperature just right, cover my lap in my favorite blanket, and set my pillow in the small of my back. That way,

discomforts do not distract me and pull me away from my writing.

11. Shut out distractions. Turn off your phone, do not answer email alerts that pop up on your desktop, and tell everyone to leave you in peace. Work in a quiet area, or put your headphones on to block out noise. Sometimes, I even use blackout curtains so I do not end up staring off into space out the window. I do not put a lot of distracting things up on my walls in my writing space, either. Distractions break your concentration and tear you away from your writing. They must be avoided at all costs.
12. When you find yourself getting tired or aggravated, take a break. Fifteen minutes should be sufficient to release your stress and approach your writing with fresh eyes again. If you must, you can stop and continue on the next day. Writing should be enjoyable—when it turns ugly, walk away for a while. No one enjoys sitting and doing the same task for hours on end—that goes for writing, too.
13. Each morning, look at your bigger goals and break them into smaller goals that you can accomplish each day. List them in pencil in the order you wish to complete them and move them around if you must.
14. As you complete tasks, cross them off, and I guarantee you will get a sense of accomplishment. When you feel as if you are making little progress, pause and reflect on these lists. See how much you really have done.

STOP MAKING EXCUSES

Okay, I have been there. I have made excuses to put off and get out of writing. I love writing, and I'm not a procrastinator. But there are days I tend to avoid it just like all writers do. I believe it is the mental exertion.

Really, there is no excuse to not write. Have a long flight? Write while you are on the plane. Have shopping to do? Write after shopping. When you find yourself justifying why you are not writing, tell yourself, "I have no excuses!" Then sit down and write, even if it is just a word! One word is better than nothing, and it gets you in gear.

Sometimes you won't feel inspired to write. After a long day, over the holidays or when you have company, you may not want to write. You are too exhausted, distracted, overwhelmed, or whatever else you are feeling. Try and take these experiences and/or emotions and write about them—even if it has nothing to do with your book.

It is okay to take breaks, as long as you have a solid plan and a specific date or time in mind to get back into it. For instance, if you take the holidays off from writing, have a plan to get back to it on a particular date after the holidays are over.

Excuses may be flimsy or valid. But they can derail your progress. Do not give them power.

WRAP-UP

No matter what—write each day. Set aside and make time when you are not busy. Budget time more efficiently now. Writing takes discipline, dedication, and time—be sure to pay attention to all of these things.

Follow my tips, like immersing yourself in writing, creating a peaceful environment free of distractions, and getting comfortable before you write, to foster the discipline you need to adhere to your schedule. Make writing a pleasant experience and you will want to commit to it. There is no need to put writing off or hate it.

Read on to Chapter 7 to learn more about getting motivated, inspired, and ready to write. Learn how to give your *procrastination* something to do! But make sure you finish your action steps for this chapter for your continued success.

ACTION STEPS

1. Determine the best time for you to accomplish productive writing.
2. Set aside time to write each day and stick to it.
3. If you cannot adhere to the time, pick another time for the same day.
4. Create a daily, weekly, monthly, and yearly plan for your writing.
5. Follow the tips above to foster discipline and sanity with your writing journey.

7
MOTIVATION, INSPIRATION, AND PROCRASTINATION

There is no greater agony than bearing an untold story inside of you.
—Maya Angelou

Are you still struggling with finding the time and motivation to write? In Chapter 6, I talked about getting and staying motivated to write by setting aside time, cultivating discipline, and applying yourself.

But there is often more to it than "forcing" yourself to write. You need inspiration for your content, motivation to push through the tough times, and tools to overcome procrastination when it rears its ugly head. This chapter will teach you how to accomplish these three things easily.

MOTIVATION

Since writing a book is a relatively challenging activity, you need motivation to get you through the tough parts. Otherwise, it is far too easy to give up when the going gets tough.

Think back to the whole reason you wanted to write your book.

- You wanted to make a difference for people and their pets
- You wanted to share your compassion for animals with other pet lovers
- You wanted to write a book based on your favorite topic—animals

Now it is time to focus on these three things to gain motivation for writing.

You may have other motives, too. Maybe you want to promote your business, or support your favorite cause. Maybe you want to be able to say, "I'm a writer," or put your English degree to good use. Maybe you promised your blog readers or customers a book, and now you have to write one. Whatever your motives are, they are good ones because they drive you to write.

When you encounter a rough patch with your writing or feel unmotivated to start writing, think about what inspires you. That should get you into an eager frame of mind for writing. But if it fails to get you writing, consider using deadlines and goals as motivation (Chapter 6).

There is no better motivation than having to complete a book by a certain date. When you feel like putting off writing, you can remember you have to finish the book in one, two, or three months. That makes you actually write because you won't finish the book on time otherwise. I often give myself fairly tight deadlines to stay motivated.

Set a writing goal for each day (Chapter 6). Set yourself up to write a certain number of words each day and complete a chapter or section by a set date. This goal will act as motivation. You want to feel a sense of accomplishment when you meet a goal and get to check it off of your list!

Now let's look at ways to inspire you to keep writing when you do not want to write. These ideas will help you if you feel like procrastinating and sabotaging your writing schedule that you created in Chapter 6.

INSPIRATION

We all have had those really blah days. Days when we do not want to write, cannot think of what to write, and do not feel excited about writing. Certain events and stress can especially rob you of inspiration.

I know after a long day of work or a long trip, I completely lack inspiration. Sometimes, I sign up to write a story for an anthology or collection. I have a deadline, but I just cannot scrounge up the inspiration for a good plot and intriguing characters. When this happens, I sit down and come up with a schedule to keep me inspired.

If you lack inspiration, you are far from alone. Do not feel bad. Here are a few things I do to get my inspiration back—I hope they will work for you.

STEP ONE: DAILY WRITING PROMPTS

To write, my mind must be in "writing mode." I am useless if my mind is in "social mode" or "playing with pets mode"—or worse yet, "watching mindless television mode." To get my mind into writing mode, I love to use daily writing prompts.

These prompts are often single sentences or even sentence fragments that compel you to create a story. The prompt may be an opening or closing sentence you must use, or simply an idea to inspire you to get started. Some prompts tell you to write a certain number of words, while others do not have a limit. You can interpret the prompt how you want and create your own unique story.

EXAMPLES OF WRITING PROMPTS

Here are a few fun writing prompts to get you going with pet fiction or nonfiction. There are hundreds of writing prompts online. Search "writing prompts for animal lovers," or a variation, and you will find a bunch to get you going.

- Write a story about your cat climbing the wall to get a moth

- Write a story about a dog who is a pickpocket
- Write a letter to your avatar (Chapter 2) telling them you are sorry
- Write about your avatar trying out a new activity

STEP TWO: WRITING CHALLENGES

Writing challenges are also incredibly inspiring. There are many you can choose from, and you can find them by doing a Google search. I would suggest finding one that fits your goals, schedule, and genre.

For fiction: "Twelve Short Stories in Twelve Months" is an example of such a challenge (Resources). In this challenge, you must create a story each month of a certain number of words (no more and no less!) centered around a prompt, then post it on the site and receive comments. You must also read and comment on the short stories other people post.

Another popular challenge is "Nanowrimo"(Resources). With this challenge, you must complete a 50,000-word novel in the month of November. There is a Facebook group with people who will support your journey. It can be fun and inspiring.

Finding a challenge can inspire you and get you into writing mode. If you do a Google search for "writing challenges," you will find groups that focus on poetry, fiction, nonfiction, short stories, etc. I listed some of them in the Resources section of this book.

STEP 3: READ OR WATCH A MOVIE

Reading and watching movies can inspire you to stay focused with your writing as well, as long as you do not use them as methods for procrastination. They are playbooks for how to create plots and characters. Plus, they can inspire you to express your ideas in unique ways.

When I feel stuck, I love to take a break and read for a while. I have several books that I am reading at a time—each one a different genre. No matter what I'm working on in my writing studio, if I feel overwhelmed or stuck, I pick up my Kindle and start reading. Every week, I try to catch a new movie, either on television or in the theater. I urge you to do the same because you never know what you may gain.

STEP 4: TAKE A WRITING COURSE

Writing courses and classes are designed to inspire you. They can be so inspiring you are almost guaranteed confidence, skills, and motivation to create your book for pet lovers and/or professionals. By taking a writing course, you will gain knowledge, camaraderie, and skills.

Some courses are in person, while others are online. Depending on your budget and schedule, find one that you look forward to. Search for a course tailored to your type of writing. For example, a mystery writing course if you are writing a pet cozy mystery. Or a nonfiction research course if you are writing nonfiction.

Look up writing courses online. Also, seek out writing groups on social media, such as Writers Write (Resources). These groups will share details of upcoming courses with you. I included a list of a few online course websites in the Resources section of this book.

STEP 5: EXPERIENCE SOMETHING NEW

New experiences in life are the fodder for books. When you take a trip to Paris, you might get an idea for a lovely romance scene as you walk past quaint coffee shops and view the Eiffel Tower. When you get together with old friends for a high school reunion, you might hear one of your old classmates share a story about how her life turned out which could spark ideas for how to shape your own character.

Try new things, meet new people, and gain inspiration when you feel stalled on a book. People watching can be an incredible resource for material and inspiration.

In pet writing, new experiences centered around pets can be helpful. Watch a dog obedience class, a team of huskies pull a sled, and/or volunteer at a cat shelter. Try to spend as much time around animals for inspiring ideas. Even trying out new pet-related products can motivate your creative flow.

I have found inspiration tends to come at the strangest times from the most unanticipated sources. Placing yourself in new situations and experiences helps you remain open to inspiration.

STEP 6: TAKE A BREAK

Sometimes we lose inspiration out of sheer boredom, exhaustion, and repetition. Working on a book for too long can drain you. That is when you need to take a break. Once you do, you can approach your writing with a fresh outlook. When you start to feel bored, exhausted, frustrated, or otherwise negative while writing, put it away and go do something else.

When you take a break, it is important to do things that do not relate to writing or your book at all. You need to exercise, stretch, go for a walk, or partake in a new activity. The key is to get your mind off of your book for a while.

A break may be a few minutes to a few days. I have taken breaks of a few months before. You need to take as long as you need to clear your head. Return when you feel ready.

A break is not admitting defeat. It is not giving up on the book, because you plan to return. But the longer your break is, the harder it can be to get back into "writing mode" and get the motivation and discipline back to sit down and write.

If you take a lengthy break of more than a day, you must set a return date. This date is nonnegotiable. When that date arrives, you must commit to writing once again.

STEP 7: MINI WRITING RETREATS

I love to schedule mini writing retreats for myself. I oftentimes go to the coast of Maine and get an Airbnb for a few days. I turn off all social media, radio, television, etc.

I even schedule stay-at-home writing retreats. This is where I stay at home and cloister myself in my studio. I do not look at social media or do things that distract me. I cook ahead and freeze my food so all I have to do is warm it on the stove.

For both of these writing retreats, I do scheduled breaks, times to talk to my husband if he is not with me, and definitely time for my doggo. Walks on the beach and time spent in nature are incredibly inspiring for me when I am on my retreat.

STEP 8: MEET SOMEONE NEW

New people form the basis for our characters—especially fiction. New people also share stories or do things that can be inspiring. As you get to know new people, or hang out with people you haven't seen in a while, you can gather a lot of details for stories and characters.

When your inspiration runs dry, I highly recommend setting up a social experience of some type. At the very least, go out to a public place and enjoy some people watching.

STEP 9: HIRE A WRITING COACH

Writing coaches have different roles and fulfill different tasks. It is one of my favorite tasks to do for other writers. In my practice, I am geared toward inspiring and motivating people to write and finish their books. I offer inspiration and strategies for overcoming the sense of being stuck. And teach people what you need to know to publish and market.

Some coaches meet in person, and others over the phone or video chat. Fees vary, but a quality writing coach is an investment. Do your research and find one that fits your personality and goals.

You can search for writing coaches online. View their reviews and portfolios to ensure they produce happy and successful writers. If they offer a complimentary session, use this to get to know these coaches better and find one who works well with you.

STEP 10: USE WORK OR OTHER MUNDANE EXPERIENCES FOR INSPIRATION

Your work can be an incredible resource for obscure or mundane material for your book. I am sure there are many other commonplace activities you engage in every day. Ask yourself how you can gain inspiration from:

- Water cooler chitchat about the weather
- Data crunching for hours on end
- Your office mate who sings to himself or herself

A true writer gleans inspiration from everything—even the mundane and banal.

I find relatable stories contain elements from the mundane. Recreating a horribly dull watercooler chat with one of your coworkers can provide priceless comedy to your story, for instance. Look at your daily experiences and see if there is something in them that you can recreate in your story in a meaningful way.

Next is procrastination. This is a real issue that many writers face. It can be easy to let procrastination take hold of your writing journey and sabotage you from moving forward. Read on to learn ways to beat procrastination.

BEAT PROCRASTINATION

Procrastination is hardly a rare experience. It is an annoying and limiting habit that many of us fall victim to. When you do not want to write, you tend to put it off, and the next thing you know, years have passed.

Overcoming procrastination can feel like beating the laws of gravity, but here are some tips I use when I want to put off my writing tasks for the day.

STEP ONE: WRITE—RIGHT NOW

When you catch yourself putting writing off or dreading it, do not wait any longer—it just lets the inertia build. No matter where you are, open up your computer or notebook and get to work. Instead of letting yourself put writing off, do it the minute you want to procrastinate and replace inaction with action.

Even if you have already missed your daily writing time, as discussed in the previous chapter, it is never too late to write. At least get a few words done before you turn in for the night.

Doing something is better than nothing! As soon as you think about writing—get to work.

STEP TWO: SET CLEAR GOALS WITH DUE DATES

It is harder to put off a clear goal than a vague one. Consider the difference between these two goals:

I want to write something today.

I want to write five hundred words by 2:00 p.m.

Which one is more motivating? Which one actually makes it clear what you must do and when? The latter goal is more likely to make you think, "Okay, all I have to do is five hundred words. I have two hours left to do it. I better get to it now!"

Each day, set a goal for your writing. Set a number, the topic, and a time. Look at your book outline and set similar goals for each part of the book. When you do this, you can overcome procrastination and complete the book by your deadline.

STEP THREE: TRACK PROGRESS

As you complete goals, be sure to check them off in a planner or to-do list or on your calendar. This gives you a sense of accomplishment and lets you see your progress. Seeing progress is inspiring and creates momentum because you think, "I already did this much, and it was not so bad!"

With each item checked off your to-do list, you will feel eager to check off more items until you are finished. You see it is possible and painless—then you want to get your writing done. Tracking your progress makes it harder to see the value in putting writing off.

STEP FOUR: CREATE A REWARD

One thing I like to do is tell myself, "I can go for an extra-long hike with my dog, Addie, only *after* I meet my writing goal today." That way, I have something to look forward to after I write. It makes me want to complete my writing faster so I can play with my best friend.

When you want to put off writing because you think you may have something better to do, make your better thing wait until you finish writing. Make writing a priority, and reserve your other activity for a reward. This tricks your brain into completing the goal.

STEP FIVE: JOURNAL OR WRITE SOME OTHER WAY

When you make your life about writing, it gets easier to find the motivation to write. Even if you are not working on your book at the moment, make yourself write a blog article, submit stories to competitions, and journals.

Also, you can read writing articles and watch videos. Attend courses and meet with other writers. Post in social media writing groups and read the posts other people make. All of these things keep you writing, and you can find it easier to overcome procrastination.

WRAP-UP

We covered a lot in this chapter, and you can refer to it often as you need help. There will probably be something new to inspire you each time you feel unmotivated.

Although, it can be hard to find motivation to write—keep in mind your motivation lies in your purpose with your pet book. Being clear with your purpose keeps your motivation alive and helps you to move forward.

There are many places you can find inspiration. Inspiration is easy to come by—even in the mundane. Be open to all possibilities. You can use your life experiences to create awesome scenes in your fiction or tips to help people with obscure issues in nonfiction.

Please, when you feel like procrastinating, do not do it. Set clear goals and intentions for writing, track your progress, journal, and do whatever it takes to overcome procrastination.

In the next chapter, learn about writing your rough draft. Remember, your rough draft is supposed to be rough! You are not ready for publication yet, so have fun with it and get your ideas down. Your final book will look better when you completely finish.

Here are your action steps to cultivate motivation, inspiration, and nab procrastination.

ACTION STEPS

1. Discover your motivation. Why do you want to write your book?
2. Write your motivation down and pin it to the wall of your writing studio where you can see it.
3. Figure out what will block or stall your writing process and determine a solution for each. Focus on those positive solutions.
4. Get inspired when you feel dull—through new experiences, new friends, books, movies, writing coaches, and writing prompts or challenges.
5. Do not let procrastination win—ever. Set goals, track progress, and make time for writing in your life.

8
YOUR ROUGH DRAFT

The rough draft of anything is garbage.
—Ernest Hemingway

Are you tempted to edit your rough draft, trying to make it perfect along the way? Please stop attempting to make your first draft a polished masterpiece. Honestly, it will drive you crazy, and you may never get your ideas on paper—or worse yet, your manuscript done.

I am going to help you write your rough draft with the tools I use myself and what I share with my clients. Your first goal after creating your outline is writing a rough draft—not a polished piece. But I promise I will help you with creating such a manuscript in Chapter 9.

A ROUGH DRAFT

A rough draft is the first draft of your book—the messy skeleton of what your book will become. It will not look great, but it is positively brimming with potential. I cannot tell you how many drafts you will write—it depends on you as the writer and your topic.

Some books may be done after one draft, while others take up to twenty. Personally, I go through my nonfiction drafts about five times and my fiction ten times. Since this draft is your creation, it will grow, evolve, and change.

Hence, there is absolutely no pressure to write a perfect, beautiful rough draft. It is called "rough" for a reason. I like to write mine quickly and sloppily—then improve upon it later.

WRITE TO GET IT DONE

The purpose of the rough draft is to get your ideas down on paper quickly. You want to get your ideas down, create some substance for the book, and give yourself something to work on and improve later.

Writing your rough draft is where you use all the tools you learned in Section I:

- Figuring out the subject or themes of your writing
- Fiction or nonfiction
- Creating your avatar

- Mind mapping techniques
- Outlining
- Developing character profiles for fiction

This draft does not need to be perfect, heartfelt, or ready for publication. But you do need to get your ideas, wisdom, and/or story written down to get your book started. Keep in mind, the polishing of your work will come later.

Using your outline, start to expand on the ideas you have already written (Chapter 4). Start each chapter with Dear, your avatar's name (Chapter 2). Using your outline, *talk* to your avatar briefly or in full detail—it does not matter. As long as you create the bulk of your content and get your ideas down on paper.

It is important to write and let the ideas flow. Do not pause to self-edit, as that can stop your forward motion and throttle the flow of ideas. Instead, ignore the mistakes and move on. I have been known to write sentence fragments to capture a main idea and move on. This is not the time to craft lovely sentences.

Of course, if you come up with a beautiful passage or lovely sentence—write it! You will forget it if you wait—trust me. As ideas occur to you, you must capture them. You want all of your ideas on paper so you do not forget them.

The length of your rough draft may not match the length you want your book to be. It may be too long or too short. That is okay. You can identify the disparity in the next draft and either add or take away content as needed.

LONGHAND

If you want to get your ideas onto paper without electronics—try longhand for your rough draft. Your handwriting does not need to be beautiful, as long as you can read it. Later, you can type and refine it. The point of the rough draft is getting everything down—longhand allows you to accomplish this goal.

Some people work better with longhand. Later, they hire someone to type their work, or they type it themselves. Authors have told me they feel a stronger connection between their brain and writing as long as they are writing by hand. If you are such a person, then go for it!

My greatest fear as a writer is losing my work if I did my rough drafts in longhand. Once you write stuff down, you never know what could happen to your pages. Scan them or take pictures as a form of backup. Store finished pages in a safe drawer, as well.

COMPUTER

Typing your rough draft is the easiest way, in my opinion. If you are not great at typing, you probably will be by the end of your book! What is nice about writing your rough draft on a computer is you have many tools at your fingertips to make the process quicker and easier.

You can use spell check and punctuation to make corrections, you are able to back up your work in different locations immediately, and you can also print your work if you feel more comfortable self-editing on paper—which many of my clients do.

If you want to be able to access your draft anywhere, consider using Google Docs or any cloud-based word processor. As long as you have Internet, you can work on your document. Plus, you can easily share the document with your team, such as editors, proofreaders, and beta readers. If you use Word (which I prefer), set it up to sync with your OneDrive or some other cloud storage. Your work is saved even if your computer crashes.

However, these documents can be hard to retrieve if you are offline. Be sure to enable offline functionality or else copy and paste your cloud document into Word to access when you are not online.

Always save often and back up your writing! There is nothing worse than working hard on a draft, then suffering a hard drive crash and losing it. Never make the mistake of saving everything in one place or this could happen to you. Imagine the setback. It may be enough to make you give up on your pet book.

Fortunately, with today's cloud storage technology, it is easy to save your work in multiple locations for retrieval anywhere, anytime, on any device. I recommend saving a copy of your draft in several databases—Google Docs, OneDrive, and Dropbox, for example.

RECORDING YOUR WORDS

Another fantastic option for writing your rough draft is to record yourself. This option is great if you are finding it difficult to sit down and write (Chapter 6). My clients love this alternative if they commute to work.

Oftentimes, my clients who record their rough draft finish their manuscripts quicker than they anticipated, and their books are finished ahead of schedule.

After you are done dictating your draft, you can transcribe the recordings or have someone transcribe them for you. Recording lets you get your ideas documented quickly when you are pressed for writing time.

I love recording my rough draft when I'm walking my dog. This way, none of my ideas are lost, and I do not have to carry a notebook. It is also convenient when I'm on the go and get an idea.

You cannot always write—but you can quickly record your ideas. Use your phone's recording app, a camcorder, or other recording device you have at hand. Store the recordings with clear labels about their content so you can find them later. There is nothing more annoying than sifting through tons of unlabeled audio files—trust me.

I recommend backing up your recordings in a cloud. That way you never lose anything important. You can also access your recordings anywhere and anytime you may need them.

When you are ready to turn your spoken words into written ones, you can hire a transcriptionist on a site like Upwork or Fiverr (Resources). Otherwise, you can transcribe them yourself.

Please remember, do not worry about self-editing until you get everything down. This is still a rough draft!

A LETTER TO YOUR AVATAR

I discussed writing a "Dear Avatar" letter to craft each of your chapters during the rough draft phase in Chapter 2. This can make your writing journey seamless once you get the hang of this tool.

Of course, you wouldn't keep the same format in your final draft, but this is a writing prompt (Chapter 7) that is priceless and a surefire way to keep you on track with your writing.

WRAP-UP

Your rough draft is your chance to get your ideas down and start writing your manuscript. It is important during this step to not self-edit or try to make things perfect. Your goal is to get your rough draft done.

You will be able to go back once completed and polish your thoughts and words. Keep in mind, shorthand notes and sentence fragments are acceptable. As long as you get your ideas down, you are accomplishing the purpose of your draft.

You can work longhand, on a computer, or by recording yourself. Find the way you are comfortable with. While I generally use a computer for my writing, I am known to jot down longhand notes or record myself in a pinch when my laptop is not readily at hand. You can thus combine methods to ensure you never forget a great idea.

After you complete the action steps for this chapter, get ready for self-editing. I love the self-editing process. I find inspiration while in this phase of creativity. Next, you will learn all my steps to getting my manuscript polished and ready for my editor.

ACTION STEPS

1. Take a look at the schedule you created in Chapter 6 and start writing without editing anything.
2. Pick whether you want to write longhand, use a computer, or record yourself to complete your rough draft.
3. Consider a combination of methods to fit your schedule and lifestyle.
4. Start each chapter as a Dear Avatar letter.
5. Always make copies of your notes, recordings, or typed documents. Save often and in many locations, online and offline.
6. Remember, the purpose of your rough draft is to get your ideas on paper by using the tools I helped you with in Section I. It is not a manuscript ready for an

editor. You will learn how to prepare your manuscript for an editor in the next chapter.

9

CLEAN UP YOUR ROUGH DRAFT

Writing without revising is the literary equivalent of waltzing gaily out of the house in your underwear.
—Patricia Fuller

Did you know you have to prepare your manuscript and perform some basic, yet rigorous self-editing before you send in your book for editing? Professional editors expect your book to be in a certain state of readability—you cannot send them your raw rough drafts.

I have a lot of respect for good editors, but I must say—editors can be tough. And we want them to be. They are not inclined to tolerate little annoyances they clearly ask you not to do in their submission guidelines.

In my experience, editors do not like staples (for a printed manuscript), small print, and terrible grammar—among many other things. To foster a good relationship with your editor, you want to get familiar with how to polish your manuscript for submission. The good news is—the more you self-edit your manuscript, the better the editing job.

Your editor will be able to perform his or her job more thoroughly if your book is already prepared. It is quite difficult for someone to slog through pages of poorly prepared and error-ridden writing. Your book does not have to be perfect—perfecting it is the editor's job—but it needs to be readable and presentable.

This chapter is about how to turn your rough draft into a final manuscript for the editor. Again, I cannot tell you how many drafts you will go through, but you will know when you have completed your manuscript. Once you feel confident your work imparts your message and is self-edited, you can move on to sending it to an editor.

Let's go over the basic steps to prepare your manuscript for editing.

SELF-EDITING

With your rough draft completed, you will start at the beginning and self-edit for the first time. This is where you fill out missing information or passages, add reference notes if applicable, and correct glaring errors. You might move sentences or whole paragraphs around and reorganize the book.

STEPS FOR SELF-EDITING

Step One: I change the font to something easy to read, like Courier or Arial. I highlight the entire manuscript and then set the font size to twelve. Next, I go to "Paragraph" and set the line spacing to double.

I save this. Now my manuscript is much easier to self-edit. I am able to spot errors that are harder to see with fonts like Times New Roman and Georgia. However, these are my personal preferences. You can play around with fonts and sizes to find the one that is easiest for you.

Step Two: Go through your manuscript from the beginning. I like to break it up into sections and do a section each day. It removes the stress from what otherwise seems like an overwhelming task. You will find what works for you. I also recommend you keep a notebook by your side to take notes, as you will probably come up with many. I like to note things that I notice or need to check on later in the document.

When you complete this part, you will be able to take a break. I recommend a break because self-editing can be vexing and time-consuming. You want to tackle it for the second round with a fresh pair of eyes. Put it down and come back when you feel refreshed and renewed. I cannot tell you specifically how long this may take, but you will know.

Step Three: You will repeat this self-editing process a second time. This time, you will be looking for errors you overlooked the first time. This is the point in self-editing where I read my manuscript aloud for the first time. Keep in mind, initially you still have to read to yourself to clean up your manuscript.

When you read aloud, you will be surprised with how much more you can pick up. Reading aloud is a tool you do not want to skip prior to sending your manuscript to your editor.

Plus, as you read through a second time, you become even more familiar with the manuscript and how to better present the information or story. You will be able to make more adjustments to have it flow soundly. Take another break, and then return for the third round of self-editing.

Step Four: The third time is the charm—usually. The third time lets you catch those little errors you tend to overlook because you knew what you meant to say.

At this point, I also like to run the book through ProWritingAid (Resources) to find any errors I still have not caught. A proofreading software is not as perfect or accurate as your own eyes or an editor. However, it can catch little things like common misspellings, misused words, run-on sentences, and passive grammar. It is an additional layer of self-editing to help you smooth out your writing.

Step Five: Watch for topic changes by reading your manuscript aloud—again! What looks good on paper does not always sound as good aloud. You need to read your book aloud at least two times in the self-editing process to make sure it flows. (I read mine three to five times.) By flow, I mean the manuscript reads cohesively, and one point leads into the next nicely.

As you read, watch out for sudden topic changes (nonfiction) or plot holes (fiction). If your work does not make sense, you are either tired, you switch topics too quickly, or you neglected to clear up something in the plot, thus creating a plot hole (Glossary). If this is apparent to you, your reader will have the same experience.

Consider adding some sort of transition sentence or paragraph signaling to the reader you are changing topics. Read it over again and notice how much more smoothly the book reads.

Step Six: Also, watch out for clunky sentences as you continue polishing your manuscript. If you lose your breath by the end of a sentence, it is too long and will lose a reader's attention. Meanwhile, if your sentences sound choppy and staccato, they are too short.

A blend of short and longer sentences provides the best cadence for the book. Some of your sentences may be worded awkwardly and need to be fixed. Read clunky sentences aloud, and if they do not feel right, then try rephrasing the sentence different ways while speaking aloud until you find the best word order.

Step Seven: Watch out for confusing pronouns. If you read "he" and have to go back to figure out who you are referring to, it is time to replace "he" with the subject's actual name. Avoid starting too many sentences with "It" for the same reason.

Step Eight: A big one to watch out for is a tautology (Glossary). This is where you say something twice in different ways. For example, "my own horse" is a tautology. All you have to say is "my horse." Adding "own" is repetitive and simply reiterates the fact that this is your horse.

You can eliminate a lot of wordiness and annoyingly long sentences by cutting out tautologies. Furthermore, you can find wordy phrases and replace them with more succinct, action-packed ones. Such as replacing "I decided to act" with "I acted." These two things exponentially improve flow.

Step Nine: Beware of passive or vague grammar. For your writing to engage readers, it must have action that is clearly assigned to a character or subject within the book.

As you read aloud, notice if you have any sentences that sound like:

"Many dogs are not taken care of, so they get sick and do not act right."

This sentence is pretty vague—who is not taking care of these dogs, and what precisely happens as a result?

Replace with:

"You may not know how to take care of your dog, which leads to many behavioral problems and health issues."

See what difference an action verb makes? The passive is sleepy and unclear—action makes your reader feel engaged.

Step Ten: Finally, try to catch when you repeat the same word too many times. A thesaurus, either online or in book form, is handy here. If you keep catching yourself reading the same word over and over, you will feel bored, and your reader will be bored as well.

Consider replacing some of the words with synonyms or appropriate pronouns. As I said before, do not start every sentence the same with "It" or "This," as that is repetitive and boring. Spicier language is always more entertaining and engaging for readers.

READY FOR BETA READERS?

If you want—when your book is smooth enough where you do not feel embarrassed to show it to other people—call on a few good beta readers. Personally, I wait until I get it back from the professional proofreader (Chapter 10).

If this is your first book—I would suggest asking a good friend, family member, or fellow writer to read and comment before you send it to your editor. Make it clear they only need to read it without editing. Their job is to ensure the book makes sense and to point out any extremely obvious flaws or issues. They are not supposed to nitpick the font or argue with you about the Oxford comma.

I suggest to my clients to offer their manuscripts to beta readers at this point in Arial with double spaces and no indents. Your preliminary beta readers can jot notes in the columns or over sentences as they read (hard copy). However, they can make comments in the margins when you put the manuscript in Google Docs or send as a Word doc.

A literary group is a great place to find beta readers and fellow writers who are eager to read and give useful tips. You can find them online or meet with them in person. The group should build you up and help you improve—not intimidate you or insult you. However, I suggest only reaching out to this type of audience when you have a final manuscript that is ready for publication or when you already have published a few books.

PREPARE YOUR MANUSCRIPT FOR YOUR EDITOR

When you write your manuscript, you can use whatever font and formatting you wish to make the book easy to work on. As you self-edit, you want to use the specifications I stated above. But when you are about to send it off for editing, you must undo any special formatting and prepare the book in a simple style that the editor can easily use.

All editors and proofreaders have their own specific formatting requirements. You can easily find these out and then make the required changes to your book. But if your editor does not specify any particular format, here is a basic one that most editors will accept.

1. Set the color to black and the font to Arial. You do not need fancy colors or fonts right now. Those are distracting to an editor, who is more concerned with

the actual content. You can add that later on in the design part.

2. Set your page size to 8.5 x 11 and set your margins to one inch on all sides. This is standard in the industry. Again, you can change all of that in the design stage.
3. Align it to left justified. This makes the left side uniform and the right nonuniform.
4. Remove double spaces after periods. Some people still type like this because that is how things were done in the days of typewriters. But now in the computer age, double spacing is unnecessary. You can easily remove this by simply going to "Find and Replace," entering a period and two spaces in the find bar, and then entering a period and a single space in the replace bar. Hit enter, and the document will become formatted accordingly. Be sure to scroll through a few pages to make sure your changes stuck. Also, be sure to save after each formatting change!
5. Get rid of tabs. Again you can use "Find and Replace" for this. Replace tabs with five spaces on the space bar. Be sure to indent all new paragraphs if your book is fiction. Otherwise, do not indent paragraphs at all. Use a single space between paragraphs to separate them instead.
6. Bold and left justify all headings. Be sure to enter a page break between each new chapter, instead of hitting the return key dozens of times to create a

new page. The page break will keep the spaces in any format, while hitting the return key will not.

7. Add page numbers. Select the option for a number on the top left of your page. Start numbering on the page your story or book starts, not on the title page. Add a table of contents at the beginning of the book with page numbers when you have finished numbering. To auto-generate one in Google Docs, you want to make each chapter heading "Heading 1" and each subheading "Heading 2." Subheadings under these can be "Heading 3."

PAGES TO INCLUDE

Your manuscript is not complete without the addition of pages called front matter and back matter (Glossary). Basically, front matter are the pages in your manuscript before the main text of your nonfiction or fiction book. Back matter are the pages at the end of your book.

Here are some suggestions of what to include—not everything is necessary. I suggest you do your own research as well. Look at some of the books you love for what the author includes in their front and back pages. Those marked with * are necessary.

FRONT MATTER

- Title Page*
- Copyright Page*

- Table of Contents*
- Forward/Preface
- Introduction*

Back Matter

- Conclusion*
- Glossary
- Resources
- Acknowledgements*
- About the Author*
- Review Request Page*
- More Books by Author*

You are now ready to send the whole document in one file. Do not send separate files for each chapter. If you print your work, do not staple them, as that is the bane of any editor's existence.

FOLLOW SUBMISSION GUIDELINES

In Chapter 10, I will go into how to find a great editor and proofreader. But for now, know this—each editor has his or her own guidelines and rules for submissions. You would be wise to follow these rules. Some editors are flexible—others not. You will find some want a printed, double-spaced manuscript delivered by mail and others want electronic submissions of .docx or Google Docs files.

The important thing is finding out what your editor really wants. He or she will usually post it clearly on his or her website and/or in your contract. Otherwise, you can ask the editor directly. Follow the instructions, and make the editorial process a smooth one by staying on your editor's good side.

WRAP-UP

To get your book ready for publication—self-edit your manuscript thoroughly. Do not skimp on this process. The more you polish your manuscript, the easier it will be for your editor to suggest changes.

I provided you with steps and suggestions in this chapter. It is important to present your editor with a polished and a self-edited manuscript. You will get a better product in return, and it may even cost you less.

If this is your first book, finding a beta reader at this point is a good idea. But if you are a seasoned self-published author, I would wait until you have your *ready to publish* manuscript.

If you want, you can ask family and friends who love animals to provide objective criticism and make sure the book makes sense. But honestly, I would not depend on them to do this for you. Instead, you might want to hire someone from Fiverr or Upwork to get the job done quicker (Resources).

After you do the action steps for this chapter, go to Section III: What's Next for Success. I will start this section by explaining different types of editors, then go on to how to design the interior of your book, create a winning cover, upload to Amazon, and market your book.

ACTION STEPS

1. Prepare your manuscript for self-editing by picking a font and size that works for you.
2. Go through your rough draft at least three to five times—rework sentences, flow (nonfiction), plot (fiction), grammar, organization, etc.
3. Read your work out loud at least twice and make more self-edits.
4. If you are a first-time writer, consider having a few friends or family members read your manuscript—ask them to comment on the flow only.
5. Prepare your manuscript to meet submission guidelines of your specific editor.

PART III
WHAT'S NEXT FOR SUCCESS

Are you inspired to go to the next step? Are you excited to be so close to self-publishing your book?

With your manuscript self-edited and ready for the editor, you can finally let out a long sigh of relief and take a break. All your hard work deserves a celebration. You definitely need to pat yourself on the back. But, as you know, this is not the end—yet.

In this section, I am going to guide you with ways to transform your book from a professionally edited manuscript to an actual self-published book for pet lovers and/or professionals. Whether you are writing an ebook or a print book, you still need to take steps to get it edited, proofread, formatted, and published.

If you do not know the first thing about self-publishing, do not worry. I did not know anything when I wrote my first book. But now I am a self-published author with over twelve best-selling books (and counting) in multiple genres. Plus, I help other writers reach their dreams of becoming a published author.

I will teach you how to find your editor, formatter, and cover designer. You will learn how to launch and market your book to pet lovers and pet professionals. From designing your cover to marketing—I will cover it. Read on to learn how to get your book for pet lovers and/or pet professionals self-published.

It is now time to take your manuscript to the next level —publication!

10
FIND YOUR EDITORS

Everyone needs an editor.
—Tim Foote

Are you overwhelmed with trying to find your team of editors? As the author, you are the brains behind your book. You definitely served an important role. But your book won't come to existence without the careful work of other professionals on your side. You must assemble a team to create an outstanding pet book that sells well—including editors.

Your team is going to consist of many different people who offer different services. It all starts with your team of editors and ends with your launch team (Chapter 13).

In this chapter, I present different types of editors available to get your manuscript finalized for publication. You may not need to hire all of them, but keep in mind each one is instrumental in your book's final success. Be sure to find great people, whether you are writing fiction or nonfiction.

DEVELOPMENTAL EDITOR

A developmental editor has a specific job. His or her main task is editing your book for structure or plot. They will look at big-picture elements such as consistency, flow, structure, readability, and clarity for your fiction or nonfiction book. Basically, they make sure your manuscript is structured properly.

Primarily, this type of editor will provide pointers and feedback on what sections or paragraphs should be deleted, revised, or moved so that your point is clear or your plot is solid.

He or she will also point out things like, "This dialogue is stilted. Perhaps try this," or "Your point is not clear here. Let's try this instead to present your point."

A developmental editor may simply help you with your final draft, or he or she may be present for the entire book from rough draft to finished draft. You need to decide when you need help and reach out to a developmental editor at the appropriate time.

Do not wait too long to get help—there is nothing wrong with seeking a professional to help make your book amazing. Especially if you are new to writing, hiring a developmental editor can make your writing process infinitely easier.

CONTENT EDITOR

A content editor is one in which you hire after you made all the changes your developmental editor has made. This type of editor will make the necessary corrections concerning the flow and paragraph-level content of your presented manuscript. Content editing does not restructure your story or chapters. Rather, they address issues of clarity and consistency within the content of your manuscript.

A content editor will go through your manuscript and correct:

- Clarity
- Syntax
- Voice
- Tense
- Flow

Once a content editor goes through you work and you receive it back from them, I can guarantee you will need to reword sentences and paragraphs to improve your final product.

COPY OR LINE EDITOR

After the structure and content are addressed, it's time to move on to the sentence-level edits. This is where a copy or line editor comes in.

They will:

- Improve phrasing and resolve incorrect word usage

- Resolve inconsistent and inaccurate punctuation
- Improve sentence flow and clarity
- Look for spelling and grammatical errors

What I love about a copy or line editor is they are laser focused. They have an exceptional talent for going through your manuscript line by line to be sure your words look polished and professional.

PROOFREADER

Finally, proofreaders. This is the stage of editing where the final set of eyes scans your manuscript for errors. They are a lifesaver in bringing your book together and making it ready for publication.

Their main job is to look for errors involving:

- Spelling
- Grammar
- Typos
- Consistency
- Punctuation

Be sure to choose a proofreader that has been formally trained and certified by a body such as the Editorial Freelancers Association or the International Association of Professional Book Editors (Resources). These associations require members to pass rigorous tests and pay fees in order to join.

Anyone can read a book and fix the glaring errors, but a true proofreader will examine your book closely in an effort to catch every little mistake. They will analyze every word and every sentence to ensure correctness.

It is best to contact a proofreading association, like the ones above, to find a vetted member. The proofreader will be able to provide you a portfolio and reviews of past work. He or she should have a professional website that makes his or her process and terms clear.

WRAP-UP

Be sure to manage your expectations for each type of editor you hire. The goal of all editors is to make your book better—but you cannot expect your proofreader to do developmental editing. A proofreader is strictly for improving the spelling, grammar, and punctuation.

To have a record of what was communicated between you and your editor I suggest using email as the primary form of communication rather than telephone or video chat. I consider it a preferred method as do my editors.

Your editor may also be open to using something like Google Docs that makes it easy to see your editor's suggestions and to share comments. You can also access it anywhere. Keep in mind, though, changing the document while the editor is working on it will only slow them down and may even decrease their accuracy.

You can find developmental editors as well as the others mentioned in the chapter on Upwork, Guru, or Fiverr (Resources). You can also look them up online and peruse their websites. A professional website that lists their credentials and best-selling books are good signs that someone is a qualified practitioner. Be sure to take testimonials into account.

Your editor must also be open to a confidentiality agreement such as an NDA, or non-disclosure agreement. This agreement states he or she will not share or reproduce your work without your written permission, not even as a sample in his or her portfolio.

He or she must be transparent about rates and what services you will receive within a specified time frame. Do not expect editors to be cheap—for quality work, be prepared to spend money for good editors.

As you can see, editors are instrumental in preparing your manuscript for publication. If you are unsure what type of editing you need, reach out to an editor and ask. Before you go on to the next step and learn how to design your book, take a look at your action steps for this chapter.

ACTION STEPS

1. Whether you are writing a fiction or nonfiction book for pet lovers and/or professionals, research various types of editors you may need.
2. Ask other writers for references.

3. Be clear with your expectations for what you need for editing. Example: Do not expect a copy editor to do developmental editing.
4. Research various editors online and review their policies, approach, and pricing.
5. Be sure you hire professionally trained editors for your manuscript.
6. Ask for a sample of an editor's work. Expect to pay for a short sample.
7. Know exactly what your editor's expectations are of you.
8. Be sure you have a contract with your editor that outlines pricing, deadlines, communication frequency, etc.
9. Refer back to Chapter 9 to be sure you provide your first editor with a self-edited manuscript.

11

DESIGN YOUR BOOK

Good design is good business.
—Thomas Watson, Jr.

Congratulations, you now have a well-edited and polished manuscript—are you ready for the next step? You are now ready to hire a formatter and the cover designer for your book.

Writing a best-selling book for animal lovers and/or professionals is not a job you can accomplish on your own. To make your book ready for self-publishing, you must hire a good team of professionals. We covered editors in Chapter 10. Now I am going to help you with hiring your formatter and cover designer.

You can attempt these things on your own, but the results will always be better with dedicated professionals who know what they are doing—especially the first time around. Be sure to shop around to find professionals who meet your needs and communicate clearly throughout the working relationship.

BOOK FORMATTER

A book formatter is a professional or a software app like Vellum (Resources). This person or app designs the interior of your professionally edited manuscript. They set the font, the headings, spacing, etc. Basically, they create an interior layout that is inviting to your reader.

Kindle and print books are formatted differently for Amazon. When you format a manuscript for Kindle or softcover, you need to know what you are doing because inconsistencies can occur. For instance:

- Spaces can become altered
- Images can become aligned weirdly
- Chapter headings may not sit where you want them
- And more

Furthermore, you will have a massive headache when Amazon rejects your images for not having the right DPI. Or when it insists a single sentence on page fifty-nine does not match margin specifications—even though you cannot see the issue on your end.

Since formatting for the first time has a huge learning curve, it is easy to become discouraged. I would wait until you have written a few books before you take this task on.

The easier way to make your book look beautiful is by hiring a professional formatter. They have the patience and expertise to deal with Word's and Amazon's idiosyncrasies. They know exactly how to lay the book out and format it across all mediums.

The formatter will size and lay out images, fancy texts, text bars, blurbs, and more. Their expertise will allow you to upload your manuscript to a self-publishing platform with no problem. You should not encounter issues with spacing, font size, font style, or images after a formatter works on your book.

If your book does not contain images, then you may be able to read up on Amazon's specifications and format your book accordingly by yourself. But when it comes to images, I do not waste any time. I leave it to the pros. Formatting requires a special set of skills that can be elusive, and even infuriating, to the rest of us.

To hire a formatter, ask your editor and author friends for recommendations. Also visit the Internet and search for book formatters. There are many formatting companies to choose from—get recommendations.

Formatters should have portfolios that display samples taken from books they have formatted. They may also be willing to format one page of your book for free to show off their skills. Look for professional, sleek formatting and great testimonials when making your decision on who to hire. Also consider rates; cheap formatters are seldom worth the money you save because you will end up having to hire another one—I've been there!

You may need to meet with your formatter in person or over a video conference to discuss your expectations. But the work can be done entirely over the Internet. A good formatter will go through your book, choose a few different formats that may suit it, and then let you decide which one you like best.

BEFORE HIRING A FORMATTER, ASK THESE QUESTIONS:

1. What is your fee and payment structure?
2. What services do you provide for this fee?
3. What is your turnaround time?
4. What is your formatting process?
5. Can you format the book for both Kindle and print?
6. Will you be able to provide more than one format?
7. How will you deliver the formatted book?
8. What is your process for revisions? Do you charge for revisions?
9. Do you have a no-risk money-back guarantee if I am not satisfied with the work?
10. Can you provide samples and references?
11. Have you formatted a book in my genre before?
12. Can you format one page of my book as a sample?

When you enter a contract with a formatter, be sure to have an NDA, or non-disclosure agreement, in place. Since the formatter has access to your book in its entirety, you have to protect your rights to the content.

Professional formatters should already have NDAs in place that establish all of these terms, and you can go through the NDA and determine what you agree or disagree with. An NDA is a legal contract, and you can use it in court if any part of it is violated, so take it seriously and never work without one.

Additionally, be sure the formatter will provide all agreed-upon services for the agreed-upon fee by a certain date. Make it clear that you will retain all rights to the book and whether or not you will credit the formatter.

Finally, make it clear if the formatter may use any part of your book for a portfolio sample to show other prospective clients or not.

COVER DESIGNER

When your first book is fully written, edited, and formatted into its full potential, you can begin the cover design stage. If you are already a pro at self-publishing, you can do this during the editing period or even before you write your book.

This is such a fun part of the book publishing process—again, one of my favorites! This is where you give your book its unique aesthetic appeal—a cover that makes your book stand out from the other pet books.

They say to never judge a book by its cover, but we all know the cover helps sell a book. Professional cover designers are experts at creating covers that sell your book. A boring, bland cover or a cover that is irrelevant to the book's contents will not entice anyone to buy it.

You want to create a cover that tells people:

- What to expect
- What your book will offer them
- What problem your book can solve

A good idea is to create a cover featuring the type of animal your book is about. A fiction cover might be artistic, while a nonfiction cover might be realistic. Come up with a concept to share with your cover designer. If you have no clue what to do for your cover, many cover designers can propose some ideas and let you pick what you like best.

Cover designers are graphic artists with massive amounts of talent. Like all artists, different designers will have different styles and skills. You want to find the one who can deliver the cover that matches your vision the best. Shop through the portfolios of cover designers and see if any of them can deliver what you want.

Do not jump into a working relationship with the first cover designer someone refers you to. Shop around. First, get referrals from authors you know, your editors, and other people in the publishing industry. Check out the designers' websites and portfolios.

You can also use a site like Fiverr (Resources) to find a cover designer seeking a gig. There are also job bid sites like Guru, Upwork, and 99designs (Resources). They host many designers from all over the world eager for work. Mark's List or Smashwords (Resources) is another source of cover designers, formatters, and others up for hire.

Finally, a simple Internet search can yield some designers with websites where you can view portfolios, rates, and reviews. When you have found a few who match the style you like, approach them for a quote. This is an interview process, so you want to ask some questions:

1. Can I see your complete portfolio?
2. Do you have any references I can speak to?
3. Have you designed covers for my genre before?
4. How will you come up with the concept for my design?
5. How will you create the design?
6. What is your fee range?
7. What is your design process like?
8. Do you do the artwork yourself or have access to a stock photo site?
9. Will you be able to create custom images that I will have full rights to?
10. Do you offer a no-risk money-back guarantee if I am not happy with the work?
11. How will you deliver the final product?
12. What is your turnaround time?
13. Are you available for additional projects if I need

them? (This can come in handy in forming long-term relationships with a great designer who can design covers for all of your books, either in a series or not.)

14. Will you give me more than a few covers so that I can change covers to boost sales at any point?

If you like the designer's work and process, can afford the fees, and see primarily great testimonials, then you should initiate the contract. Each designer is different with how he or she likes to handle contracts.

Your contract should outline expectations, types of files, payment schedule, copyright to images, deadlines, etc.

Clear communication is also essential. Cover designers may be experts in the field of cover design, but they are not mind readers. You cannot expect them to know what you want unless you state it clearly. If you do not like a cover concept that someone submits to you, be sure to tell him or her why so that he or she can fix the issue and meet your expectations.

You not only need to communicate your vision for the cover, but you also need to communicate the format and size of your book. Designers can create different sizes and covers that are formatted for ebooks and softcovers. You have to specify what you need.

It is perfectly possible to do this part yourself. But you must become familiar with how to use a design software and size the cover image to fit your book properly. I always leave this part for the pros—I don't want to risk having an unprofessional-looking cover.

WRAP-UP

Writing a best-selling book for pet lovers and/or pet professionals is not a job you can accomplish on your own. To make your book ready for self-publishing, you must hire a good team of professionals—including formatters and cover designers.

You can attempt these things on your own, but the results will always be better with dedicated professionals who know what they are doing—especially your first time with self-publishing. Be sure to shop around to find professionals who meet your needs, communicate clearly throughout the working relationship, and establish an NDA and clear contract before you start working together.

Read on to learn how to create a website to help market your book and boost sales. In this modern age of Internet, you must have a web presence to make it as a pet writer—or any type of writer. But check out your action steps below to be assured you hire the best formatter and cover designer for your masterpiece first.

ACTION STEPS

1. Research formatters and cover designers by asking

your editors, fellow authors, and using the Internet for referrals.

2. When hiring your formatter and cover designer, be sure to acquire an NDA and contract.
3. Ask your potential formatter and cover designer for samples of their work.
4. Ask them for testimonials from other clients.
5. Be clear about your needs, expectations, and deliverables at the beginning of the hiring process.
6. If you have published books before, consider using an app called Vellum (Resources), which is especially great for fiction. If you know what you are doing, it works with nonfiction as well.

12
CREATE A WEBSITE AND LANDING PAGE

Do not think of your website as a self-promotion machine, think of it as a self-invention machine.
—Austin Kleon

Have you created your website yet? If you are not a tech-savvy person, you probably groaned when you read this chapter title. But never fear, creating a website for your book is not terribly difficult! In fact, it is fun and straightforward once you learn how.

You may want to create a website on your own, or you may want to hire someone to do it for you. That is your prerogative. However, you must have a website dedicated to your pet book. If you already have a website, that is great. What you will need to do is create a landing page for your book—just as you would for a service, event, etc.

You might think you do not need a website. But sadly, you are missing out on a huge market and great marketing opportunities. Creating a web presence is essential to helping you get the word out.

I created my own website with Wordpress and the Avada theme. I go into how you can do this in my first book in this series:

> *Pet Blogging 101: How to Start a Riveting Pet Blog and Gain Loyal Followers* (https://amazon.com/dp/B07XWRS95W).

I won't go into the technical aspects here, as I want to focus on what you must include in your website. Please check out the Resources in the back of this book to help you out as well.

A WINNING AUTHOR WEBSITE

First and foremost, your website is a form of marketing. You must treat it as such. The purpose of your site is to provide a place where readers can go to keep track of what you are publishing. A website is a tool where you make an impression, convince readers to read your book, and also tell people a bit about yourself.

You can create a site using your author name or the name of your book. I recommend going with your author name. Especially if you plan to write more books. Using the name of your book or series can be extremely limiting. However, if you write one book or a series—and that is all you plan to do—you can dedicate an entire site to either your one book or series title.

FEATURE AN "ABOUT THE AUTHOR" PAGE

This is where you talk about who you are. You include a biography and at least one picture of yourself. Pictures of your pets will sell even more copies! Try to show readers the image you want them to see and will best sell your book.

For example—a loving, compassionate veterinarian, a fierce opponent to habitat violation, a charming fiction writer. These are images your readers get from your books—depending on who you are. Uphold that image in your biography by sharing information with your readers. I talk a bit more about how to build a good biography in the "Amazon Author Central" section in this chapter.

FEATURE A LANDING PAGE

This page shows your book cover, description, reviews, and where to buy it. You may include an Amazon link here. The purpose of this page is to convince people why your book is worth reading.

A landing page is a page on your website dedicated to your book. Creating a landing page for your book is a great idea if your book is part of your business. I have landing pages for all of my books on my websites:

- centerforpetlossgrief.com
- centerforanimalcommunication.com
- wendyvandepoll.com

For Center for Pet Loss Grief, LLC, my actual site is centered around the subject of pet loss grief. I feature a home page where I share the basic premise of the site and what users can expect. But I also have a clearly visible list of links at the top for my products. It makes it easy for people to enter my site, know what it is about, and navigate to what they need. Only people who need my resources are likely to visit my site. I market to them by showing how I can help them.

Nonfiction needs to sell the book by showing how readers will learn from it. Make the biggest promise that you can keep here.

Some examples:

"Are you at your wit's end trying to house-train your puppy? In my book, I offer a twelve-step system you can use to train your puppy in a week!"

"If you are debating about adding a snake to your family, you probably have many questions. I answer all of them and more in *There's a Snake in the House*! By the end of this book, you will have the confidence to purchase your first reptilian pet."

See how these promises are specific? They tell a reader what:

- The book is about
- They will learn

- Benefits they will gain
- Time frame they can expect to see those benefits

Meanwhile, fiction needs to include a power-packed description. Bryan Cohen's book, *How to Write a Sizzling Synopsis,* is another great one about creating descriptions especially for fiction. With your fiction, you want to share what the book is basically about, while leaving a lot of suspense in the reader's mind. I have found this book helps me write my nonfiction descriptions as well.

When you do this, the reader (your avatar from Chapter 2) is eager to buy it and find out how it ends. You want to create a brief description or even share a sample of the book that acts as a sort of teaser. If this book is part of a series, mention the series title and include what number in the series the book is.

Be sure to feature clear links to your book on your home page and a menu bar item that takes users to a landing page marketing your book.

INCLUDE A CONTACT PAGE

This page will include a contact form for people to contact you directly with questions. Have a sign-up form for people to subscribe to your emails. Include social media links to all of your social media profiles (which will be covered more in Chapter 15) and information about your pet business, if you have one.

This page is important, since readers may have questions or concerns after reading your book. Or they may have questions before they read it. By being available and open to chatting, you make them feel supported and inclined to become your biggest fans.

Always answer all emails and respond to comments on your site and social media accounts. If you cannot keep up with all of the emails you get, then consider hiring a virtual assistant (Glossary) to help you. Some email programs also automate your reply. An automation can let people know you received their email and will be responding soon.

Each person who visits your site is a potential lead, or customer. You want to sell your book to them. With that in mind, think how you can make your site stand out and entice people to read your book. Great critical reviews, photos of you signing your book at a big bookstore, and a tantalizing description will entice readers.

FEATURE A BLOG

I believe it is necessary to have a blog as an author. Publishing books, especially on animals, is competitive. In a blog, you can post new and relevant things relating to your book.

For instance, if I write a *new* book about managing pet loss grief, I'll want to create a blog post about it. The article shares what the book is about, but also shares twenty percent of the book's secrets so readers want to buy it and learn the other eighty.

I'll also want to post other relevant content and articles about pet loss grief on my blog that does not have to do with my books. This strategy keeps people visiting my page and keeps me relevant in their minds.

Furthermore, it entices people to sign up for my email lists. I can send them free gifts, book announcements, and notifications that will get them to buy one of my books or other products.

The first book in this series, *Pet Blogging 101: How to Start a Riveting Pet Blog and Gain Loyal Followers* (*https://amazon.-com/dp/*B07XWRS95W), goes into great detail about this topic.

SEO

To rank highly in searches and help people find your book, you must use search engine optimization, or SEO. I also covered this extensively in *Pet Blogging 101: How to Start a Riveting Pet Blog and Gain Loyal Followers,* but I will go over the basics here and in the Glossary.

It is easy to get buried in the mountains of content on the web. That is why you must utilize SEO. Throughout your content and site metadata (Glossary), you must include keywords that people are likely to search related to your book. To find these words, be sure to do some research.

Google Keyword Planner (Resources) is one of many ways that you can research keywords and find out the most popular, or high-ranking, ones. Use a mixture of high- and medium-ranking keywords (Glossary) throughout your website content and in the page and site descriptions. That way, people will find you.

AMAZON AUTHOR CENTRAL

On top of having a website, you want to create an Amazon Author Central page (Resources). This page highlights who you are as an author and allows you to claim all books you have self-published on the Amazon platform. Readers can visit your profile and see your other books, if you have published more than one.

Amazon Author Central has a great help section, and the customer service crew is awesome and helpful. But I will sum it up in this section for you.

- Visit Amazon Author Central and sign up.
- The sign-up process is quite self-explanatory.
- You will want to claim your books on Amazon.
- Fill in all the options to inspire potential readers to buy your books.
- Finally, you want to post a profile picture and write a riveting biography.

For your profile picture, choose something that represents your love of animals. For dog books, you want to be posing with your beloved dog, for example. Make sure the photo is well lit from behind the camera and shows your face. Do not hide your face with sunglasses or a hat. A smile is most inviting, but you can also wear a serious expression if that is your brand.

For your biography, share something that makes people feel connected to you and able to trust your knowledge. If you are a licensed veterinarian with a specialty in exotic animals, for instance, be sure to say so. If you run a rescue, tell people why you do this type of work. You want pet owners to read your biography and think, "Wow, this person is someone I can relate to and trust on the subject of pets."

You also want to seem like a real person. You want to talk a bit about yourself. Include:

- Where you are from
- Where you went to college
- If you are married
- How many kids you might have
- Talk about your pets and how many
- List your hobbies
- Talk about foreign countries you may have lived in or visited
- Share what you do for a living
- Reveal some of your passions

Think of what makes you unique and human, then add to your Author Central biography. When you present yourself as a real person, you can allow readers to connect more with you.

For example, I include fun facts like:

1. As a wolf biologist, I was followed by a wild wolf in minus sixty below weather.
2. When walking my dog, Addie, I was hissed at by a wild bobcat.
3. Hiking with Marley one morning, I was huffed and chased by a momma bear.

WHAT IF YOU HAVE OTHER BOOKS THAT ARE NOT PET-RELATED?

There are a few ways to go about this. The simplest way is to publish all of your books under one name and feature them on your page. Give a general biography that touches on your expertise in all areas of the subjects you write about.

If you write fiction, talk about where you are from, what you do for a living, and maybe if you have a family or pets, as well as anything interesting about yourself. A fun fact is not a bad idea to include as well.

But you can also publish in different genres under different names. Your nonfiction pet books might be under your real name, while your romance is under a pseudonym, or vice versa. You can create different pages for each name in Author Central, claim the books you publish under each name, and then link them so that you can access and control them all from one account. There is no need to create multiple Amazon Central accounts.

Be sure to update your biography as soon as changes occur in your life. You can use these biographies as "About the

Author" sections on your books and update them with each new release. You should also feature this biography on your website. The same biography creates consistency so that people remain sure you are the same person.

WRAP-UP

A web presence is essential for any author. You can build a site yourself or hire someone to do it for you. Be sure to feature your book prominently on a landing page on your site and also on social media.

A blog is an effective tool to promote your book. You can reference your publication within a blog article, send potential customers to Amazon to purchase, and also grow your mailing list by offering a free gift in exchange for an email.

I have found many authors do not make use of their Author Central account. This is a wonderful resource to gain followers, clients, and/or book purchasers. This platform is free and is instrumental to your success as an author. Be sure to fill out all the options. Do not leave anything blank. You want your visitors to become followers and purchase your books.

Are you ready to get your book out there? Then read on to start building your launch team. Treat your team well and they will help create interest for your book! But first, check out your action steps for this chapter so you are well prepared.

ACTION STEPS

1. Create a website yourself or hire someone to do it for you.
2. Include an engaging biography and photos with you and your animals.
3. Create a landing page dedicated to your book(s).
4. Try blogging to gain followers and increase your visibility on Google.
5. Design an easy-to-understand contact page for people to get in contact with you.
6. Set up the SEO for your website and your landing pages.
7. Create an Amazon Author Central page and fill it out completely.
8. Keep your biography updated over time.

13
BUILD A LAUNCH TEAM

If you have a dream, do not just sit there. Gather courage to believe that you can succeed and leave no stone unturned to make it a reality.
— Dr. Roopleen

Have you ever heard of a launch team? Your launch team, also known as your street team, is a group of people who spread the word about your book and encourage others to buy it. They are your first step in marketing your book.

The great thing about your launch team is they can help you spread the word, get people excited about your book, and generate sales for you. Word of mouth is always the best and most trusted form of advertising, and your team can help.

Your launch team will accomplish this by:

- Downloading, reading, and writing reviews for your book on Amazon and other platforms
- Sharing your book to their following, friends, and family
- Creating and sharing social media posts with their following
- Hosting ads on their websites and blogs

They may also be able to put you in touch with major social media or publishing influencers. These platforms and/or folks can offer significant traffic to your book and website with their endorsements and reviews.

A huge part of launching your book is networking with other people. Other people can open up opportunities, provide marketing, and help spread the word for you. You do not have to do all of this work on your own—a great launch team can help you. When you communicate your expectations, educate, and stay in touch with them, your book will sell.

A launch team does not have to be made up of expensive professionals. Rather, it can consist of your friends, family, business followers, clients, and members of your local circle. It can include those who follow you on your author Facebook page and writer's groups. It can even include the employees of local pet businesses, libraries, and bookstores. Read on to learn about how to build a great launch team.

ENCOURAGE WORD OF MOUTH

When you first get ready to publish your book for pet lovers and/or pet professionals, you should consider giving free copies to:

- People in the pet industry
- Your friends
- Local pet businesses
- Acquaintances, etc.

Ask these people to spread the word and recommend your book to others. Word of mouth will encourage many people to read your book who might not otherwise give it a chance.

THINK ABOUT IT

When you see a new restaurant open up in town, you might not give it a try unless a friend tells you, "It is really great food!" You do not want to risk wasting your time and money trying something unless someone you know and trust tells you that it is worth it. The same goes for your pet book. People may not read or consider it—unless they hear from trusted sources they should.

Another consideration is to launch your freshly published book with your own expanded social circle. People who know you are already more likely to share your interests and trust your book is worth reading. Then they will spread the word and share it with others they know who might like it. This is how your book starts to gain notoriety and sales.

Sadly, many people overlook this free form of easy marketing. They do not want to bother their friends and family by asking them to read their books. They feel shy or worry their close friends won't enjoy their books.

Take advantage of your friends, family, acquaintances, local pet businesses, and bookstores to help spread work of mouth for you. This marketing is free and also effective. You have vast resources at your fingertips at the local level if only you take advantage of them!

EARLY ACCESS

Right after you upload your book to a self-publishing platform (Chapter 14), you absolutely should offer free or low-cost (I suggest $.99) Kindle copies to gain momentum in the Amazon algorithms (Glossary).

Your supporters can be the word-of-mouthers discussed above. But do not rely on your friends and family exclusively. You need social media influencers, pet bloggers, and avid Amazon book reviewers. When you reach out to them, in exchange for free or inexpensive access to your book, these people will spread the word and post reviews on your book.

By giving your book out, you incur the rule of reciprocity. People will hopefully feel obligated to do something for you in exchange for something you do for them. That way, you can ensure at least a few people actually read your book and leave reviews—directing other people to read it. Reviews will definitely boost sales.

Furthermore, if any of these people leave negative reviews early on, you can take their words as constructive feedback.

1. What did they not like about the book?
2. What could you improve?
3. Did you forget to include something?

Most often, negative book reviews are because the book was not clear, the book did not have good grammar, flow, and/or plotline. Or the book failed to address and/or provide what it promised it would. You can work on these things and then re-release the book.

You can also reach out to your followers on social media. Tell your followers that the first twenty, fifty, or hundred people to sign up for your newsletter will get a free copy of your book. Then you hope they give you a review.

Is this foolproof? No, it is not. You might send several people copies and never hear from them again—this is normal. While this can be disappointing, you will get some reviews to show for your efforts. Plus, you got your book into the hands of more people! This is a good thing.

REVIEWERS

Many professional book reviewers are admired and respected in their industry. People may not even become aware of books until they read reviews under popular columns and/or a popular reviewer.

A great form of marketing is to get such acclaimed critics to read your book and review it. You will reach many people this way, people who may never otherwise learn of your book's existence.

Look up bloggers and book reviewers in your particular pet industry and genre. Next, view their website and review policy. Book reviewers should have them clearly posted. If not, you may consider contacting the reviewer and politely introduce yourself, pitching the book in a few sentences, and asking how you can submit it for review.

Some reviewers want print copies, while others want ebooks. They will have rules about where and how to submit books, what to include with your submission, and even the dates when they accept new submissions.

Write the reviewer a personalized letter or email. You can create a form letter that you use again and again—be sure to tweak it for each reviewer. Address the reviewer by name and with a polite salutation. Do not waste time with words—be succinct and get to the point.

1. First, introduce yourself and state how you located the reviewer.
2. Then, launch into a brief description of your book, what it will do for readers, and why it is worth reading.

3. Finally, offer to send a free copy in the format the reviewer prefers and thank him or her for their time.
4. Sign it "Sincerely" and with your full name.
5. Before you send the letter or email off, be sure to proofread it. Errors look quite amateur and decrease your chances of hearing a response.
6. When a reviewer responds with interest in your book, be sure to send it promptly. Thank the reviewer again for taking the time to review your book.

As you collect reviews, be sure to share them on social media, Amazon Central, and post them on your site (with the reviewer's permission, of course!). The more attention and mention your book gets, the more people will feel comfortable reading it. The law of social proof means, if at least a few people read your book, then others will feel comfortable trying it out themselves.

Again, negative reviews may be hurtful or even crushing, but use them constructively to improve your book. Professional book reviewers are people with their own personal opinions—do not take every review to heart. Unless a critic offers some truly valuable advice on how to improve your book, or several people review it negatively for the same reasons, you do not need to follow the guidance of every negative review.

Definitely do not hold off on publishing your book just because of a negative review or two. Not everyone will love your book. This is a reality that comes with self-publishing. Writing scathing replies to negative reviewers may be tempting, but it will only make you look bad in the long run. Handle negative reviews with grace and move on.

SOCIAL MEDIA INFLUENCERS

Social media influencers are people who have amassed hundreds of thousands of social media followers and use social media to promote products or brands for money. They have a huge platform and audience to market to, and they have access to many people who may read your book.

Find literary and pet influencers on social media. These would be pages and people who have thousands of followers and mostly promote books or pet products. Watch a few of their videos and read their posts to see what their approaches are. Then, reach out to them with personalized emails, inviting them to read and promote your book.

You can also try a marketing device like BookTweeters (Resources). For a small fee, these services will post daily tweets about your book for a set period of time. They can place your book in front of the right readers and spread your marketing throughout the social media world for you.

INFLUENTIAL ENDORSEMENTS

What are influential endorsements? They are the people in your pet community who have clout. They may include veterinarians, veterinary technicians, groomers, pet store owners, shelter owners, boarding kennel owners, competitive owners of show animals, judges, and the like. Check out my book, *Pet Jobs 101: How to Choose Your Dream Job and Thrive in the Pet Industry* (https://amazon.com/B08478K-MYD), for a list of all potential influencers in the pet industry.

Celebrities are also excellent endorsements, if you can convince one to endorse your book. Even if you cannot get an A-list movie star to endorse your book, you can ask local celebrities, such as local news anchors or spokespeople for major local organizations. Bloggers in your area of pet expertise who have lots of followers are also excellent influential endorsements.

Reach out to influential people. You may visit them in person or write them letters. Always be direct and polite. Point out:

- Why your pet book is good
- What it is about
- How it will help pet owners in some way
- What you hope to accomplish with your book

This will convince influential people, who are probably busy, to take some time out of their day to promote your book somehow.

Find people who care about the same pet-related things you do. If you wrote a book about shelter dogs, for instance, you would want to find people who donate to or run shelters. If your book is about lizards, you would want to reach out to people who are well known among reptile owners—such as reptile product company owners or reptile store owners.

WRAP-UP

Gathering a launch team is a critical step in your self-publishing journey. Honestly, work on building your team before you publish (Chapter 13). Have your team prepped for the date your book is live on Amazon. The more preparation you do by following my advice, the more downloads and reviews you will get.

Keep in mind you will *not* get one-hundred percent participation from your team, but you will get about thirty percent activity. This is why you have to keep working on keeping your book prominent on social media (Chapter 15) and events (Chapter 16).

Your launch team will help get your book out there! You can turn to friends, book reviewers, local celebrities, clients, and business owners to get the word out. Never underestimate word of mouth! This is one way to market your book even before you release it to the public. Offer people free copies in exchange for word-of-mouth advertising.

There is a lot that goes into gathering a launch team, and it would take an entire book to explain the subject. The information in this chapter gives you a solid premise on what to gather, what you need, and what you can expect.

Now it is time to learn how to upload your book to Amazon. Read on to the next chapter to find out how to do that! But check out your action steps for this chapter first.

ACTION STEPS

1. Encourage worth of mouth.
2. Get some early reviewers by offering free copies of your book.
3. Get influential endorsements.
4. Take advantage of a social media influencer's following.
5. Enter partnerships with other writers, bloggers, and pet business owners.
6. Collect book reviews to be posted on the day you launch by your launch team and to use on your Amazon Central page.
7. Be sure to use negative reviews constructively, and do not let them discourage you. Never respond to them on Amazon.

14
KINDLE DIRECT PUBLISHING

A professional writer is an amateur who did not quit.
— Richard Bach

Are you ready to hit publish? With your book edited, formatted, and with its cover designed, you now need to upload your book to a self-publishing platform. The one I use and strongly recommend is Kindle Select, which puts your book in the Kindle Unlimited store (if you so choose).

Being part of Kindle Direct Publishing allows users to find your book when they search for your book's subject on search engines and within the Amazon site. As long as you completely fill out the options for your book—keywords, description, etc.

If you do not already use Kindle Unlimited yourself, it is a massive ebook store where users pay a monthly fee to get access to hundreds of thousands of titles.

You can pick a book in the Kindle Unlimited program and download it to your Kindle app on any supporting device. Kindle is the current trend in self-publishing and lets you get your book in front of millions of users.

Amazon gives you the option to place your book in Kindle Select or not. I highly suggest you do because Amazon will promote your book. At least enroll for the first three months of publication. Kindle Select allows you to run promotions within the platform. Because of the scope of this information, I suggest going into KDP and learn more about Kindle Select and Unlimited.

But let's get your book published. Read on to find out what you need to do to become a self-published author.

CREATE A KINDLE DIRECT PUBLISHING ACCOUNT

To upload, you first need to create a Kindle Direct Publishing (KDP) account. Go to https://kdp.amazon.com. The platform in KDP is extremely easy, and they also have a help section and an easy-to-reach customer service department.

Note: I recommend you sign up with KDP using a different username/email and password than the one you use if you already have a personal Amazon account. I like to have two separate accounts because it keeps my business history separate from my personal buying history. This makes tax time easier.

TIME TO UPLOAD

Now you are ready to upload!

1. Sign in to your KDP account.
2. Click on your "Bookshelf."
3. Click on "Create a New Title."
4. Click on "Kindle ebook."
5. Select "Kindle ebook Details" and fill out *everything*.
6. Next, go to "Kindle ebook Content" and follow the prompts.
7. Then save and continue, and proceed to "Kindle ebook Pricing."
8. Be sure to fill out *everything*—and refer to the detailed help section in KDP.

IMPORTANT CONSIDERATIONS

When you choose "Upload ebook Manuscript." It will pull up a window of your computer files, so locate your manuscript and select it. Hit "Open." It can take a few minutes, but you will receive a confirmation your book is uploaded. Next, you want to preview the book to ensure nothing went wrong.

You can also repeat this process when KDP provides a pop-up to create a print version. You can offer the same book in both ebook and print if you want. Follow the directions as you did above.

When you are asked to proof your book, definitely order an author's proof for a softcover. You want to be sure your soft-cover book is perfect. I covered formatting and cover design in Chapter 11; please go back and review if needed.

Be sure you have your softcover and your digital cover formatted to KDP's specifications. I always get an author's copy because it is so much easier to check a book in print format than on the computer screen. Plus, Amazon does make mistakes.

Definitely do some keyword research using Google Keyword Planner or a similar service to find keywords people might use when looking for books like yours. You want people to find your book easily. Do not skip this step.

To set the price, you first must pick a royalty plan. After you choose your royalty plan you will then set pricing. You will be given a list of currency options and the ability to set your desired amount.

Be sure to specify in your Kindle account how you want to receive your royalties. Also, learn the royalties schedule so you know when to expect payment. You will need to file for an EIN (Resources) and report your royalty earnings to the IRS.

After your book is live, you want to sign in to your Amazon Author Central and click "Add Book." Search by your book's title or ISBN. When you find it, hit "Claim." That adds the book to your list! You can refresh the page, and it should be on your page. You also want to post links to the book on your website and social media so people can start buying it!

This whole process is free! And it puts your book in front of countless readers. Your only job left is marketing.

WRAP-UP

Launching your book after all the work you put into it is an exciting feeling when self-publishing—especially the first time. It is the ultimate accomplishment, the moment when you can honestly say, "I am an author!" With Kindle Direct Publishing, or KDP, self-publishing is easier than ever. Just follow the directions KDP offers.

Familiarize yourself with the KDP platform. Read the helpful articles that are available to you in KDP's help section. Although this process can be stressful—uploading your pet book to KDP gets easier with each book you publish.

Be sure to have your manuscript formatted correctly (a professional formatter makes this part so much easier) and your cover properly designed to fit the template that KDP provides. I recommend a professional cover designer as well.

Upload the ebook and/or print versions and fill out the relevant information. Pick a royalty plan and set a price for your new book. Then watch the reviews and earnings flow in! Do not forget to claim the book on your Amazon Author Central account (Chapter 12).

This is not the last step, however. First do your action steps for this chapter. Then go to the next chapter and learn how to get more reviews and increase your earnings. Continued marketing of your book is critical.

In the next two chapters, I cover the basic yet crucial forms of marketing you must do to sell your book. After all, no one can read your book if no one knows it is out there!

ACTION STEPS

1. Make sure your manuscript is properly edited and formatted (Chapter 11).
2. Get your cover design .jpg finalized to fit the template that KDP requires.
3. Create a KDP account.
4. Upload your ebook and print versions.
5. Fill out *all* the book details—do not skimp.
6. Pick your royalty plan.
7. Set your price and currency.
8. Preview to make sure it looks right.
9. Order your author copy for the softcover.
10. Alert your launch team to download and leave their reviews (Chapter 13).
11. Read on to start marketing your creation to pet lovers, influencers, and professionals.

15
INTERNET MARKETING

Content is King, but engagement is Queen, and
the Queen rules the house!
—Mari Smith

Are you ready to influence the pet industry with your message? Since many folks are online these days, it makes sense to market your book using social media. You will reach a wider and possibly international audience with Internet marketing. It is possible to build a huge following and get many readers with the right kinds of channels.

The first thing you must do is establish yourself on social media. What are the most popular ones in your area and/or for your brand? Twitter, Instagram, LinkedIn, and Facebook are the big ones right now. If you do not sign up for any other social media, at least sign up for those four.

Chances are you are already on social media, but you want to keep your author accounts and personal accounts separate. That protects your privacy and lets you market to the right audiences. Read on to learn how to take advantage of these sites for marketing purposes.

FACEBOOK

Facebook is huge all over the world, and many businesses have used this platform to their advantage. You definitely want to create a business page for yourself as an author. This will begin your strategy for the online promotion process.

Your business page is your headquarters, with statistics about audience engagement, easy access to ad creation and posting, and a means to post new content.

You can also pay Facebook to promote your page. This is where Facebook places your page ad in front of people who have liked related pages in the past and thus are likely to like yours. As you incur likes, you will grow a wider base of people to put content in front of.

Another great thing about Facebook—you can join groups related in some way to your book. It is a great way to find people who will read your book. You can engage through thoughtful comments and let people see your page name. They will then be more inclined to check out your page, like it, share it, and hopefully buy your book.

Start by inviting your friends and family on your personal Facebook to like your page. Ask them to invite their friends and family. As they invite more and more people, you begin to grow a decent fanbase of people who have never even met you before. They are new potential leads for your book.

Post content every day. About twenty percent of your content should actually be about your book. You can post:

- Blurbs
- Book deals
- Reviews
- Promotional deals
- Upcoming appearances on local cable television news
- And more

But the rest of your content should be relevant and interesting—providing equal parts of informative and entertainment value.

You can also post some funny memes, a few cute animal videos, and then a couple insightful articles about canine nutrition and/or behavior to inspire users to keep following you. Post engaging content that is fun, educational, and relevant to your book and/or brand (Glossary).

INSTAGRAM

Instagram is about posting great photos. You may think this would be difficult to translate into promotional material for your book, but you can definitely use your creativity to market using this platform.

Here are examples of the types of posts I do. Depending on your genre, you can post photos of your:

- Own pets or pet products
- Followers and influencer interacting with your book(s)
- Pets alongside of your book(s)
- Newest articles on your blog
- And other relevant things that entertain and educate

With over seven hundred million users on Instagram, it is the most popular social media site right now. You would be missing out if you weren't on it! Instagram marketing is powerful.

Start by setting up an Instagram business page. Your business page could be specifically for your book (not my recommendation, as you may write more books in the future), or better yet—you as an author.

Use your page's built-in insights to understand your audience better. Remember, insights only come with business pages, not regular personal pages. Be sure to utilize them to create ads that work, posts that get more likes, and allow visitors to contact you directly.

A thirty/thirty-five/thirty-five rule is ideal for Instagram. Thirty percent of your posts should be promoting your book. Thirty-five percent should be educational (educational links to blog posts and insightful videos, for instance) and thirty-five percent should be to entertainment (cute puppy videos, for instance).

Be sure to post every day. And avoid those glaringly artificial stock photos. Take your own photos if you can. Nice mobile photos of your pets may not look polished and professional—but they do look refreshingly real. Instagrammers appreciate that! Be sure to engage with your commenters and thank them for checking out your stuff.

Be sure to use hashtags (Glossary). A hashtag is a keyword phrase without spaces with a pound sign in front of it. For example: #petauthorpreneur, #petloss, #petsofinstagram. I cover hashtags in more detail in the Glossary and in my book, *Pet Blogging 101: How to Start a Riveting Pet Blog and Gain Loyal Followers* (https://amazon.com/dp/B07XWRS95W).

To get followers, you must be a follower. Follow the people you admire, like other authors or pet business owners. Engage with their content so they notice you. Following those with pages related to yours can help you grow and expand your followers by putting you in line with people who will like your content.

TWITTER

To use Twitter as a marketing strategy, you want to tweet something at least once a day. This helps readers feel connected to you. You might tweet a sentence from your book, a quote about pets, and or a quote about writing—

always add a link to your book. Tweet when you are appearing in:

- An ad
- A critical review
- A podcast
- Or some other online or in-person event so your readers can attend

Always provide links and hashtags (Glossary) to whatever you are talking about—be it your book or a podcast you will be a guest on.

Twitter posts move fast. Therefore, create captivating copy that is short, to the point, and fast to read. When you provide great information in a concise and captivating manor, it increases the odds your tweets will be retweeted. Your efforts will reach a broader audience and earn you more followers. Quotes or short teasers are also ideal.

When someone shares your tweet, be sure to thank him or her. This can be time-consuming. But it helps you stand out from the crowd and incur loyal fans who feel valued by you. The more personal interaction you have with your readers, the better.

An especially good move on Twitter is to befriend and talk to people whom you want to get to know. You can make a list of famous people, pet lovers, business owners, authors—and then follow them. Once you get to know them, you can glean helpful information from them. They may even retweet your posts about your book and spread the word to an even larger group of people!

You should also be helpful to others. Retweet their books. Post links to articles and products other authors and pet lovers could appreciate or use. These things make people feel as if you are worth following.

It is best to use the 4:1 rule here. For every four things you post that are helpful or useful, post one thing that promotes your book. This keeps followers from unfollowing you. You do not want them to get tired of reading about your book and nothing else. Most people do not enjoy monotony or being spammed (Glossary)! Especially on social media, where trends fade in and out within days of each other.

Every so often, you should host Tweet chats where you chat directly with your readers and future readers. Create a hashtag specific to your chat and then encourage readers to use it during the event. Clearly post hours and be present for it. This is a chance for you to talk about your book and answer questions.

LINKEDIN

LinkedIn is a social networking site for professionals. To promote your pet book business—definitely create a LinkedIn profile. On the profile, talk about your expertise and feature a link to your book(s).

As you add new followers, be sure to send an email greeting to each new member by name and then invite them to look at your book(s). Talk about what your book features and how they will benefit from following you.

It helps to create a basic email template. Copy and paste it to each new email you send out. Customize the name, and you are good to go.

Post every day or every other day. Talk about your book, blog posts, or a book event you will be attending. This way, LinkedIn users can follow your book launches.

As with all social media platforms, add a LinkedIn button on your website to your book Landing Page, About Page, and Contact Page (Chapter 12).

AMS ADS

Amazon Market Services, or AMS, ads are a great way to drive people to your book on Amazon with little effort on your part. Go to https://advertising.amazon.com to set up your account.

The key to AMS ads is to first research keywords (Glossary) and gather the maximum of one thousand words that will do well according to your SEO (Glossary) research. Then create an ad with Amazon and enter a clear description—Amazon will pull an image from your book listing. As a beginner, set a bid for ten cents per click and a cap of two dollars a day.

It takes time and knowledge to build successful AMS ads, and I would need to write an entire book on the strategy. Plus, Amazon is always changing the way they do things. I love and recommend Bryan Cohen's book and course on creating AMS ads (Resources). You could also purchase Publisher Rocket (Resources), which is an app you can download.

Keep in mind as you set up your ads—clicks cost you money, so you want them to lead to sales. If you are getting a lot of unproductive clicks, perhaps improve your book description or your keywords. Review your keyword traffic and eliminate the words that seem to be getting the most unresponsive clicks. Unresponsive clicks are part of the business, so you will get some, but do your best to avoid them.

GREAT PLACE TO FIND KEYWORDS

You know the list of books that appear under any book on Amazon, "Customers who bought this item also bought..." This is a great place to find relevant keywords.

The way to do this is to take a look at each book. Ask yourself, "Are these books bestsellers, have great ratings, have over fifty reviews?" If so, add the title and the author's name as a separate keyword in your list of available one thousand words.

When you do this, you are treating authors in your genre and niche who are bestsellers as potential leads for clicks and hopefully sales. When you show up in the "Customers who bought this item also bought..." recommendations, readers will then likely click on your book, buy it, and hopefully leave a review.

WRAP-UP

The Internet is a fantastic place to put your book in front of many people. On top of a website (Chapter 12) and a launch team (Chapter 13), you must use AMS ads and social media to build your brand and sell your book.

I always recommend designing a plan when you are developing your social media strategy. Having a plan and checklist can keep you accountable for creating new posts, engaging with your followers, and general marketing of your brand and books.

Your goal as an author is to gain loyal followers. Social media will help you collect emails, inspire people to buy your book(s), and engage with you.

Be sure to give pet lovers, influencers, and professionals great content so they are loyal to your brand. Your posts cannot be *all* about your book! Be sure to post at least three or four posts that entertain and/or educate before you try to convince them to buy your book(s).

Even though there is a learning curve with AMS ads, do not delay in starting the process as soon as you are live on Amazon. Check out Bryan Cohen's book and course. If you are patient and do your research, your ads can be extremely profitable.

Go over your action steps below to help you with your strategy for online marketing. The next and final chapter is about the old-fashioned way of self-promotion—in-person marketing. This approach is an effective way to put your book in front of new readers who might enjoy it or need it.

ACTION STEPS

1. Set up a business Facebook author page.
2. Set up a business Instagram account.
3. Set up a Twitter business account.
4. Set up a LinkedIn account.
5. Decide which day(s) you are going to post on your accounts.
6. Engage with followers and the people you follow on a daily basis.
7. Find people you can follow with all four accounts.
8. Join Facebook groups.
9. Start a Twitter chat.
10. Sign up for AMS ads by going to https://advertising.amazon.com, do your research, and watch closely—you have to pay attention to your AMS ads.

16

IN PERSON MARKETING

You cannot expect to just write and have visitors come to you—that is too passive.
—Anita Campell

Are you concerned that Internet marketing is the only way to promote your book? As popular as the Internet is—meeting people in person and forging personal relationships is still an effective way to market your book.

When people meet you in person, they feel connected to you and are more likely to read your book. You are not a faceless, anonymous stranger selling your book online—instead, you are a real person who makes a certain impression.

But how do you accomplish this and go out in public to promote your book? There are actually a few simple and fun events I want to share with you. These options are excellent ways to show people the real you and raise awareness of your book. Garner the attention and interest, make an impression, and sell your book with these public appearances.

BOOK SIGNINGS

One of the best ways to raise interest in your book is to go on a book tour. With a book tour, you make in-person appearances at bookstores and libraries. It gives you a chance to interact with people by offering book signings.

In traditional publishing, your literary agent will set you up to do this. In self-publishing, you have to set it up for yourself. But it is worth it and not as hard as it may sound!

You may consider only local businesses or those in cities that you will visit soon. The first thing to do is to locate:

- Bookstores
- Pet supply stores
- Shelters
- Pet events or fairs
- Pet bazaars
- Local community colleges
- And other places that would attract the types of people who would read your book (remember your avatar from Chapter 2)

Then, approach these locations several months in advance to give them time to accept your proposal and promote you. You will pitch the store owner or event/festival planner. If there is an upcoming event or festival, see if you can fit in a reading or presentation during it.

Keep in mind your host must see the worth of your book for their customers before hosting you. Be sure to immediately state in your proposal something of value to their customers.

Try and get your book on the shelves prior to your visit to a bookstore or library. This can help with promotion and marketing ahead of time. It can also decrease your luggage load if you are traveling a distance.

When you set up a signing, be sure to run an ad in the paper and on social media. Have the store post signs and mention it in their newsletter to generate more interest. Pin up notices in other local businesses with their permission. Definitely mention it on your author website. You want to spread the word.

What if your first book signing is a bit of a sad affair? No worries—I have suffered through many book signings where people weren't interested. This is no reason to give up. Keep posting about it and sharing photos of your books. This is a great use of your time when your event is a flop. Keep in mind the event still:

- Gives you material to post on your social media
- Assures people your books are being read
- Gives you social proof

PODCASTS

Even though a podcast is not technically an in-person event, they are extremely helpful, and I wanted to include them in this chapter.

A podcast is another fantastic and fun way to get people to follow you and buy your book(s). You do not have to start your own podcast—although it certainly is not a bad idea! Rather, you want to find related podcasts that will have you on as a guest to talk about your book and your pet business. The podcaster will interview you, and you will get to share a bit about why your book is worth buying.

It is useful to listen to podcasts in your field of pet expertise and find the ones you want to be on. Reach out to the podcaster with a personal letter and pitch explaining why you are a great guest for their listeners.

You want to show your host the value of your message for their listeners. Before you go live, you also want to prepare some material. This way, when you get nervous you won't forget what you wanted to say (trust me, it happens to the best of us!).

Be sure to alert people to your upcoming podcast interviews on your social media and website. This lets users tune in and boost the podcast's listeners. This way, you give the podcaster something in return for the great marketing and promotional opportunity you got from him or her.

Some podcasters are happy to interview over the Internet or phone. Others will want to meet in person. Look into how the interview will take place to make sure it fits into your schedule.

BOOK GROUPS

Also try out a book group as a chance to promote your pet book. Book groups are groups of people who love books and often love to host authors. They can also offer honest and helpful reviews (Chapter 13).

Some book clubs meet in person, while others are members of Internet clubs. Your best bet is to find local and regional book clubs and learn when they meet. Contact the club's president and convince him or her to let you present your book during a club meeting.

Like a book signing, you will set up a table with several copies of your book. You will present your book for a few minutes to the club and then answer questions for a few minutes. You will sign copies as you distribute them to the club members. You will charge whatever you have priced your print copies at on Amazon.

The beauty of these clubs is the members like to read. While only a few may buy your book at your actual presentation, they may tell their friends about it. You can easily get expanded sales from just five attendees at a book club meeting.

If a book club loves your book and presentation, they will welcome you back if you write anything else. You have an easy source of promotion and word-of-mouth marketing at the same book club for the length of your author career!

If you cannot find a book club that is keen on your nonfiction or fiction pet book, you can try to reach out to other types of pet clubs. If you wrote a book about sheep herding, meet with a group of sheep herding trial competitors, for instance.

You can also look into online groups. You may want to post a video or use a live function on Facebook to present your book to the group. Post a link to your book on Amazon and watch the sales increase!

Do not forget your pets are an excellent source of promotion! Attend pet events with your book and your companions. This is a great way to get people to meet you and learn you are a trustworthy voice on the subject of pets.

PET SPECIALTY GROUPS AND EVENTS

As a pet author, this audience is priceless and not to be ignored. Rescue organizations, breed-specific groups, and/or training groups oftentimes host fundraising events to support their cause. Research the groups in your area first—in my experience, the local groups love to support other local people.

When I find a group or event that is promising, I reach out to the director with a brief email. I explain who I am, what I do, and provide the links to my website and book(s) on Amazon.

At the beginning of my email, I explain the benefit to their members of having me at their event or group meeting in two sentences.

For my books, I have found this to be one of the most successful ways to market and gain loyal followers, reviews, and future buyers of my books and services.

WRAP-UP

Do not ever underestimate the power of marketing in person! People will love to meet you and learn what inspired you. This alone can help with sales because potential customers are experiencing a real person.

Start making a list for appearances on podcasts, bookstores for signings, book clubs, pet specialty groups, and events to promote your book and raise sales. All of these venues are perfect for authors.

Keep in mind, people love local authors and are usually enthusiastic about hosting you at an event. There are probably a good number of pet events in your area where you could show up to do a book signing.

You have now reached the end of this book—but not the end of your new journey as an author. You have many years of success ahead of you. While the work may never truly end, the rewards do not either.

You will love the sense of accomplishment you will feel from having written your book, and you will love the way your book can earn you a great income while you lounge at home in your pajamas.

I believe in you. Now believe in yourself! Apply the tools in this book and you will not regret it! But do not forget your action steps for this chapter and my Pep Talk in the next section!

ACTION STEPS

1. Make a list of all bookstores, pet supply stores, libraries, pet specialty clubs, events, and festivals in your area.
2. Arrange book signings, talks, and personal book sales.
3. Research and reach out to podcasters. Some will want to meet and record you in person—others will not.
4. Become a special guest at local book clubs and be available for questions.
5. Get featured on online book clubs as well—like Facebook live book clubs, etc.

PEP TALK!

If writing has been on your list of things to accomplish for years, *yet* you did not have a clue on how to start—*now* you have the tools to create a winning, best-selling pet book.

There is no need to wait or procrastinate any longer. It is time to jump in and make your dream come true. Most people want to write—you will be one of the few who actually does!

Writing in the pet genre can be daunting and even scary at first. But as you can see after reading this book, the entire process is fairly straightforward, exciting, and life-changing. Just take your time, set reasonable and specific goals, and celebrate your achievements.

A good team is the single best way you can accomplish your goal without failure. A team motivates you and helps bring your book to fruition. Find good, reliable people to edit, design, and format your book before you complete your rough draft.

You must also use a great launch team. Your best friend or local pet store can be a part of your launch team. There is no need to spend a fortune on securing an expensive publicist. You can market yourself online, in person, and through word of mouth.

Were you worried about sales? Now you know how to boost sales with the tools in this book to raise awareness about your book(s) for pet lovers and professionals. Remember, no matter how great your book is, no one will buy it if they do not know about it! Get out there and share it.

Furthermore, do not shy away from creating a website. A website markets your book while you are asleep, eating, or away on vacation. With a few simple steps, like social media marketing and SEO, you can ensure that your website drives sales and coverts visitors into leads. You must have a web presence to survive in the literary industry these days.

Self-publishing is hard work, and it can be expensive, but you do not have to go into debt to accomplish your dream. You will certainly love being an author. Sharing your knowledge and passion is a heartwarming feeling.

> ***How could it not be—you get to write about the best topic ever: pets!***

I believe you can do this and reach your goals. You just need to believe in yourself, learn as much as you can, and put yourself out there.

At first, I struggled with self-doubt about becoming a successful Pet Authorpreneur. I was petrified when I wrote my first book. I kept asking myself, *Will anyone be interested in what I have to say? Will my books find their way into readers' hands?*

My first review on Amazon secured I was on the right track, and I reached my goal for becoming an author. I wanted to help people, and this one book led into over a dozen best-selling books and counting.

Get *ready* for your journey. Do not forget to *set* your goals and plan for success. Then write every day to get your book done.

You can do this! I believe in you!

Warmly,

Wendy Van de Poll

January 1, 2020

All books in The Pet Biz Series

- Pet Blogging 101: How to Start a Riveting Pet Blog and Gain Loyal Followers, (Book 1) - https://amazon.com/dp/B07XWRS95W
- Pet Jobs 101: How to Choose your Dream Job and Jumpstart Your Business. (Book 2) - https://amazon.com/dp/B08478KMYD
- Pet Authorpreneur 101: How to Become a Successful Pet Author and Grow Your Business, (Book 3) - https://amazon.com/dp/B0852QD6DH

GLOSSARY

Affiliate Links — Or affiliate marketing is a marketing strategy in which one business rewards another business (affiliate) for each visitor and/or purchase by that visitor. It is up to the affiliate to market. A special link is provided by the company the affiliate is promoting.

Amazon Algorithms — A complicated system by Amazon. Their layers of algorithms determine how books are ranked in the best-seller charts, popularity list, which books appear in the keyword search and the order in which they appear.

Avatar — Your avatar is like a real person—they have a name and family status. They live in a particular place and have hopes and dreams. An avatar is a detailed profile of your ideal customer. The avatar focuses on one person and outlines everything about them.

Back Matter — The book elements that occur in the back of your book after your body of work. Includes acknowledgements, appendix, glossary, resources, bibliography, references, illustration credits, and index.

Backstory for a Character — Basically the history of a fictional character. Their experiences that help to explain their desires, fears, motivations, etc.

Beta Reader — A person who reads a work of fiction before it is published and suggests improvements. They are not editors.

Branding — The marketing practice of creating a name and logo that identifies your product from others. A great brand strategy gives your business a major edge in a competitive market. It is your promise to your customers' needs.

Character Profile — A detailed description of a fictional character's life and personality. A quality character profile helps the author get into the mind of the character and make them come alive for readers.

Front Matter — The elements that occur in the front of your book prior to the body of your work. Includes series title page, title page, copyright page, dedication, epigraph, table of contents, list of illustrations, foreword, introduction, and abbreviations.

Google Keyword Planner — A tool that provides keyword ideas and traffic estimates to help you build traffic to your website.

Hashtags — A hashtag is a label for content. It helps others who are interested in a certain topic find content on that same topic. A hashtag looks something like this: #wendyvandepoll or #dogsoninstagram. Hashtags are used mostly on social media sites. They rocketed to fame on Twitter.

High Ranking Keyword – When your chosen keyword on your website or in your blog article ranks with Google on the first search page.

Keyword/ Short-tailed Keyword – Short tail keywords are search phrases with only one or two words. Their length makes them less specific than searches with more words. "Pet" (one word) is an example of a short tail keyword, whereas "holistic raw cat food" (four words) is a long tail keyword.

Long-tailed Keyword/ Keyword Phrase – A keyword phrase is two or more words typed as a search query. For example, "What is the best way to feed my senior cat" is a good example of a keyword phrase.

Manuscript – This is essentially the earliest draft of your book. It is unpublished and the document that gets submitted to editors.

Medium Ranking Keyword – Same as a high ranking keyword but your chosen keyword may not be on the first page. More commonly found on the second page of a Google search.

Metadata – Is a series of micro-communications between your website and search engines. It lives and works behind the scenes in the HTML of web pages. It drives search engine optimization or SEO (see SEO).

Mind Map – A mind map is a visual representation of writing prompts that includes a central idea surrounded by connected branches of associated topics/chapters/characters/plots, etc.

Plot Hole — An inconsistency in the narrative or character development of your fiction manuscript.

Premise — In fiction it is the foundation of your story or the underlying idea of your story. It is the foundation that supports your entire plot.

SEO — SEO or Search Engine Optimization is the name given to an activity that attempts to improve search engine rankings. In search results Google™ displays links to pages it considers optimal according to your keywords.

Spammed — Is when you send your email subscribers too many emails advertising for them to buy your product. You must send email that educate your readers to give them value rather than trying to sell them all the time.

Tautology — Writing the same thing twice in different words.

Virtual Assistant – An independent contractor who provides administrative services to clients while operating outside of the client's office. They are able to do social media management, the management of appointments and calendars, sending and answering emails, etc.

Working Title – Also known as a production title or tentative title. Basically, it is a temporary title used during the development of writing your manuscript.

Writer's Block – Is when an author loses the ability to produce new work, or experiences a creative slowdown. The issue ranges from difficulty in coming up with original ideas of being unable to produce work for a certain time period.

RESOURCES

A FREE GIFT

A Winning Checklist
~ Become a Successful Pet Author and Grow Your Business ~

Here is your link to download:
https://wendyvandepoll.com/pet-authorpreneur-free-checklist

AFFILIATE SITES**

ConvertKit - email provider
https://wendyvandepoll.com/convert-kit

Kylitics
https://wendyvandepoll.com/k-lytics

ProWritingAid - editing software
https://wendyvandepoll.com/pro-writing-aid

Self-Publishing School – self-publish your book platform
https://wendyvandepoll.com/self-publishing-school

Siteground - website host
https://wendyvandepoll.com/siteground

AMAZON LINKS

Amazon Author Central
https://authorcentral.amazon.com

Kindle Direct Publishing (KDP)
https://kdp.amazon.com

ASSOCIATIONS

Editorial Freelancers Association
https://www.the-efa.org

International Association of Professional Book Editors
https://iapcollege.com

National Association of Independent Writers and Editors
https://naiwe.com

GRAPHIC DESIGN SITES

Canva
https://canva.com

PicMonkey
https://picmonkey.com

MARKETING

BookTweeters
https://literatureandlatte.com/scrivener/overview

PHOTOS

Deposit Photos
https://depositphotos.com

Librestock
https://librestock.com

Pixabay
https://pixabay.com

SERVICES

99designs
https://99designs.com

Fiverr
http://fiverr.com

Guru
https://guru.com

Smashwords (Also known as Mark's List)

https://smashwords.com/list

Upwork
https://upwork.com

Vistaprint
https://vistaprint.com

SOCIAL MEDIA ORGANIZATIONAL TOOLS

Agora Pulse
https://agorapulse.com

Buffer
https://buffer.com

Hootsuite
https://hootsuite.com

Later
https://later.com

ShareCount
https://www.sharedcount.com

WRITING COURSES

Writer's Digest
https://writersdigest.com

Writer's Write
https://writerswrite.com

Udemy
https://udemy.com/course/writing-with-flair-how-to-become-an-exceptional-writer

WRITING CHALLENGES

12 Short Stories in 12 months
https://writerswrite.co.za

NaNoWriMo
https://nanowrimo.org

NaPoWriMo
https://napowrimo.net

StoryADay
https://storyaday.org

Word of the Day
https://wordofthedaychallenge.wordpress.com

WRITING TOOLS

ProWritingAid (affiliate)
https://wendyvandepoll.com/pro-writing-aid

Scapple
https://literatureandlatte.com/scrivener/overview

Scrivner
https://literatureandlatte.com/scrivener/overview

Vellum
https://vellum.com

OTHER

Best Page Forward (Bryan Cohen)
https://bestpageforward.com

EIN or Employee Identification Number
https://www.irs.gov/businesses/small-businesses-self-employed/apply-for-an-employer-identification-number-ein-online

Google Keyword Planner
https://ads.google.com/home/tools/keyword-planner

Publisher Rocket
https://publisherrocket.com

DOWNLOAD YOUR FREE GIFT!

A Success Checklist to Become a Successful Pet Author and Grow Your Business

https://wendyvandepoll.com/pet-authorpreneur-free-checklist

***The **recommended sites** are products that I use and highly recommend. They are affiliate links which means if you purchase the product, I receive a small commission (which helps me greatly as an author.) You are not charged more because of the affiliate link.*

ACNOWLEDGEMENTS

I would like to thank all the animals who have trusted me to be their advocate and voice. They inspire me to be the best human-being I possibly can.

Many thanks go to my followers, students, and clients. Thank you for pushing me to write this book and others to follow in this series. It takes a team to put together a book and I would like to extend my appreciation to all that have helped along the way.

A huge hug goes to my husband, Rick. He is a remarkable animal lover and human being who dedicates his life to the animals and the environment. He inspires my soul. You can find his books on Amazon, as well.

ABOUT THE AUTHOR

Animals are Wendy Van de Poll's passion. Any chance she gets she is hiking with her dog, observing wildlife in her backwoods, and listening to their wisdom.

Wendy Van de Poll is an award-winning and International best-selling author of thirteen books and counting. She has been working with animals in various capacities for over forty years. With her success she is passionate about helping others achieve their writing and pet business goals.

Wendy has helped people around the world start their own blogging sites, pet businesses, and write best-selling books. Her clients describe Wendy as a "dedicated partner who helps get your ideas down on paper, your work (blog, job, or book) done, and in the hands of readers and customers who want more."

She is the founder of the CenterforPetLossGrief.com. Her website and blog provide a safe place for dedicated pet parents and pet professionals who want support and guidance with pet loss grief, hospice for pets, and coping with the loss of their pets.

Wendy is a certified end-of-life and grief coach and a tested animal communicator and medium.

She holds a Master of Science degree in wolf ecology and behavior and has run with wild wolves in Minnesota, coyotes in Massachusetts, and foxes in her backyard.

Wendy also coaches people who want write their own books about their pets and other topics.

Her articles can be seen on Medium.com as well as her own websites.

Her articles can be seen on:

Wendy Van de Poll, Bestselling Author, Influencer, Animal Advocate: https://wendyvandepoll.com

Center For Pet Loss Grief, LLC: https://centerforpetloss-grief.com

Medium.com: https://medium.com/@wendyvandepoll

Click Here to Get Your Free Gift

https://wendyvandepoll.com/pet-authorpreneur-free-checklist

THANK YOU FOR READING!

As the author of this book, I appreciate you buying and reading it. I hope you found the information useful and are on your way to becoming a successful pet author.

I would be grateful if you would leave a helpful book review, either with your favorite book distributor or with Amazon.

Thank you,

Wendy Van de Poll, MS, CEOL

Best-selling and Award-winning Author, Writing Coach, Animal Advocate

www.wendyvandepoll.com

For all of Wendy Van de Poll's books, please visit:
https:amazon.com/author/wendyvandepoll

Check out my Free Gift that Goes with This Book
https://wendyvandepoll.com/pet-authorpreneur-free-checklist

ALSO BY WENDY VAN DE POLL

THE PET BIZ SERIES

Pet Blogging 101

Pet Jobs 101

Pet Authorpreneur 101

PET BEREAVEMENT SERIES

My Dog Is Dying: What Do I Do?

My Dog Has Died: What Do I Do?

My Cat Is Dying: What Do I Do?

My Cat Has Died: What Do I Do?

Healing a Child's Pet Loss Grief

The Pet Professional's Guide to Pet Loss

Pet Loss Poems: To Heal Your Heart and Soul

HUMAN-ANIMAL BOOKS

Animal Wisdom: Conversations From The Heart Between Animals and Their People

FREE BOOK

Healing Your Heart From Pet Loss Grief

CHILDREN'S PICTURE BOOKS

The Adventures of Ms. Addie Pants Series

The Rescue

The Ice Storm

New Friends

Off to School

To receive notification when more books are published, please go to:

https://wendyvandepoll.com

We will add you to the mailing list after you download your free gift.

A Success Checklist to Become a Successful Pet Author and Grow Your Business

https://wendyvandepoll.com/pet-authorpreneur-free-checklist

You can also find my books on Amazon:

https://amazon.com/author/wendyvandepoll

Made in United States
North Haven, CT
04 November 2026

21768317R00323